Golriz Ghahraman made history as the first refugee to be sworn in as a Member of the New Zealand Parliament in 2017. Iranian-born, Golriz arrived in New Zealand with her parents seeking asylum as a nine-year-old. She studied human rights law at Oxford and has practised as a lawyer in New Zealand and for United Nations tribunals in Africa, The Hague, and Cambodia. Golriz is a member of New Zealand's Green Party.

KNOW YOUR PLACE

Golriz Ghahraman

HarperCollins*Publishers*

HarperCollins*Publishers*

First published in 2020
by HarperCollins*Publishers* (New Zealand) Limited
Unit D1, 63 Apollo Drive, Rosedale, Auckland 0632, New Zealand
harpercollins.co.nz

HarperCollins*Publishers*
Unit D1, 63 Apollo Drive, Rosedale, Auckland 0632, New Zealand
Level 13, 201 Elizabeth Street, Sydney NSW 2000, Australia
A 53, Sector 57, Noida, UP, India
1 London Bridge Street, London, SE1 9GF, United Kingdom
Bay Adelaide Centre, East Tower, 22 Adelaide Street West, 41st floor, Toronto,
  Ontario M5H 4E3, Canada
195 Broadway, New York NY 10007, USA

A catalogue record for this book is available from the National Library of New Zealand

ISBN 978 1 7755 4142 4 (pbk)
ISBN 978 1 7754 9173 6 (ebook)

Cover design by Damon Keen, adapted by Megan van Staden
Front cover photo by Nick Gill
Unless otherwise credited, all photos are taken by or are from the collection of
  Golriz Ghahraman
Typeset in Adobe Garamond Pro by Kirby Jones
Printed and bound in Australia by McPherson's Printing Group
The papers used by HarperCollins in the manufacture of this book are a natural, recyclable product made from wood grown in sustainable plantation forests. The fibre source and manufacturing processes meet recognised international environmental standards, and carry certification.

For my parents, Maryam and Behrooz, who lost their home, family, friends, professions, and even language, because they were not willing to raise a little girl in oppression.

Contents

1

Flight

My life, as it is now, began the day I left Iran at the age of nine. I've spent my adult years protecting that little Iranian girl from being erased, because that day was also the day life as she knew it ended. She never saw her friends, her cousins, or her school again. She had to learn most truths about daily life over again. Little of what had shaped her as a person — who she was or wanted to be — would exist in her new home. In fact, she would only encounter a small roomful of people who looked like her, knew her language or world, either in person or in fiction.

I think of that nine-year-old girl often and wonder where she would be now had her life not been unhinged so suddenly, so deliberately, when she boarded that plane. Still in Iran, now in her thirties, she would speak and think and dream in Farsi, abilities I lost so fast it was almost traumatic once I realised they were gone. She might be a lawyer too. That much is possible. Maybe the urge to rebel and speak out is innate in us, so the oppression would be too hard for her to bear in silence. Maybe that oppression has made her stronger, a real-life freedom fighter, which I can't claim given that all this freedom I'm now afforded in Aotearoa takes some of the rebellion out of the outspokenness. Maybe she paid that terrible price we were all fearful of: ending up in the notorious Evin prison.

Or perhaps, under the weight of convention, she would be married and have children now. I wonder, does knowing what is expected of you make it easier to feel contented or complete?

I recall that nine-year-old's strong sense of self, which has never been whole in me again. Leaving my homeland as a child has suspended me between worlds, so it is never possible for me to be fully Iranian — but the experience of having fled Iran is exactly why I will never be 'fully' anything else either. The experience of leaving makes the identity of a foreigner forever more acute. It binds us to other children of foreign origin as a tribe, more so than to our own original or adopted cultures. Given I will never know who I would have been had I not left Iran, I must have begun existing the day we flew out of our then homeland, never to return.

That day was greeted as a triumph. It wasn't an ending; it was a fresh start. Getting out was something everyone around me spoke about for as long as I could remember. Enforcement of what the regime called Islamic law had begun in earnest the year I was born, as did the bloody eight-year war waged against Saddam Hussein's Iraq. My childhood was peopled with a generation of adults in a state of perpetual shock as new oppressions and indignities flooded their lives, as an army of amputees returned from war, as weeping mothers mourned their martyred sons. Once in a while, people would disappear. That meant either exile, prison, or, as we'd discover some time later, death at the hands of the regime. For us, it was exile that released all that pressure and fear that had defined our daily lives. No wonder then that I walked onto that plane determined to shed everything, the good with the bad. What wouldn't you give to be free from fear?

My memory of that morning in late September 1990 begins with waking up in my uncle M'ammad's apartment in Tehran. It was before sunrise, cold and half-dark. We were drowsy automatons, going through the motions of getting dressed and putting the last of our things into already-packed bags, while being careful not to wake M'ammad's daughters, who were around my age and had school later that day.

Tehran traffic was notorious even then, even at dawn, so we were leaving hours before our flight. Driving in my uncle's car, I remember the grey smoggy sky, the crush of apartment blocks, and roads with so many vehicles jammed on them that the lane markings were meaningless.

I hadn't grown up in Tehran. I had spent my childhood moving between Mashhad and Urmia, where my dad's and mum's families were, and thought of these places as home. Mashhad in the north-east — near the border with Afghanistan — is a big dusty suburban city, nothing like the cosmopolitan Tehran. It's famous as the second city of Shi'a Islam. Urmia is right across the country in the north-west, almost bordering Turkey. Green and lush, it's home to an open secularism that comes with diversity, where Sunni, Shi'a, Jewish and Armenian communities happily mingle. But the final scenes of Iran in my mind are of that tense drive in the grey Tehran dawn.

Tehran was the last of three rounds of goodbyes we made. At no point did we tell anyone of our intention to flee, but no one was in doubt about that. It was an extraordinary expense for people like us to go on an overseas tour to begin with, and truly bizarre to go around conscientiously saying a fond farewell to people in person before what was supposedly just a two-week trip. In Mashhad, where I was born and we lived, we took a few days to visit my parents' best friends and close relatives, including my grandma and two uncles' families. I remember the extended tight hugs; the kisses on each cheek, then each cheek again; the squeezed hands; the welled-up tears fought back. These goodbyes were profound for their permanence.

I know the hardest goodbye that round was my dad's to his mum, Maman Naz (lovely mama), as she was to me. He had been a self-professed and proud mama's boy his whole life, and they remained close until she passed away in October 2017. Since we never felt safe enough to go back into Iran, he never got to see her as her health declined, even when she was moved to hospice care. He couldn't go home for the funeral.

As difficult as those Mashhad goodbyes were, they were a picnic compared to the harrowing scene at Urmia airport before we flew to Tehran for our final leg.

My mother is the middle child of seven. They grew up largely on vineyards in Western Azerbaijan, which my grandma's family had owned for generations. The women of my mother's family are passionate people, remarkably loving and extraordinarily close to one another. We split our time between Mashhad and Urmia during my childhood in Iran, because my mother could hardly bear to be apart from them. That closeness seems to be deeply rooted in their Kurdish heritage and a deep connection with their homeland — the vineyards of Western Azerbaijan. I always felt like an observer of this, since I never became proficient in their native dialect. But even being a little on the outside, the warmth of their familial culture was always electric.

Even though Iranian vineyards couldn't make wine after the revolution, my grandmother held on to them as well as growing other kinds of fruits and walnuts. We spent a lot of time there on the land, the whole family chatting and preparing food, eating and laughing hysterically at a series of much-repeated in-jokes. There was generally a party on weekend nights. Members of the enormous extended family took turns hosting, and we all danced the traditional Kurdish line dance with scarves. All this happened at fever pitch on our last short visit before leaving the country.

My mother always said she married a man from across the country so she could get away and find her independence, but I think moving to Mashhad only intensified her sense of belonging to her own people, and they to her. When we left, the tears came hot and fast. Almost the whole family was there: her two sisters, her brother, all their children, her aunts, and their adult children. My grandmother's two youngest children, my aunt and uncle, had escaped the country soon after the revolution. She hadn't seen either of them for a decade, and still felt that loss keenly. At the airport, she was visibly distraught, though trying hard to hold it together for my mum as we said goodbye. It was a whirlwind, given the number of people. I felt overwhelmed, as I usually did with the emotional openness on that side of the family. I'd never been too demonstrative, and I remember feeling guilty that I wasn't crying and clutching at everyone the way they were all doing. I also remember, most vividly, that my little grandma had to be restrained by security, because she kept walking through the barriers beyond where only ticket-holding travellers could go. She kept ignoring everyone and walking faster, calling for my mum to turn around so she could get a final look at her face. They were speaking in their dialect, Azeri, which I understood enough to know that they were reassuring each other, laughing about the next time we would all sit and eat my grandma's giant Turkish meatballs together. I felt lucky to be permitted in that inner sanctum; it was unconditional love made palpable, so it was harrowing to have it ripped away. We never ate meatballs with my grandma again.

For my part I was acutely aware of the fact we were leaving for good and prepared for it silently in the weeks preceding. I had listened to those whispered conversations about fleeing, about seeking asylum, and about the few people we knew who had made it out. I knew it was a kind of salvation. I wasn't afraid of it, but I knew people didn't really come back.

I made a concerted effort to take snapshots in my mind's eye of every special place and person I was parting with. I still carry these with me. I would sit on my bed and look in each direction for a few seconds, without blinking. I wanted to particularly remember the white-and-pink closet wall unit across the back wall of my room, which we had painted ourselves only a year or so earlier. I was proud of the colour scheme, which I had chosen myself.

On its shelves was an overflow of books, ranging from picture books to young adult books, which I had just begun reading and loved, all in Farsi. The last Farsi books I read were a biography of Helen Keller and a little compendium of the biographies of important historical figures like Gandhi and Abraham Lincoln, illustrated with watercolour portraits. I would lie on the floor in a sea of chaos, switching between different books, which would inevitably be left strewn across the carpet. (I never did learn to put things back once I was done playing with them. It was the bane of my mother's life.) It wouldn't be until twenty years later, when it was finally safe for my aunt to send them, that I would get to see and hold a few books from my precious collection again.

On the top shelf above the books sat dozens of tiny glass animals. I had been collecting them for a couple of years with my pocket money. They weren't expensive, but it would still take me a few weeks to save up for one. Then I would go to the mall and spend hours examining all the animals, from exotic lions and tigers to farm animals like little pink pigs, before very carefully choosing my next purchase. It was a whole production marked with build-up and ceremony.

I'd sit on my bed, looking at all these objects to memorise their places, textures and colours. This slow, deliberate process of letting go was necessary. It meant that, even now, I remember how everything sat around our home, and in my friends' rooms. I even know what times of day we visited significant people in our lives before we left, because I remember how the light hit people's faces.

I couldn't take any of these things with me, because we couldn't let on that we were leaving forever. That would have set off alarm bells.

We were lucky that exit visas had become more available in that winter after the war with Iraq had ended, though they were still limited. They came in the form of lucrative tours to select countries that allowed Iranians entry (read: other Islamic states or those who were not themselves signatories to the Refugee Convention). We were booked to take some kind of luxury tour of Singapore and Malaysia that, for a holiday, cost a huge amount. I assume this was how the tour operators could secure the exit visas, through some serious kickbacks up the chain. We had spent almost our entire life's savings and abandoned everything for the tickets out. We looked at it, though, as an investment in our freedom. It was a secure way out, in among a group, organised by people who had a business interest in getting us out. But there was no guarantee until that plane was in the air with us on board.

We had to look the part, so packing for this trip was as bizarre as the journey itself. We knew we would be searched and questioned ad nauseam as we left the country. We couldn't risk any sign that we were leaving for good. We bought new clothes to wear on the plane to look the part of international travellers. We packed light bags. I was only allowed a couple of toys, and about ten days' worth of outfits. I chose two of my favourite tiny china figurines, a cat and badger, gifted by my friend Jeiran, and two soft toys, a scruffy yellow teddy-bear and a fluffy elephant.

No one tells you how warped life has to get before you realise you have to leave forever. Leaving Iran was such a long time coming that it already felt historic in the chronology of my nine-year life, even as it was happening. Maybe that's why I remember it with such filmic detail and in bursts of significant scenes.

My uncle dropped us off at Tehran Airport, which was chaotic and overflowing with people. I was constantly being pressed into a towering adult in front of me — not my mum or dad necessarily — as entire families hustled past nervously. Everyone was either a uniformed official or travellers in their best curated Islamic dress, in black, grey, brown, with maybe white or navy thrown in. No one dared stand out. For women, there had been a decade of tugging forward hijabs, checking and re-checking if their outfits were loose enough, long enough, didn't look too expensive or 'foreign'. I'm always shocked and fascinated by how Iranian women have pushed back those first overbearing dress codes to a place where they can now wear jeans in public.

There was immense tension in every encounter with officials in that first post-revolutionary decade. The airport embodied the absolute pinnacle of that tension. Not only were we coming face to face with a wall of regime officials, searching every inch of our belongings and person, but we were seeking the most contentious of privileges — to leave the regime's realm of control. This was a realm where everything from phone lines to private conversations in places of work were surveilled, where everything from the evening news to the strands of hair on a woman's head was jealously watched over by the 'Guardians of the Revolution'. Leaving could be considered high treason. Of course, just about anything could be considered treason, and anyone could disappear into a torture chamber or quietly appear in a shallow grave for just mouthing off to one of these officials. Playing the wrong music at a wedding, reading the wrong book, wearing a tie — any of these things could indicate your allegiances were offside. It was that constant state of terror that marked my childhood. I felt it too with all the adults at that airport. It meant I wanted to leave as badly as my parents, who were escaping a much more tangible personal danger.

There was an inexhaustible variety of officials to placate: immigration officers, ordinary guards, Pasdars (the regime's moral police or, more accurately, militia). We were separated by gender and strip-searched in little curtained cubicles. I kept close to my mother and silently let the woman in the black shroud inspect my shoes and pat under my clothes. Then there was the grilling. They spat questions at us, at everyone, and moved us about the place. They used the demeaning familiar tense, which in Farsi is used to denote hierarchy akin to a master addressing a servant, and is rarely used between strangers except by adults addressing children. That's how the regime spoke to its public: '*Biya*,' '*Boro*,' '*Baz kon*,' '*Bedeh be man*' — 'Come,' 'Go,' 'Open this,' 'Give me that.' They demanded women hand over jewellery, separated families for interrogation. Women tugged their hijabs forward on their foreheads and tried not to make eye contact. Everyone made appeals to God and the prophet, his daughter Fatimah, in rhythmic chants. At the airport, stakes were high. Everyone involved knew what the right answers were, how to give them, the personas to adopt, but the power of forcing the charade was enough for the officials. The anxiety and contempt we all felt was not enough to stop them.

Once all the searches and questioning was over, we were ready to push on, but not before I caused a near disaster that almost changed everything. My dad had given me a small zipped bag to hold, a man bag if you will. He told me to hold on to it for a minute, to not put it down. Then he turned to deal with the man searching our final bag. By this stage, I had been up since dawn, and was drowsy and overwhelmed. I must have put that little bag down the moment he passed it to me. When he turned back to grab the bag, I didn't have it. It wasn't on the ground, not on the counter next to me. It had vanished. Panic set in. He became frantic, asking me where I had put it. My mum got involved, telling him he shouldn't have given it to a child, interrogating the guards nearby. It turned out that little zipped bag, which I can still somehow see so vividly, held all our passports, documents and whatever amount of cash we were allowed to exchange and take with us. No one standing near me could tell us where the bag had gone. Within a few minutes, they put a call on the airport intercom and threatened to close the exits in the main area. Then, the guard standing next to me reached up to a cubby hole above the security check line and pulled the bag out. He could suddenly see it, he said. We thanked him, but not without shooting accusatory looks at him. We were close to tears and shaking.

We boarded the plane and sat with me between my parents, busily straightening ourselves out, buckling seatbelts, performing a shaky calm. The plane finally took off, but that isn't the end of it for Iranians. The real collective sigh of relief comes when the pilot declares us in international airspace. Back then at least, many women would defiantly pull off their hijabs; my mother did. Despite the curated boarding process, she didn't miss her first chance at shedding the possessive control of the regime. I promptly fell asleep and woke up just before landing as dazed as I was that morning, but we hurried through a far simpler airport experience, and finally into the colourful balmy new world. That initial joyous escape has drawn me back to South-east Asia again and again, but it was short lived during that first trip.

Our brief visit to Malaysia and Singapore was tense. It felt like an eternity of holding our breaths and trying to act natural, waiting for the moment to skip out to our real destination. Hilariously, none of the other Iranians on that tour were there to explore South-east Asia either. No one had any interest in sampling the local cuisine or seeing the water puppet shows on our schedule. Most of them were there to buy electronics to import back to Iran, breaking trade sanctions. There was almost no attempt to disguise this once we landed, and the tour organisers didn't seem too worried.

We knew the right to claim asylum was not available in Malaysia or Singapore, so we couldn't stay. We were there to play the part of tourists while we secretly invested all we had in flights to anywhere with a stopover in Auckland. A cousin of my dad's lived in New Zealand with his family, which was why we were trying to go there. Complicating matters, we needed the flight to leave at around the same time as our return flight to Iran so the tour organisers weren't alerted to our leaving early. I can barely imagine the fear my parents lived under. Iranians weren't supposed to do anything without regime approval, least of all move freely outside the regime's realm of power. Everyone could be a spy and a fair few were.

At some point, my dad managed to buy the tickets we needed, headed to Tonga with a stopover in Auckland, where we planned to claim asylum. Claiming asylum is the process by which a refugee applies to have their refugee status recognised, once they enter a country like New Zealand where the Refugee Convention is law. Before that, we are 'asylum seekers'. Claiming asylum is not only legal in New Zealand; it is a fundamental human right. The right was recognised in the aftermath of the Holocaust, after the 'civilised' Western world reckoned with the harrowing reality that it had blocked its borders and actually turned back ships loaded with asylum seekers escaping Nazi persecution. We collectively recognise that refugees have a right to claim asylum, because without that right most other human rights they hold are undermined. In fact, it is specifically illegal to sanction refugees for being without passports or using false travel documents, since the first step to persecution is usually to make travel impossible for the persecuted group. The Third Reich cancelled Jewish citizenship rights well before the death camps came to be, making the killings possible, as it made it possible for the world to turn its back. For refugees lucky enough to escape or even to afford travel, leaving solves only half the problem. Arriving in a country that recognises those rights is an equally formidable obstacle to safety. Even though the *St Louis* made it out of Nazi Germany with thousands on board, the fact she was not allowed to dock once she made it to the United States is why around a third of the returned refugees on that ship were later murdered in the death camps.

Landing in Auckland Airport without visas to enter New Zealand meant we had to escape from the transit lounge to access our rights. The anxiety of our time in that white transit room was a whole fresh hell. Stakes were far higher now — we were actually in danger of being returned, which would mark us as dissidents attempting to flee. I knew we could lose everything, that my parents could be imprisoned. I knew that in Iran people were tortured and killed in prison. Everyone talked about the number of dozens of lashes people were given for infractions like drinking alcohol. Everyone talked about executions as a pretty common end to an arrest or disappearance. We knew at least two people who had met with that end already. So I sat silently as my parents tried to figure out the exits. At least at the gauntlet of Tehran Airport, we knew the rules. We knew what to say, how to dress, what to hide. Now in an unfamiliar place, we were suddenly helpless. That was the first time I realised that, from now on, my parents would not have the answers to most of our everyday problems. They had no experience of the systems or social protocol, and only basic English they picked up in university courses years ago. It was useless to tell officials we were refugees in the transit area because we had no right to claim asylum outside of New Zealand (which technically the transit area was) and no right to enter. That would, in fact, ensure we were watched and sent away.

So we sat and waited for an eternity. Finally, we got up the courage to walk out toward the escalator, but we were intercepted. It makes me laugh to think of it now. The person stopping us was trying to be helpful. He asked if we were lost, because we were leaving the transit lounge. We assumed he was there to make sure people didn't escape, so we thanked him and went back to our seats. After another lifetime of staring at the clock and straightening our clothes nervously, we made another dash for it. This time we weren't stopped. I still think about that moment when I stepped on the escalator separating international space from New Zealand soil. The set-up is completely different now, but I like to think it's the same cosmic stairway.

Once we reached the ground floor, we scrambled for the first official-looking person and told him we were refugees and asked to be processed. We were taken aside to a desk where two people in uniform interviewed us. Their manner was warm and casual, without alarm or hostility. My parents were audibly relieved and grateful. Their first question to me, half mimed and translated back by my overwhelmed parents, was, 'Are you hungry?' I still can't think of that moment without fighting back hot tears. I said

I was fine. Then they asked us if we were carrying any fruit or plant products. We said no, but my shoe had come off and there was a leaf in it, which was taken away for scientific study or cremation. Then we were given the opportunity to exercise our right to speak with a lawyer. Our relations here had given us the name and phone number for Coral Shaw, later Judge Shaw, who spoke to Immigration and agreed to help us.

We made one more phone call, to my dad's cousin. He came to fetch us from the airport. That's right: we were released into the wild, having been given access to food, legal rights and community support within the first hour of being in this new place. It felt like landing on a warm beach and taking a deep breath after almost drowning. We were exhausted and elated. The adults talked and talked in the car ride home. My parents exchanged stories with my dad's cousin about all the luck we had had making it here. He told them a little about Auckland, about the roads, or shops or whatever we happened to pass. I sat quietly behind the driver's seat, taking in the scenery. Auckland was cool and humid after some rain. I thought the houses looked like the thatched houses from cartoons, with the pitched roofs we didn't have in Iran. I had been drawing houses like that my whole life even though Iranian houses had flat roofs. I remember the colours and the light were so different than in Asia. The blues seemed lighter, more aqua; the greens were almost in soft focus. Mostly, I remember that there was just so much green — open lawns in front of every house, more parks and reserves than I'd ever seen in my life. It felt profound to me that the place that had become synonymous with freedom would be filled with nature. I knew immediately that I was going to like it here. That I was going to be okay.

2

After the revolution

It was a decade of upheaval that brought us to Tehran Airport that grey morning. Understanding our flight means knowing also what we lost and gained thereafter. My childhood years in 1980s Iran saw the inception of images and rhetoric about us as angry 'Islamists' which allowed current perceptions of the Middle East, but particularly Iran as embodying some 'Axis of Evil', inherently aggressive and at war with the West. Meanwhile we lived the lives of ordinary people under so much frightening oppression that we ultimately abandoned our home forever. It is important to know what that looked like from the inside, because, for most refugees, that part of our lives is what is lost to the world. The tragedy for my family — for refugees the world over — is that our nation's descent into fundamentalism, violence, and general instability was not only the basis for our flight, but the basis of the prejudice against us in our new lives.

By the time I was born, in January 1981, Iranians were in the eye of the storm. The 'Islamic Revolution', as the post-revolutionary regime came to call it, was over, but the reality of its aftermath was yet to set in. For secular Iranians like my family, it felt like my generation were born into a hyper-politicised world experiencing a catastrophic downward spiral. But there was that tiny window immediately before and after the revolution when the best was possible. Our parents had changed their world, toppled the old guard. They were empowered and brave and, in that moment, free. That was the Iran I was born into.

What ultimately shaped my childhood was the panic that set in as that idealism and fervour turned into confusion and defeat for the adults around me. That played out against the backdrop of a bloody war against Saddam Hussein's Iraq.

Only eighteen months or so before I was born, almost everyone in our vast, diverse, ancient country was either directly affected by or personally involved in a colossal uprising. I have realised that what I know of the revolution is reflective of the sentiment held tight by my parents' cohort of secular university students, Leftists, who marched against the Shah but did not see the Islamic regime as its end point. Their memory is not uniformly representative of Iranian revolutionaries, certainly not of the vast numbers who did march for Islam, the poor Shi'a majority who were in different ways lifted by the regime that came. The Iranian Revolution was one of the largest popular revolutions in modern history. Millions of people from all walks of life put their bodies on the line to protest the authoritarian monarchy and nationalise the oil resource. The revolutionaries were students, Socialists, Communists, Islamists, and ordinary people aching for change. The thing that made their revolution both incredibly special and deeply tragic is that it was a true grassroots movement, driven by the desire for democracy, social justice, and independence. It came as a total shock to the rest of the world, because Iran was not experiencing an obvious financial or political crisis that would necessitate regime change. Revolutions ordinarily follow economic collapse, unsuccessful war, or military coup.

That this revolution was driven by the people and during relative calm betrays an uncanny level of socio-political awareness among a huge proportion of that now-oppressed people. They didn't accept what the Shah had offered. They were not satisfied with mere secularism, a halfway democracy, or just a bit of access to their nation's great oil wealth. They rejected the corruption and violence by the Shah's own secret police, the SAVAK, who killed and tortured dissidents. They revolted, screaming for public services like education in the provinces and quality public healthcare, and protesting against government spying. They understood the way foreign interference and internal nepotism was affecting their democracy. They weren't giddy about the embrace of American presidents and European monarchs. They were not content with wearing mini-skirts and listening to The Beatles as if they were Westerners. They wanted substantive equality with the West; a democracy in function, not just form. It is important to remember that the revolutionary generation of Iranians were Middle Easterners who revolted because they had an understanding of their place in the international world order as equals. They believed themselves deserving of representative democracy and human rights.

That they were successful in bringing regime change is magical. That their revolution was so completely hijacked as to leave them far more oppressed than ever before is a heartbreak that this generation has never overcome. In triumph, they became the forgotten voices of their generation, of Iran, and of the Middle East. They then watched the world reimagine them as a faceless mass of 'backward' Islamists holding the US Embassy hostage, perpetually at war or endlessly ignorant, a humiliation that shaped my life as it became my parents' burden. We have been defined in varying degrees by the idea that we are fundamentalists or violent as we interact with the world around us as refugees. We remain simultaneously victim escapees and suspects of collusion with our own abusers.

By the time I was old enough to remember, all that was left of that enormous popular uprising were comically large and inescapably recurrent images of the Ayatollah Khomeini overwhelming every public space. His brow, always in a knit, and his eyes, scornful, presided over our lives. He was in every classroom, above the counter at the corner store, always in the background of whatever was on TV. The image of Khomeini with a black turban and a piercing stare is burned in my mind's eye as the defining image of my childhood in Iran. It still makes me shudder to think about, as I suspect it was designed to do. By then, it was *his* revolution and *his* Iran. The narrative was simplified to one of an Islamic Revolution aimed at bringing the Ayatollah to supreme power, and sold, lock, stock, and barrel, by both the regime itself and the Western media.

This was what created the panic in my parents and their contemporaries. They were on the outside with all the world, and outsiders in their homeland. They were written out of history and driven underground in Iran itself, even as they were part of a victorious majority only moments earlier.

*

I learned a different narrative about the revolution from those idealists parenting my friends and me. They frantically told us their story, over and over, looking to set it straight. They were looking for redemption. They needed us to know that they had not meant the harm that came.

Once the Shah was deposed, a gaping power vacuum emerged and was filled at whirlwind pace by the charismatic Ayatollah. He had been exiled as a dissident by the Shah years before and had become a dissident leader to various extents since. But the revolution was in no way a monolithic movement of his followers. So how had the Ayatollah emerged and consolidated power so thoroughly?

A big part of the problem was inequality. I think what the students and Leftist revolutionaries like my parents had underestimated is that the working-class masses were not being brought along by the political movement that purported to represent their interests. That is a common blind spot I can now see in Leftist politics from first-hand experience. So while the secular revolutionary groups were fighting to nationalise oil and end imperialism in order to address poverty, those actually living in poverty resented them. They were seen as part of the same elitist class structure oppressing the poor.

The Islamist wing of the revolution spoke directly to the working classes, who were broadly more religious, and had suffered discrimination and abuse as the Shah's 'modernisation' agenda was imposed upon the country at a fast pace. Women of my grandmothers' generation had in fact been forcibly stripped of their hijabs, which must have felt similar to Muslim school girls when they were forced to remove their daily garb under French law in 2004. While the secular revolutionaries were wearing the latest '70s protest wear and dancing in co-ed clubs, the religious poor felt excluded from modern cultural and economic development.

Eventually, the imposition of Islamic rule was successfully framed by the regime as a class win. In a solidly Trumpish move, the Islamic regime told us it was ridding Iran of elite cronyism as it appointed its own thoroughly underqualified people to high office in every arena of life. In turn, it won an army of working-class defenders. The religious poor were called upon to impose strict Islamic codes, whether as moral police, or in any leadership role previously closed off to them, including at universities. The vetting of institutions was done swiftly and caused a mass exodus of intellectuals, experts and others with actual experience in every sector. Thus, as has happened again and again all around the world, a revolt against inequality was transformed into a culture of anti-intellectualism via an appeal to pseudo-religious rites.

It is important to note that even those who did support or admire the Ayatollah before the revolution mostly had no idea of his intention to lead the next regime as an Islamic dictator, which he quickly became for all intents and purposes. Yes, Iran is a constitutional democracy in name, with regular elections and high voter participation. In reality, the Grand Ayatollah has the final word on most things, including who may run as a candidate in elections. That, at least, is specified transparently in their system. But even where the constitution safeguards democracy, like the separation of powers between the courts and government, these laws have never been upheld.

A parallel 'Revolutionary' system, imposed in the earliest days of the revolution, trumps the law of the land, from the Revolutionary Guard who police dissidence with total impunity to the Revolutionary Courts who impose harsh sanctions extrajudicially and in secret. To what extent democracy can be said to exist in the context of a moral police and torture chambers is not really a question for most of us. None of this was ever part of the revolution's purpose, or foreseen by the vast number screaming against the Shah's own corrupt political crackdowns.

Having inherited the need to make these points at every opportunity, I devoted my Master's thesis at Oxford to exposing this constitutional hypocrisy. The Iranian justice system enforces the death penalty at one of the highest rates in the world. I set my mind to a study of what defines an institution as 'judicial'. Transparency and independence from political entities came up in every human rights–based definition, in every region. We are taught that human rights and justice itself is a Western ideal, but, from the African system to the Koran itself, the basics of what we see as fairness in modern Western judicial systems appear again and again. My study concluded that there is a broad consensus that an institution can't call itself a 'judicial institution', a court of law, unless it is politically independent, transparent, applies pre-existing law and provides for effective defence against its accusations. Iranian executions emanating from the Revolutionary Courts are not exercises of judicial sanction. They are targeted political murder.

As the new regime revealed its brutality, it quickly eclipsed the Shah's tyranny in every way. For one thing, it never made the mistake of sending opponents to exile only to have them reemerge some time later. If they got away, it followed them. Even in Europe, Iranian refugees were being assassinated for their political affiliations in the 1980s. Back home, the population lived in confused terror. The nation that had just led a record uprising for democracy now grew mass graves of Communists, Socialists, Mojahedin (anti-government rebels), teenagers who handed out political flyers. It felt like everyone had family and friends who had been captured, lashed, tortured or killed. Those conversations became the norm, including among my parents and their friends. They inevitably would not realise that we children had emerged for a snack or forget we were nearby playing, so we could often overhear such conversations. They were in shock. That much was obvious. It became normal to be afraid for your parents, your older siblings, your cousins, your friends' parents. By the time I have a living memory of life in Iran, Iranians lived in constant fear of their own government.

Worse still, the regime itself formed the same old allegiances, propped up via cheap oil sales for weapons bought from the USA, even Israel. All the while it forced us all to chant death to both those nations before class every morning and on TV every night. Like the Shah, the Islamic Republic was an oppressive regime backed by foreign powers, while Iranians fell to new depths of inequality.

The regime is one thing, but we know as Iranians that Iran has been constantly under siege, from the Iran–Iraq war to the ongoing US sanctions, renewed aggressively by the Trump administration with the persistent threat of war. Iran is held back, as its neighbours have been, by internal dictatorship and deliberate external oppression.

In 2011, when the Arab Spring first hit the news in New Zealand, my dad asked, 'So who's behind all this?'

I responded, 'Students. It's a popular uprising.'

He smiled a father-knows-better smile that made me feel naïve. 'That's what we thought in 1979. It's either Islamists or the army, propped up by the West,' he said. What he meant is that, as opaque and complex as politics is in the Middle East, we can't know for sure who the political actors really are. I didn't disagree.

The experiences and trauma of my parents' generation marked the lives of their children. My parents were actively involved in the protest movement of the revolution. Both in their early twenties, idealistic and political, they marched every day during the height of revolt. My friends, cousins, and I all grew up with stories of those mass marches, the chanting, the violence. It sounded scary, but also exhilarating. The stories were sometimes told with breathless excitement about just how many people turned out to march, or how the Shah couldn't subdue them even when the army was sent out, even as tanks rolled out. They kept marching and chanting in the face of death because they wanted freedom. They wanted the West to know that Iranians could see through this crony Emperor, that they could take their country back. Other times, the tone of their stories was sombre. There was an apologetic resentment about the outcome. They shook their heads at their own dumb idealism, at the fact that they thought they would ever be able to take their country back, at the notion that the West would ever let the Middle East own its own resource. Our revolution had happened soon after the oil price hikes in the 1970s, which lost our Shah a little of his Western support base. It all seems so clear now. Maybe the West was ready to deal with a real dictator rather than a halfway one. Either way, whether the overthrow of the Shah was really led by the people or nudged along by external forces, what was clear in 1980s Iran was that they had not chosen their new leaders. They were confused and panicked, never sure how it had all gone so wrong.

They asserted over and over that they were marching against corruption and not for religion. They talked a lot about the Shah selling their nation off to the West, about the huge gap between the haves and have-nots in such a rich country, about the lack of regional infrastructure. They gave far too much detail, truth be told. That was because the Shah years were fast seeming like a lost paradise. They wanted it noted that he was brutal and ineffective, but they did not revolt against his secularism. They didn't mean for women to be forced into Islamic dress. They weren't savages. They didn't say that part out loud, but they seemed very concerned that the world and their children would think just that, because the revolution had done a lot to take the country backward. The history books were closing in around them, blaming them for dragging one of the most advanced and stable countries in the Middle East 'back to the dark ages'.

Much of the retelling was about their 'free' lives before the revolution. They were telling us who they were, who they had been, hoping the oral history would protect them from complete erasure. That generation — at least the middle-class student revolutionaries around me — retold stories about wearing the latest mod styles, indulging in hippy culture with flared jeans and long androgynous hair, at parties with any manner of the latest Western music or the likes of Googoosh (the Iranian queen of pop) playing, as if they were creation myths. Without them, we might forget who we really were and suddenly believe in the Ayatollah.

When I read Shirin Ebadi's autobiography, *Iran Awakening*, I smiled reading over the descriptions of how Westernised life in Tehran was, how Ebadi and her fiancé met in cafés where young men and women mingled freely. I was struck by the similarity in tone and detail to the stories my parents told. Even to the renowned lawyer and Nobel Laureate, it was important to remember how 'modern' and 'normal' Iranians would be were it not for the current regime. To that generation, painting that image was as urgent as exalting the true purpose of the revolution. It is important to note that the Islamic Regime's interpretation of Shi'a Islam or its enforcement were not based on what the majority of those responsible for revolution had understood to be Iranian culture, although most did identify broadly as Muslim, whether practising or not, and as nationalists.

The compulsion with which these stories are told betrays a sad truth that, as Iranians, we need to tell stories about how Westernised Iran was, in reaction to prejudice that portrays being Middle Eastern as somehow backward and repressed. Central to all this was the affirmation that Iranians were part of the contemporary world. There is truth to the descriptions too, though the experiences were not universal to all Iranians; in fact, the majority were not indulging in lifestyles or fashions that get trotted out now to prove how great Iran was before the revolution. But it was a bit true, and constantly retold to me. My dad was well into The Beatles, and he's still pretty committed to Pink Floyd and the Eagles, though to mid-twentieth-century Iranians, European cinema and music were just as engaging as American pop culture.

Given everything had to be dubbed anyway, the Anglo world didn't have a huge advantage in reaching Iranian audiences. To my parents and their set, the sky-high hairstyles and knee-high boots were Brigitte Bardot references. Their own cutting-edge popular music and cinema interwove and built upon Western themes. Women in Iranian magazines and pop culture embraced everything from 1960s mod to flowing hippy styles mixed in with their own signature coaled eyes and gold jewellery.

My mother and her three sisters were big into cat-eye make-up and perilously high hemlines. They wore their hair in razored layers or flat with a centre part — some fusion of Euro-mod and Middle Eastern hippy. A lot of their photos from this time show them dancing in big groups of young people in a line, as Kurdish people do, wearing mini dresses, bright patterns, and laughing brightly. Maybe there's some fancy shisha in the corner just out of shot. My mum talks about how they all went off after school on Thursdays to buy cheap bright fabrics, so they could sew new dresses to wear out that night. Friday is the end-of-week holiday in Iran so Thursday night was prime time. They would go to parties, cafés or music joints with all their friends and relatives. As long as I can remember, Mum would recite these stories of how they would all dance with boys and wear the latest fashions. She had anecdotes about the boys sometimes falling in love with her or one of her sisters or friends. They would sneak their phone numbers into the girl's coat pockets. Then she would talk about where each person ended up. This person escaped to Canada. This one didn't get out in time and skipped the draft, so they were in hiding. That one became a Mojahed and was living underground in Germany. These were my fairytales.

My dad had been just such a boy at some point, joining their group one summer when he came to town to stay with his older sister. He was studying engineering at Shiraz University, and wanted to be with family over the holidays. His sister and her husband and children, who were around my mum's age in their late teens, were renting the upstairs flat from my mum's family. My dad had been played up as their young, fashionable uncle. Photos show him sporting a grown out flop hair-do and on-point side burns with a distinctive moustache, which he didn't shave off until his fifties, here in New Zealand. He wore a lot of fitted button-down shirts in various patterns and huge 1970s-style collars. He also seemed to have gone on frequent co-ed ski trips with his brothers and their girlfriends. There were photos of snow fights and women wearing jeans, walking around with their male cohort, everyone's floppy hair flying around their heads. I remember all these photos with enduring detail, because, to my post-revolutionary Iranian child's eye, they were extraordinary. The images of the girls in the outdoors, at school, in cafés, wearing dresses and flowers in their hair, standing next to male friends and boyfriends were mesmerising. They were from a time and place, a utopia, that could not be.

I know all my friends heard the same stories. These tales became essential myths to us kids, told to us so that we could retell them, as if our own identities as civilised members of modern human society depended upon preserving those memories.

I think the stories they told us focused on dress and gender interactions because that became the immediate frontline of oppression under the Islamic regime. For women, the frontlines were our bodies and how much we surrendered them to the will of this new patriarchy. Of course, the frontline of most feminism has been women's bodies, but this patriarchy looked different to what Iranian and Western feminists had thus far encountered. We were no longer being judged by how attractive we were to men, though our outward appearance remained the centre of dispute. We were not expected to adhere to common beauty standards or accept objectification. This was the exact opposite of the battle being fought by second-wave feminists in the 1970s. Iranian women were forcibly *de*sexualised, stripped of colour, and made shapeless in public life. The female form was effectively outlawed, shunned from view altogether. An affirming interpretation was that a woman's value must not lie in her physical allure to men, and the regime would protect us against that. In part, the idea was that objectification of women was an evil begotten of Western imperialist influence. The covering was itself presented as a nationalistic win.

The way this law was explained to me in Iran, by teachers and self-appointed guardians of that law, was through the Koranic verse that told women to guard our modesty. It's a simple verse that also instructs men to avert their eyes. As has often been argued, it is very unclear whether any particular kind of covering is required here, or whether it should cover women's hair or bodies, but many Muslims and enforcers of various types of Sharia have interpreted this to mean a head covering or full-body cloak-like cover. It's worth noting, though, that covering a woman's hair for religious modesty is not exclusive to Muslims, and probably arose from regional culture, since we see it in other Abrahamic religious practices.

To me, whatever the covering, the risk comes from interpretations of the verse that say a woman must guard her modesty or she may incite sinful thoughts and actions in men. The idea that we might 'incite' lust, adultery, or even sexual assault, and that we are responsible in part for minimising that risk, is not only found in interpretations of Islam. As women, still responding to questions about the length of our hemlines in court, we know they exist in all cultures. In Iran, the proponents of this law openly espoused that it was necessary for a woman's safety and respectability to keep herself covered. In effect, our bodies were being kept from sight for the pleasure of our husbands or future husbands alone. Our government treated us as temptresses, capable of being party to our own objectification, and a risk to public morality.

The immediate and indisputable wrong was that women were no longer allowed to choose for themselves. The reverse of this imposition came a generation before it when women were stripped of their right to wear the hijab — something modern Western and non-Western nations are now adopting under the guise of protecting women's rights and advancing cultural unity. At the time, a majority of women had voluntarily moved away from the practice of wearing hijabs, but a large number of women chose to wear the covering. The forcible removal of that right was equally traumatic and deeply degrading to those who did believe the covering to be part of their religious duty and culture.

A perhaps unforeseen and little studied effect of the post-revolutionary imposition of Islamic dress was the rise of feminism among working class and religious sectors of Iranian society. Those women were suddenly empowered to take part in public life with far fewer restrictions than before. Devoutly religious families were suddenly able to send their daughters or wives to work and study in environments where they were now safe to practise their religion through dress. A different demographic of women was suddenly gaining university degrees and holding positions of authority. Of course, that change would not become apparent for some years. In the immediate post-revolutionary decade, the crisis was in the regime's overwhelmingly strict and often violent imposition of control over women's bodies and behaviour.

My generation, and those who came after, never got to see women and men interacting freely in public. That was something we only knew from bootleg films. We never got to see women's hair completely uncovered, or their bare limbs, in public. We never saw men and women hug or hold hands without some trepidation.

That being said, Iran, even under the Islamic regime, has never required women to wear a full-length shrouds (chadors) or cover our faces. We were never banned from higher education or any particular profession. Women continued to work as doctors, police officers, and even parliamentarians. I know, too, that things are different now, far freer in some ways, certainly in the clothes women wear, than when my family left. I know that the spirit of secularism and gender equity never died, and Iranians never forgot that the controlled reality in which they live is not necessary or normal. I know that Iranians have inched their way toward freedom in various ways, and — at least in urban centres — young men and women can sit in pretty familiar-looking cafés drinking cappuccinos. And yet, for all the surface shifts, young people can still disappear into torture chambers for filming dance videos and posting them online.

Even in my childhood years, as the most drastic changes came and were so brutally enforced, there also came small heroic acts of daily resistance. Walking out of the house became a daily ordeal. The extra layers of clothes that women were required to wear included a headscarf, and a 'manteau' or long coat (a few French words are in regular Farsi circulation since the French came through centuries ago) so their arms, legs, and hips were covered over their trousers. Some chose the full-length chador. All the outerwear had to be in dark or subdued tones, so black, grey, navy or dark brown were really all anyone was allowed to wear in public. But despite these restrictions, women found ways to express their individuality and dissent in different ways privately and in public spaces. All our photographs of the time show intense shoulder pads and metallics, purples and pinks from the neck down. From the neck up, women sported booming perms of varied lengths with details like a headband or pushed-up bubble fringe. Those bubble fringes were the weapon of choice against the hijab, becoming increasingly ambitious in height and outward protrusion from the headscarf. Fuchsia and frosted pinks came out via lipsticks. So, at the risk of torture or lashing, Iranian women pushed back. To be colourful or even sexualised was a way to express dissent against the regime, not just in terms of the hijab but as an identity point against religious rule altogether.

For many of us, childhood in 1980s Iran meant accepting that the adults around us were in shock. They were anxious, depressed and stressed to the point of being physically ill. In fact, it became a bitter national joke that doctors regularly diagnosed people with almost any physical ailment, from a heart condition to chronic pain in any given part of the body, with 'stress'. Much of the stress came from having to edit our behaviour and politics in public, lest we disappear into Evin Prison. Subtle rebellion in clothing, or lack thereof, became a way people recognised each other as either comrade or regime supporter, though the very real fear of spies meant strangers could never be trusted. That coded division was another way our world closed in around us. Pre-revolution friendships and activist connections solidified as the only safe associations for my parents.

My parents and their friends would get together to talk about politics ad nauseam. It wasn't a grim obsession. They mixed it with dark humour and slow informal dinners in each other's kitchens. I remember a summer when they made a lot of pizzas, which we would then eat out in the garden. My parents got very into figuring out the recipes for the dough and the perfect sauce. Their friends, at that point all in their late twenties or early thirties, would sit around listening to music, offloading about the state of the nation, and chopping piles of pizza toppings. There was always some kind of sausage, grated cheese, mushrooms and onions on a tomato base with a handful of dried oregano scattered over. Sometimes they went overboard and threw on capsicums or shrimps, but for me they were always best scantily topped so the delicious crispy base and sauce could shine. They would roll out huge uneven blobs of dough that were in no way circular and a nightmare to cut into easy-to-eat slices. They probably thought themselves culinary artisans.

I generally had at least one friend at these gatherings, though not all my parents' friends had children my age. It was normally one of two little girls: Aida or Venus. We would hang around the kitchen, coming and going from my bedroom, or, if the weather allowed, we'd take a blanket and picnic on the tiles in the garden. Every so often a new pizza might appear for us to eat. Summer nights were long and children in Iran didn't really have the strict bedtimes we tend to impose in the West. We'd stay up until about 10 pm easily, then doze off, to be carried off to the car at the end of the night.

My dad would brew beer and distil what he called 'vodka' (which I've come to believe was actually moonshine) in our basement. I'd often help him with brewing or testing the alcohol levels, to my mother's great dismay. He must have learned how to do this almost immediately after the revolution, because some of my earliest memories are of hanging around in that basement with him.

His approach to life was to enjoy it. This is a common trope that gets thrown around, but I don't know that anyone has kept to it through the tumult of revolution, theocracy and exile as well as my dad. That he brewed beer and made moonshine at the risk of torture, so he and his friends could sit around our kitchen, laughing and drinking like life was normal for a minute, is a thing I marvel at and carry with me today. My dad and I have always had an easy, economical communication between us, so when he leans back with an absolute smirk on his joyous, worn face and tells me to eat more cheese or a sliver more cake, or to drink a splash more wine in the face of any societal or existential adversity, I know he means so much more than that. It's what kept a generation of worn revolutionaries going. It's what keeps Iranians celebrating their ancient Godless festivals, as much as what keeps us inching back our civil rights from that violent regime.

When it came to me, my parents both had a relaxed approach to alcohol, in that they believed being around people drinking recreationally and seeing it as a natural part of life, rather than an escape or rebellion, was the best way to go. My dad applied that philosophy to all drugs — not that my parents or anyone they knew took hard drugs, but we were able to openly speak about drug use. The cultural reference point for my parents was the same as what I came to know of boomers in New Zealand, pot smoke had been around as part of the 1960s and '70s counter-culture and their generation's sense of self was related to being accepting of that. I was basically taught that drugs were a curiosity I may encounter, and if I ever wanted to try anything, I should do it around friends or family, where it was safe and someone would look after me.

Within the oasis of acceptance and social progressiveness, I remember my childhood in Iran as filled with birthday parties, summer stone fruit, and snow fights (because of course Iran is not a desert, as I've realised many believe it to be). There were dinner parties too. These were late-night productions, held at the risk of raids, disappearances and torture. Still, we had them. Dinner was a massive feast served at around 9 pm, if not 10 pm, with Iranians arriving notoriously late. There was music and dancing and boisterous laughter — often at bitter political jokes about our country's so-called state of affairs. There was always bootleg alcohol of some sort. Those parties were pure Iranian, so much so that even this acute level of peril didn't manage to suppress them.

As jovial as these parties were, the risks created an omnipresent tension, shrouding us ever more in precautions and defensiveness. No one could be trusted off-hand. There was always a chance that neighbours might be listening out, and they might decide to call the Pasdars to win brownie points. Homes were regularly raided, and it wasn't unheard of for these raids to occur during parties with gender-mixing and alcohol. These urban myths, based no doubt in truth, stuck with me as nightmares of raided wedding parties, of brides having to escape through the window or hide on the roof while the grooms or even elderly family members were dragged away to be lashed. No one knew exactly what this all was worth to the whistle-blowers, but the result for those on the outs with the regime machinery was devastating on a personal and societal scale.

It seems wild to me now that my parents' circle continued to have political gatherings, to listen to music and dance at the risk of torture. They never stopped finding bootleg music. I remember in particular the 1980s Madonna music videos, just loud enough for joyous dancing in our living room. The women wore their own Madonna-esque matching permed hair and bright headbands. But things were tense. They were scared. They would turn down the music. They jolted a little and their ears pricked up if there was a noise, a knock on the door. We could be raided at any time. What would we hide first? The alcohol, the literature, the fact that men and women sat uncovered together? Any of those things could lead to at least the men being taken to be whipped. That might be the best-case scenario, because what if they took the women? They did flog women too, but a lot worse could happen. That was my understanding even as a child. So in our homes we lived our real lives in constant terror, and talked about freedom. Outside we hid our true selves. Our culture was pushed underground and we became unintended dissidents.

*

I remind myself with some amazement that my parents were in their twenties and thirties, adapting to these imposed identities. My mother attended university and gained her degree in psychology after the revolution. Her dream had been to become a professor, to do her own research and write books. But from the start, it was clear she could never function in the new religious context of state universities. She couldn't help but fight every battle against what she saw as grossly dehumanising violations of her rights. From the dress code to the seating plan, the university became her protest ground. They began to impose segregated seating, with women made to sit at the back of the lecture theatres. Every day, my mother would defiantly sit in the front row until she was politely asked to move. Even then, she might not go straight away — she needed them to say 'please' first. It was a small gesture, but it gave her agency. The lecturers weren't immediately regime plants, so maybe they felt a sense of vindication in being part of the protest, given they too were now trapped in this alien oppression.

Once she graduated, she applied for research jobs and got several offers, but then overtly refused to sit the required Islamic exams. She wanted that refusal on the record, as a point of protest, dangerous as it eventually got. As a result of this defiance, she never worked as a psychologist.

After university, my mother poured all the focused ambition of her stolen career into being a housewife and mother. It was important to her that she contribute to the household economy, so she sewed and knitted and baked constantly. She bought patterns and modelled our style on illegal copies of Madonna's music videos. We weren't going to descend into colourless compliance on her watch. My birthday parties became a production. Truth be told, I felt pretty alienated from the uber-extroverted Iranian party culture of dancing and singing with full abandon. The other girls and boys would arrive in their best and brightest outfits, compete to dance in the middle of the room, sit for endless photos. I would often escape to my room with one or two close friends to play quietly. But for my mother, every party was a show of her success as a mother, maybe even as a child psychologist.

She settled into being a full-time mother, but I wasn't her only outlet. She continued to speak out, forming groups and book clubs with other women to access and share discourse. I remember her friend Giti in particular, a dignified academic who had lost her job after the revolution because she was Bahá'í. Her husband had been forced to publicly denounce their religion in order to retain his job in the Ministry of Agriculture, where my dad also worked. I remember the humiliation of that time for Bahá'ís who chose to reject their faith to protect their families, and the sheer violence faced by those who didn't repent.

Giti and my mother began interviewing women about domestic violence in an effort to produce a book. I would play for hours silently on the living room floor at her home while the two women went through their case studies. Their purpose was to lift the veil of shame that women lived under, and talk about violence as the responsibility of the abuser. Despite the outlets they managed to create for themselves and their work, I remember that they were palpably angry. Everything elicited a bitter reaction. Every aspect of their lives was a struggle. They kept reading academic literature and feverishly searching for different news sources. As the rest of the country settled into passive obedience, they kept trying to keep the dissident political momentum going. My mother became an outsider even among the educated ex-revolutionaries, as fewer of her circle kept up the will to rebel in the face of harsh crackdowns.

The understanding that the 'news' wasn't always an impartial source of information stayed with me for life. There was always hushed chat at home between the adults as they exchanged information and leaflets, and tried to tune into banned radio stations, huddling around to hear what was 'really' going on. There was also perpetual talk of how much we needed to get out of the country. It went from a question of will, to one of necessity, then urgency.

My father had a government job in agricultural research. He was an engineer working on energy extraction from sugar beets – an early green-energy project. For him, the pressure came from refusing to edit his life, politics or friendships in any way while in government employment. My dad was a socialist too and politically active in his own way. But what I remember most was his resistance by living a defiantly unchanged life. He's always been a hedonist, so the pleasures of life became the frontlines of the political battle for him. Men faced different dangers under the Islamic regime. Apart from brutal punishments for alcohol consumption and political dissidence, the main cause for alarm was forced conscription into the war. While oppression was normalised, the war broke through as the dominant force of terror in our lives, competing with food insecurity and hyperinflation as sources of mass anxiety. Anyone from teenaged boys to middle-aged men were all under threat. People began planning their sons' escapes. Would they pay off officials or pay human traffickers?

Both were a risky gamble, and most tried to wait for it all to end. I remember seeing vans stop on the street and load up a group of boys playing football one day. My mother stopped, stunned, and I asked her what was happening. She said aloud inadvertently, 'They're stealing children for the war,' then hustled me on. My dad escaped conscription for medical reasons, but I remember the terror of that risk hanging over our heads, among the other terrors during the war years.

That's when the cult of the martyr began. Streets, monuments, even schools were renamed with the names of dead young men. Their soft-focused pictures competed with images of the Ayatollah himself in overwhelming the public consciousness. The streets were also slowly filling with a sea of amputees. They would beg on the street in such great numbers that people began to wonder if it was all real. Myths about fake amputees vying for sympathy in the begging game emerged. That's the level of depravation to which we had sunk.

I remember crying over something trite like a lost toy once. My mother stopped and told me to save the tears for something worse. She gestured to a young man with no legs on a street corner and said, 'You never know how hard life will get. He didn't know he would lose his legs, and he has to get through that now. So you can't fall apart every time something unexpected goes wrong.' It was a harsh lesson for a seven-year-old, but it was the new reality we had to process.

Like women, men had to dress as supporters of the regime to avoid harassment, though they faced nowhere near the scale of force for disobedience. They hid away their neckties, which the regime had declared an offensive sign of Western influence. Some had let their beards grow out, a sign of alignment with Islam. My dad staunchly continued to sport his '70s moustache. He wore enormous bell-bottoms to his wedding a year before the revolution, darned if fundamentalists were going to tell him to mess up that high style.

Aesthetic cues became an important part of the way people interacted and kept safe over that first post-revolutionary decade. They could win a promotion or otherwise mark one as an agitator. With that came deep rifts and suspicion in the community. There was resentment against those who grew their beards out to win favour with the regime. They were benefactors of the persecution that saw so many others lose jobs, face prison sentences, or submit to flogging for failing to fall in line. Worse, we were always looking out for spies, active participants in that persecution, so even a clean-shaven tie-wearer couldn't be trusted if we didn't know his bona fides. Those same fractures mark Iranian diaspora communities in the West, even in New Zealand.

My friendships lay with the children of my parents' closest friends or relatives. We played into the night as our parents ate late dinners and talked around the table, or moved into the basement for more serious chats. My two closest friends were both children of my dad's cousins. Jeiran was half German. She was endlessly enchanting to me, the only foreigner I had ever met. But Jeiran and I felt like soulmates and formed that sort of easy wordless intimacy that children have almost instantly. Her mum, Gunhilde, embraced Iran and Iranians with a kind of fetishism that was a great relief to us. As Iranians we were increasingly embarrassed of our nation's backward image on the world stage, from the still-recent hostage crisis in 1979, when fifty-two Americans were held at the United States Embassy in Tehran for 444 days by a group of Iranians identifying as the Muslim Student Followers of the Imam's Line, to having religious leaders present as our politicians. Meanwhile, Gunhilde was busy learning to cook Iranian cuisine and studying Iranian art with a deep respect that some of us lacked by this point in our shaky history. Their house regularly hosted enormous Christmas trees and gorgeous painted wooden Easter decorations. My mother found a soulmate-ship of her own with Gunhilde. They would sit with tea and cake, talking for hours about their lives as unexpected housewives. They analysed culture and talked about raising girls in that 'difficult context'. We girls would play quietly with our toys for hours. I remember we often swapped our toys with an easy unguarded generosity. When it was time to go home, we would desperately beg for five more minutes, then say slightly teary-eyed goodbyes.

My other dominant friendship in those days was with a little boy, another relative, who lived a block away from us. Sadra was a couple of years older than me, but we talked and played for hours, mostly building things out of Lego. When we were slightly older, I would sneak out to go watch him play football on the street, as boys do in most of the world where football is a national passion. Our families spent a lot of time together. In fact, my parents were at Sadra's house when my mum went into labour, so his family was at the hospital when I was born. When my mum was at university, his mum, Shiva, picked me up from kindergarten most days, so I was a little bit the daughter she never had. My mother was eternally grateful that she could study while I was still so young. This formed a strong bond between the two women. Shiva was 'Khaleh Shiva' to me, *khaleh* being the word for maternal aunt in Farsi, a term of huge endearment that children give close female adults. Our families had the kind of relationship where impromptu visits would turn into dinners that went late into the night. I knew they were part of the trusted group around my parents, because I would overhear them talking about intimate things like relationships, which Iranians keep hidden from gossip. Their talk of politics went beyond lamenting the price of petrol to discussing people we knew who had been arrested. They talked about how they might escape the country as things heated up around us. From the intimate to the political to actual life or death.

What I'll never forget is the harrowing plight of Sadra's teenage cousin, a political prisoner at the age of sixteen. I heard this unsettling tale as it happened over the course of a few years by way of whispers and questions I asked that my mother struggled to answer without causing too many nightmares. Khaleh Shiva's beloved nephew was caught by regime officials spraying graffiti. The incomplete sentence he had sprayed read 'Death to …'. He was asked what he was going to write. He could have easily said 'America', 'Death to America' being a common chant and the subject of much regime-sponsored graffiti art. But he was an idealistic rebel, probably taken with the Mojahedin resistance movement against the regime. He looked those officials in the eye and told them he was going to write: 'Death to Khomeini'.

He was arrested and taken to prison. It was months before his family got word of where he was. He could have been conscripted into the war, but this was worse. I remember hearing the adults talk about his fate for years afterward. There were always whispers about distant family and friends who had been conscripted into the war or arrested. That was normal. I think this one stayed with me because he was so young, so close to us, and his fate was the cruellest. In the end, his mother was allowed to visit him. He asked her whether it was night or day. He had been held in darkness for so long, he could barely remember the light. He asked if his father had been arrested, because he had been told during his interrogation that the screams he was hearing of a beating next door were from his dad; in fact they were not, but the intended anguish was effective. He apologised for causing so much hurt.

His family continued to ask to see him and I think they did once more, a year or two later. Twice they were told a visit was booked, but when the family turned up, they were declined entry, after waiting for hours for their turn. His mother continued to drop off care packages and letters as frequently as allowed. Then, without warning, the family were sent his execution notice. He had been killed almost a year before, while the authorities continued to accept the letters and packages lovingly prepared by his heartbroken mother.

All the anxiety and humiliation wrought by the Islamic regime was always presented to me as part of a continuum of trauma that came with being not only Iranian, but Middle Eastern. It was true that the repressive retrograde culture of the regime was not ours, though it was undeniably administered by Iranians. But it was also true that the reason we were in that mess was, as it had always been, that our oil resource was needed by the world. We knew the Shah's dictatorial rule, including a very real spy agency and the same torture chambers that the Islamic regime now use, existed with the support of Western backers for oil. And soon we knew the same was true of the new regime. The Iran–Contra scandal drove it home. We found out the United States had secretly sold weapons to both sides of our war with Iraq. Our leaders had bought the means to wage war in exchange for our oil money, and our lives.

At some point during the war came the sanctions. As the West secretly sold weapons to our Ayatollahs, it openly backed its ally, Saddam Hussein, and imposed sanctions on Iran to 'help end the war'. Of course, we now know there was no incentive to end that war, given it was an industry unto itself. Meanwhile, Iranians bore the brunt of its violence and collateral economic collapse. The war brought widespread scarcity, the erratic availability of basics like medicines and rationed food items. Even petrol came to be available to ordinary Iranians by rationed coupons. In one of the world's most oil-rich lands, we had to beg to buy our own resource. That had been the basis of most of our problems to begin with.

The daily frontlines were the interactions with our fellow Iranians, any of whom could be regime agents. The double life we learned to live was predicated on the new unfettered cruelty of the regime, but also the two worlds that quickly emerged, one benefiting from and emboldened by the new order, the other displaced by it. A segment of society, who had genuinely suffered inequality and prejudice under the Shah, formed a deep allegiance with the regime. For religious, working-class families, it was an honour to give up their sons. The dead were honoured as martyrs by the regime. There was a newfound respect in being devout and poor, which had been robbed of so many Iranians under the previous regime. That marginalised demographic could finally hope to work in positions of power. They could even allow their daughters to take part in public life or higher education, since it was all a safe Islamic space. But this new order of things created new nepotism and corruption. Favour could be won by pretending to be religious, and giving up others as dissidents.

The constant weight of that degradation is always with us as Iranians. By the time I was old enough to absorb the existential chatter of the adults around me, there was an air of acceptance that Iranians were second-class citizens of the world, so we weren't allowed democracy. Our lives were cheap, and our story forgettable. I eventually lost that feeling of being 'less-than' and without control of my identity after we moved to Aotearoa, but there were times when it would wash over me. In 2002, in the middle of Auckland's IMAX cinema, I remember suddenly bursting into uncontrollable sobbing while watching Michael Moore's documentary *Bowling for Columbine*, where the deposition of Mosaddegh appears on a list of American assaults on democracy around the world. In that moment, I realised there were Westerners who knew who we were.

Prime Minister Mohammad Mosaddegh took office in 1951 but was removed by a US- and UK-orchestrated coup d'état in 1953. A democrat and socialist, Mosaddegh introduced unemployment compensation and benefits for sick workers, and gave land rights to peasant workers. Most offensively to the Shah's Western backers, he nationalised the Anglo-Iranian Oil Company. The bitter loss of that moment of hope in our history was still palpable during my childhood. Mosaddegh served as a rallying point in anti-US protests during the revolution and remains one of the most popular figures in Iranian history. He stands as proof of what Iranians would have had, if we were allowed to choose. It was overwhelming to have that sense of injustice validated that night in the dark cinema, confirmation that we were not just inexplicably backward, but that our will had been violently and unjustly overborne by greater powers, over and over again.

For me, the story of modern Iran is the ongoing story of the people of the so-called Middle East — itself a twentieth-century Western construct which ignores that some of us are and culturally associate as Asians and some are African nations — turned caricatures in the world's consciousness. We have little say in devising our own nuanced identities, either inside or outside our homelands. We are conveniently presented as a homogenous mass of fundamentalists again and again by foreign powers who would profit from our oppression. We are 'othered' on the international stage as endlessly primitive or brutish, because that makes it easier to justify the violent dictatorships the West happily deals with in the arms trade and oil-for-food programmes. Our lives are cheap because we are not seen as capable of sharing the hopes and dreams of the rest of humanity. Our celebrations are bombed and our children are thrown on the frontlines of perpetual wars. It feels like no one bats much of an eye, because we are assumed less capable of ordinary human experiences like having high-school sweethearts, planning weddings, and expecting a peaceful life raising children who grow up to play sport rather than fight in militia.

What is important to understand is that, as we sit trapped in that nightmare, we are well aware that it is happening to us. I knew, growing up in Iran, that no one on the outside cared about our plight, and that seemed natural, because we were Iranians not Westerners. We knew it was Ronald Reagan and George Bush Sr who sold those weapons to our leaders and to Saddam, trapping us and our neighbours in eight years of violence for profit. We knew our oppression would not continue but for the West's need for our oil. We knew we were lied to by both sides. We also knew what rights we should have. My parents talked endlessly about equality between men and women, not as a Western ideal but as ours. They saw gender inequality as imposed by an illegitimate regime. But that part of our culture, those voices, were erased. What emanated was the feeling of being second-class citizens in a world where our lives and our stories mattered less. And yet, Iranians persisted. They continue to persist; the culture speaks of celebration and fortitude even under the black veil of imposed theocracy.

3

Our landing place

Those first days in New Zealand were a haze of blue-green. This wasn't just a different place. *We* were different. You would think that would be unsettling, that we would feel a terrible longing for home, but there was something else, at least at first, which meant we didn't miss anything from Iran. We lived without fear. We had shed the ever present anxiety that comes with living under a violent dictatorship. We walked outside without covering our hair or our skin. We moved about in wonder. We smiled more easily. Such was our eagerness to be here, to be *of* here, to fit in. Although our situation was uncertain, things made sense.

What strikes me when I look back with the distance of twenty-eight years is that we didn't know anything about this place other than it was a free Western country. We encountered New Zealand as a Pākehā nation. We did not have a strong sense that we had moved to a South Pacific island nation, colonised by the British Crown. Instead, just as we looked at our own culture under the Islamic regime with a little disdain, we glorified a lot of what we encountered here as superior because it was Western and we embraced it fully. We were in the lavender fog.

What struck us back then was the New World egalitarianism. What made us feel free, other than the legal protections, was that people here were diverse in their aspirations, the kinds of homes they lived in, their family structures. There was less pressure, in every way, to conform.

We got to see what those legal protections — those rights we were so desperate for — looked like on the ground. As we waited for our asylum claim to be investigated, we had access to social welfare benefits straight away. We had had no experience of government income support before. Even more incredible was that this was not yet a point of shame or scorn in New Zealand culture. We were given what we needed to survive before benefits crept under the subsistent levels they are at today. We were deeply moved and relieved. It's still very emotional for me to think about the basic dignity we were afforded when we needed it. The fact is that my parents had watched their lives turn into a harrowing nightmare, but they could actually pack up, bundle up their child, and find refuge here. We were poor, but we weren't destitute or humiliated. That is, of course, as it should be. I know the basics of life and dignity are not a privilege for any human being. I know that it shouldn't be extraordinary to say a person can escape persecution or war, but millions can't. And today our welfare system leaves so many behind, leaves them hungry and degraded. The truth is that anyone can at any moment need that help, when life takes an unexpected turn for the worse. Disabilities happen, marriages break down, mental health declines. It was part of what made New Zealand safe and free, to know that the safety net not only existed but was never weaponised against those it served. We were certainly not made to beg. Though we felt the urgency to repay the debt of gratitude, it was never an imposed degradation.

Almost as soon as we stepped off the plane, we started to make a life in New Zealand. We rented a modest two-bedroom unit in Kelston. We bought groceries, scrounging for bargains. We got a little obsessed with the inexhaustible variety of junk food to try as part of our commitment to cultural integration. My parents tried to give me 'normal' food by buying mini packs of chips and chocolate bars for lunches. Encountering 'chicken'-flavoured potato chips was, and still is, baffling. We learned that ketchup tastes far too sweet. None of the spices we normally used were available in quantities and prices that made sense for daily consumption — saffron was a rare gem — so we adapted the recipes and trained our taste-buds. Eventually, someone told my mum how to make 'mouse traps', so grilled cheese on toast became a staple. I was enrolled in school with no questions asked and my parents started English classes.

Our lawyer, Coral Shaw, interviewed my parents and we passed on the documents we had smuggled out of Iran to support our claim. After some months, the investigation was complete, and we were recognised as refugees based on political persecution. In law, that means it was established that we had a 'well-founded' fear of serious harm, akin to torture or persecution, because of our political affiliations. We felt like all these rights were connected to the 'humanity' experienced by citizens of the 'free world', which was lost to us in Iran. The inalienable right to legal representation, which really is the right to be heard, became particularly important to my life as I forged my career.

I don't remember feeling homesick. It was springtime in this upside-down part of the world. The air was chilly, but bright. The greens in the grass and trees were brand-new mints. Everything was constantly washed in sun showers. That's Auckland: always bright, warmer than it should be, and always a five-minute shower away from ruining your hairdo. I walked around taking mental snapshots of the new things around me, like the memorial snaps I had stored away of the things we had left behind. I would look at the big tree outside my school, the unfamiliar row of shops up the road, and think, 'That will just be "that tree", "my school", and "our local shops" soon.' I daydreamed about how I would walk by these things, all without even thinking about it. I imagined the gaggle of girlfriends I would soon have at school. In time, we would share memories of the funny things that had happened while we were sitting together on our school's lawn, under the huge tree, walking past our local shops. I tried to remember how big it was to start school in Iran at first, and how small it soon became, how I became a part of the old guard as new kids came through. I thought about that happening here in Auckland one day.

One thing I'll always cherish about New Zealand is that we arrived here with nothing, and that didn't seem to matter. On St Leonards Road, where we lived, no one had a whole lot more than anyone else. Many were renting. There were only a few large opulent houses, like middle-class people might try to build in Iran. People always bought used cars, rather than flash new ones. No one dressed in fancy clothes, no matter the occasion. Bare feet were summer wear. This was mind-blowingly casual to us. I remember the number of times people asked us things like, 'Did you have refrigerators/cars/microwaves in Iran?' and we would glance down at their bare feet, thinking, *'You're not wearing shoes!'* But this was liberation.

We owned no more than a few travel outfits and some toiletries. We had no books, no photo albums, no heirlooms. I had the two animal figurines and my teddy-bear to decorate my room. We had the job of rebuilding our lives from scratch and we were in a hurry about it. I suppose we wanted to prove that we were capable and worthy to no one in particular. It is an ambition often shared by the dispossessed. The tip from other refugees was to buy the *Trade & Exchange*. We pored over the giant classified list every Thursday, looking at all the different things people were selling at a bargain, trying to find items that we may or may not have needed. It was a thrill. My dad meticulously marked garage sales that were on. We would wake up extra early and traipse through the city at the crack of dawn every Saturday and Sunday morning, restocking our life. We would bargain down the sellers. A dollar or two saved was a huge prize to us. This must have been strange to my parents, if they stopped to let it sink in. They had never bought second-hand appliances or clothes in their old life. That was the reserve of the truly poverty-stricken in Iran. That would have been greatly humbling. When I think about it now, it's surprising that they took to it with great humour, never shame or sadness. At least, that was how they presented to me.

Eventually we managed to buy everything from tables and chairs to dishes and a toaster. What my parents couldn't buy second-hand, they made. Mum bought fabrics to make curtains. She reupholstered an entire lounge suite using garage sale–sourced fabric and an old sewing machine. I remember she was so proud of that feat. We got to be house proud again. This was a hopeful, happy time for us, because we were making so much progress. Our focus was on the microlevel of basic needs.

I bought old and still-boxed-up Barbie dolls, teddy bears, trinkets, and loads of old books to rebuild my little world. I remember the winning feeling that came with spotting something on a table or in a box of junk, beelining for it and getting a decent price. Nothing ever cost more than a dollar or two. Mostly it was a couple of bucks for a box of the stuff, or I'd buy one thing for a dollar and get an extra, less-desirable trinket or doll for free. My parents suddenly became focused on buying a piano so I could learn to play, to 'keep up' with the cultured Kiwi children they imagined would be my peers. Thankfully, we never did find a garage-sale piano, because, honestly, I never would have learned it. I also never met another child who was a musical prodigy. My peers, happily for me, were far more committed to sitting and chatting over food than anything methodical like sports or music.

Soon, my parents made a few 'Kiwi' friends, neighbours and people they had met through the Salvation Army who had reached out to help us resettle. Their new friends started inviting us over for barbecues and birthdays. They asked us to 'bring a plate'. This concept was only equal in its otherworldliness to leaving the house without shoes. Every non-Western migrant has a story about the first time they encountered the 'bring a plate' bombshell. We either turn up with a literal empty plate, wondering what interesting purpose this rare custom would have, or — having done some research and found out this is a food-sharing ask — inadvertently cater for the entire party with enormous arrays of intense homemade dishes harking back to the motherland, only to find everybody else has brought a single bag of chips or a plate of sausage rolls. The 'bring a plate' conundrum often escalated to being asked to bring not only 'a plate' and drinks, but to bring any combination of extra cutlery, dishes, music, even literal furnishings like chairs or a table. We obliged and wondered why we were leaving the house with half our belongings. Kiwis don't realise what a gorgeous abomination this is in most other cultures. But this brand of Kiwi ingenuity is also emblematic of the openness people have to not having everything sorted yet. There is a nonchalance in having such a total lack of concern for impressing guests, especially compared to the almost-competitive opulence of Iranian dinner parties, no matter the host's actual means. It was a new-world approach in a young country, where 'making do' was nothing to be ashamed of.

We were also suddenly surrounded by all sorts of family units, divorced and reconstituted, unmarried life partners, solo parents on the Domestic Purposes Benefit (DPB), and the rainbow community. My parents had to explain all this to me in a burst. Their take was always, 'That's normal. It's nobody's business. What's terrible is a culture that pressures people to be one way or another. That's what was wrong with Iran.' For some reason, I remember being most scandalised when one of my friends told me her parents had never been married. She must have read the look on my face, because she asked if I still liked her. I quickly shook off the shock, smiled and nodded reassurance. In Iran, I only knew one little girl whose parents were divorced. My mum had been helping her mum get custody of her kids in the Islamic family court system, which had automatically given them to her drug-addicted, abusive husband. The heartache went on for years. In Iran, at least in those days, divorce was a scandal. In fact, most domestic issues were deeply guarded secrets.

My mother's view on unmarried couples, when I finally brought it up with her, was that it made no sense to marry unless you've lived with someone for a long time: 'How can anyone promise to do something for the rest of their life when they've never done it before?' Her view on divorce was that every break-up is a triumph: 'You're moving forward from something that wasn't working.' After university, my mother had worked with a Bahá'í friend, who lost her job as an academic after the regime's persecution of the Bahá'í minority set in, to document women's experiences of abuse in the new system where divorce was only permitted through the husband's permission and custody of children fell to their father by default. This was dangerous work for both women, but they felt strongly that their alienation from mainstream means of work and research gave them a certain freedom to work on what the regime would not have allowed in their research institutions. She knew that for many women marriage in Iran was a literal prison, and her generation of feminists certainly saw it as a subjugation tool. This was all pretty abrupt and hard-nosed for a nine-year-old to hear, but to that Iranian feminist it was somehow urgent to pass on those truths in a place where she could see so many alternatives suddenly possible for the little girl she had rescued from oppression. She wanted the alternatives properly glorified. 'Every break-up is a triumph' was an answer to a culture that crushed women under the burden of being nothing but successful brides. It wasn't her and darned if it would be her daughter.

During the 2017 election, I ran as a candidate in West Auckland. It felt like a defining choice. I returned to the street on which my family and I had first lived to shoot a spot for TVNZ's *Neighbourhood* programme. This was part of the colourful snapshot collection from my nine-year-old mind, filed away and almost forgotten. There I found things starkly, wonderfully unchanged. There were the two little convenience stores and a couple of food outlets, all run by people of South Asian heritage, the same as I remembered it. The storefronts were filled with South Asian snack foods right next to all the old Kiwi-brand lollies, toffee chocolate slabs, sour balls, and pick-and-mix baggies. This was the place where I first encountered diversity.

Today, when I comment on issues of race or immigration as a politician, I come to that from the lived experience of a first-generation refugee, a migrant of colour, arriving in New Zealand in 1990. It is a useful point of reference, anecdotal as it is.

My family and I were simultaneously the subject of the migrant race experience and objective observers of it. We didn't expect much by way of a welcome or even equality. We were grateful. But we didn't come with a sense of degradation, which is borne from experiencing generational racism. We didn't yet carry the burden of feeling inferior or resentful. Indeed, we weren't forced to carry the deep sense of rage and grief that must come from the intergenerational trauma of colonisation. Over time, there comes to be that internalised self-hate and systemically imposed inferiority complex from knowing certain doors will never be open to you. It comes from living with knowing that people like you probably won't be getting the job, and if you do get the job, you probably won't be promoted, and if you're promoted, you'll likely never be the boss, not in an established institution. So migrants give up trying to compete against the status quo in the job market, and start businesses and drive taxis instead. We learn to make self-deprecating jokes about our food and accents. We have to own the exclusion or it will crush us. We didn't learn that until later. In those early days, we walked around with our heads high. We felt a kinship with all other persons of colour, who we assumed were migrants, even Māori.

When I think back to that first encounter with 'multiculturalism', I'm struck by how monocultural the society we encountered in fact was. As much as we saw other migrants and persons of colour coexisting around us in West Auckland, in terms of dominant cultural cues, Aotearoa as we experienced it through the 1990s was a starkly Pākehā society. Pākehā culture and history dominated the national identity and was presented to us as 'Kiwi'. 'Kiwi food' was pies and lamingtons. The language was English. Kiwis loved rugby in winter and cricket in summer. Even the books I read through my school years were mostly by English or American authors, with a bit of Katherine Mansfield or Janet Frame on the side, and one short story by Patricia Grace.

The striking thing for me now is that there was no strong indication of the special cultural place or rights of Māori as our indigenous people. Back in Iran, one of my older cousins, who had heard we might be going to New Zealand and looked into the place for us, told me the creation story of Māui fishing up the North Island. But since Māori myth or culture wasn't highlighted at all to us once we got here, this was diminished to an obscure, quirky story, detached from New Zealand's modern-day myths about the All Blacks and who invented the pavlova. In that context, we saw Māori as another ethnic minority, like the few New Zealanders of Indian or East Asian origin we encountered, and inseparable from the Pasifika community, with whose culture we were equally unfamiliar. Te reo Māori was certainly not taught, at least not in any school I attended until high school, where a separate class existed teaching a te reo Māori curriculum separated from the mainstream curriculum. I feel embarrassed now knowing we entered a colonised land without appreciation of its tangata whenua. That migrants regularly integrate into the Crown's New Zealand without this understanding is to me a breach of Te Tiriti o Waitangi. It's also a huge loss to all our communities. Since learning about the New Zealand wars, and the violence and repression of Māori culture motivated by resource grab, I see how much our refugee experience might have helped us relate to Māori and understand the history of our new refuge.

Instead of this, we focused on merging into the Kiwiana around us as well as we could, ignorant to the deeper obstacles ahead.

What I remember from those early months in Kelston is venturing out barefoot to walk to the shops for ice blocks in the summer. I remember savouring the warm, rough concrete footpath, and breaking it up with the relief of the cooler grassy berm when it was too hot or a particularly rough patch of pavement approached. The ice blocks were forty to sixty cents. They coloured your tongue fluoro shades of green, orange or red. I remember deliberately delighting in this ritual walk as my 'new normal'. 'Eventually,' I thought, 'I won't be mimicking this at all. I'll just forget to wear shoes and I'll be going up the road to join a group of friends like everyone else.'

Over the years, as I got to live as an urban native in Auckland, I'd think back to that little girl deliberately learning to embody her new life: standing outside looking in, scratching at it, trying to get into it and eventually finding a little hole, sticking her elbow in and figuring out how to step through.

These days, I frighten my mother by wearing pre-loved clothes. She's flabbergasted that a professional adult person who can afford new things would deliberately buy their wardrobe second-hand. Even when everything we owned had to be scavenged at flea markets and garage sales, my parents never could bring themselves to buy anybody else's old clothes. Instead we bought cheap, brightly coloured clothes from Kmart and DEKA. We still have photos of us in matching loud teal tracksuits at Lynn Mall in West Auckland. The mall was a new experience to us. The infinite variety of life and all the buzzing activity seemed to distract everyone else from our weirdness, so we thought we fit in. We took a photo, like tourists, but I know we were revelling in how much we could just merge into it all. We even got that wrong. Bright was what fashionable Iranians would wear. It turned out that Kiwis did nothing but understated. So we adapted. At least, I did, swiftly, in the face of impending peer pressure and the smell of teen spirit wafting with apathy and angst. It turned out that while dancing in loud showy circles at birthday parties had never seemed right, grunge culture was where I finally felt comfortable.

Going through that transition, though most of it was mercifully subconscious, has made me far more aware of how much of human behaviour is dictated by cultural constructs. In court, that means reminding juries that people from different cultures, or even socio-economic backgrounds, don't always behave the same in a formal setting, nor react similarly to trauma. We're reminded that looking downward and avoiding direct eye contact is a sign of respect, not evasiveness, in many cultures. In Islam, men and women who are not close relations don't touch at all, out of respect, not degradation. Even shaking hands in a formal setting would be enormously disrespectful.

In 2018, an Iranian delegation to the New Zealand Parliament didn't shake hands with my colleague Jo Luxton. The press reported on this as a sign of disrespect, a sign of misogyny, that women were considered 'lesser' by the delegates. I checked on Jo — this could have been a distressing position to be in — but she was only a touch annoyed about the lack of cultural briefing and the distorted commentary. I found myself in the uneasy position of publicly correcting this misinterpretation, not because I wanted to defend the delegation, who I see as part of a corrupt and murderous regime, but because the false narrative played into prejudice against Muslims generally.

Sometimes, when I catch myself effortlessly tackling some daily rite, I'm a little startled. It can happen when I casually communicate a nuanced issue in English, because the words are there in my subconscious like a native speaker. It can be a throwaway comment about politics, a bit of legalese about trial procedure, a colloquialism like 'mansplaining' or particularly Kiwi jargon like describing something as 'naff' to mean lame or un-cool, then realising there's no word for that even in other dialects of English. I remember for a split second that at some point I thought and dreamed in Farsi, then translated that into English every time I spoke. Now I wouldn't easily know the Farsi way to express most of my own thoughts, outside of food and family chat.

Or it can come with unconsciously tackling a social situation, walking into a bar, ordering a drink without the menu, bantering with the bartender, casually waiting alone for friends, not feeling remotely out of place. Even knowing what to wear and when is a cultural learning point, as we found when we retired our fluoro trackies. Knowing whether to wear jeans to a party is huge. Taking cues on giving people a hug after a first encounter, especially when gender norms are involved, takes years. Successfully swearing casually and in the right circles are all things that don't cross cultural boundaries well. For my parents, these things will always be uncertain. For me, navigating these situations is a bit like driving halfway across town without ever consciously braking at the lights or deciding on the route. At some point, I stepped through the wormhole and I won't ever get back.

That's the startling part of it. I know there's a parallel world with different rules, different ways of expressing friendship, different ways of being a 37-year-old woman in private and in public, but I wouldn't be able to navigate that world easily. There is a world where streets don't have grassy berms, where feeling that cool grass between your toes on the way to the local shops is unthinkable. Knowing when and where to wear shoes was at some point tricky to me. Now if I went back to Iran, I might laugh too loud or show a bra strap in the wrong company and be considered an unsavoury character. Deciding to partake in that bit of barefoot exoticism was declarative of my belonging. It proved I knew something, something more than the newer arrivals, maybe. It was also sharing in a collective experience with the locals. We all knew what the hot pavement felt like, what relief the cool grass brought, how sticky the drips of ice block made our chins. I was creating childhood memories that my parents didn't have. Memories which my own contemporaries in Iran (or those scattered around the globe as post-revolutionary Iranians) won't have. This collective memory is what all my other casual signifiers of belonging are built on.

But what I didn't realise is that sharing in this experience meant losing another experience, which in turn meant becoming less Iranian, and, slowly, not really that Iranian at all. It feels good to be safely on the inside, an insider, being in on the jokes. But it feels a little traumatic too. Remembering Iran is like an ache from an old wound. It's knowing where the pound of flesh was that we've paid in exchange for belonging elsewhere. Some part of me might be living out there somewhere, but I'll never get it back.

Starting school was a huge moment in mimicry and genuine nine-year-old excitement. I was enrolled at Chaucer School, a tiny primary school in West Auckland, and it was a total blessing. I remember walking onto the school grounds that first day. There was a narrow driveway winding past an old pine tree, but what struck me was the seemingly endless field. I had never been at a school with green open spaces. In Iran, though I was at a relatively populous urban all-girls school, the schoolyard was concrete and tiny by comparison. Not so small that we didn't manage some running around, though, and I had been the inventor of a popular 'cops and robbers' game the previous year. We ran and hid up and down stairs, screamed with the thrill of being caught by the opposing team. I was always in the robbers' team because I was obsessed with Robin Hood. We were probably a bit of a nuisance to all the kids trying to walk around and eat their lunches, because the space was too small not to crash into people. Dodging bodies in an overpopulated concrete jungle was half the fun.

But no amount of subversive anti-authoritarian horsing-around in wartime Iran could prepare me for New Zealand's school physical education regime. Running sprint relays or doing laps of that field were cruel and unusual punishment. I was distressingly unfit and uncoordinated beyond belief. As it turns out, those were not cultural indicators, since I never did manage running even as an adult. The sports we played, however, did pose a distinct cultural challenge. I had never seen a game of rugby, let alone a cricket bat. I spent a lot of time looking aloof around sport activities, hoping no one would pass me any kind of ball or pick me for their team.

The only thing that terrified me more than that massive field was the fact that we had living, breathing boys in our class. Not only was I suddenly sitting next to strange boys, we had to do folk dancing together. The absolute horror was that on some rounds, girls were required to ask the boys to dance. That killed me. I did not know how to deal with that move at all, and I always took an eternity to pick someone, drawing more and more attention to myself and whichever last man standing was waiting to be asked. I wish now I could remember what the boys' responses were to these interactions. Mercifully, I must have been too young to be concerned with their reactions to my awkwardness and focused solely on my own end of the transaction. I remember telling myself this was all 'normal', and my segregated life in Iran was what had always been unnatural. That's what my parents had drummed into me. After all, they had mixed friend groups, and they talked endlessly about how wrong the gender segregation rules of the new regime were. I knew this was part of why I was at this new school at all. So I'd take a deep breath and approach the boys with curiosity and a bit of excitement. Despite all the alien games and gender-mixing, I found my classmates friendly and approachable.

In the beginning, I was put into a 'special-needs' class (as they were called for a while when they first arrived) for children with disabilities, presumably because of the little English I had beyond what I had learned in six months or so of children's English language classes in Iran before we moved, and also because there was no other resource. This wasn't unusual — I know other migrants who also attended special-needs classes. I sat with a younger boy with Down's Syndrome. I was moved to a mainstream class with children of my own age after only a few weeks.

At first, I would wander around the school during playtime and lunchtime, eating on benches near enough to the other kids to be able to hear them, but not quite able to engage in more than a few words of conversation with them. I picked up the language fast, as kids do, and, because the other children were open to it, we started to have little conversations soon enough.

My class was made up of children from various ethnic backgrounds, mostly Pākehā, but, importantly, most of us were essentially poor. There was a sense that everyone's family was scraping by. There was an openness about this, because no one could afford flash clothes. Children talked about their dads leaving, their mums losing their jobs, and I could openly say we bought my toys at garage sales. Even having a pair of new shoes from Kmart elicited happy congratulatory greetings for me at school. There was no façade of perfection over anyone's life, so the fact that my parents looked different and barely spoke English was just accepted as part of the general understanding that none of us had it too easy.

I compared this to the double identity a lot of us lived as children in Iran. At school there, I wore a grey uniform of trousers, a sort of button-down long overshirt and matching headscarf. Each morning we lined up in our class rows, heard a Koranic prayer followed by a blessing to the Ayatollah, and chanted regime-mandated slogans. Picture hundreds of little schoolgirls standing in a concrete yard, chanting things like 'Death to America'. The chant sometimes changed to include various other 'enemy' nations. I remember America and England were permanent fixtures in our burn book. But sometimes France, Russia and Israel had mortally offended us too. The chants were meaningless to us, as was all the regime propaganda about martyrs and keys to heaven. Those of us from anti-regime households knew it was all a charade. But we also knew never to question anything taught at school, never to let on that we were non-believers, not to the teachers or each other. Even at that young age, we knew about the raids, the disappearances, and people being lashed. We had to know, or we might slip up and the unthinkable could happen.

While I experienced absolutely no hostility from my schoolmates at Chaucer School, the barriers were tangible, until they broke down with the start of my first real friendship. I was in a small corner garden, tiptoeing around the little brick garden path, when a girl from my class approached me and struck up a conversation. Her name was Karen, my soon-to-be first-ever Kiwi best friend. Karen was a striking child and noticeably popular in the class. Her hair was golden, not a typical hay blonde, but shimmering gold. It was straight and cut in a careless bob that she flopped to one side. Her clear-blue eyes set off the look. Karen's family had lived in the neighbourhood a while, and she already knew all the kids, having been at the school since preschool. She was confident and jaunty, moving around with her head high and a matter-of-fact stare. She was curious about me. She wanted to know where I had come from, what I was about, what we had in common. Soon we started walking off to share our secrets. We spoke quietly about our families, things we would do when we grew up, our reckons about our classmates. I told her about Iran. We climbed the big tree out front, criminal as that was, so we could sit in it and talk alone. We got into trouble for that and made an example of by our teacher. Mr Smith wanted to exhort the dangers of tree-climbing, but all the seriousness was hilarious to us. We barely held in our giggles as we stood in front of the class, red-faced and grinning.

I don't really remember how we communicated, but we certainly understood each other. Karen started coming around for dinner, which my family ate just after school. We were still on the Iranian schedule of eating an elaborate late big lunch and lighter antipasti meals in the evening. Soon I was an ingrained part of her broader friend group. We had sleepovers, boys included, went on school camp, shared ongoing in-jokes. I never really looked back.

While I was busy being validated and finding my new self at Chaucer School, my parents' adjustment was profound in very different ways. For my dad, that meant going from being an educated professional working in green-energy research and providing a comfortable life for his family, to accepting that he would never be an engineer again and asking strangers if they had any kind of unskilled work he could do. He went from having the status that came from being part of an old, well-regarded family to having no social standing and no contacts or support networks to draw from at all. He went from being at the centre of a close-knit boisterous group of friends, to nodding and smiling as conversations he barely understood passed him by. What I noticed and still find painful is that my dad lost his keen, well-known sense of humour. In Iran, he was known as the funny one in his circle. He would do hilarious impersonations of his self-important Dervish uncle for his cousins during late-night sessions at our house. I remember them all doubling over in laughter. He came up with witty nicknames and taglines for every situation. The dark developments in Iranian society or politics would turn into tragicomedies, a survival tool that made him the centre of attention. These would become ongoing insider jokes in his circle. He was always hilarious for us kids too. He joined in on our games, took on funny characters, put on funny voices, and made us laugh till we had tears rolling down our faces. I was so proud of having the cool, fun dad. After we moved, he was still very funny, but, other than my mum and I, no one around him could tell. Humour doesn't translate, so he mostly stopped trying.

My mother was an educated, politically minded woman, deeply into literature, involved in women's issues, and passionate about her chosen field, psychology. Suddenly, her university degree, like Dad's, was unrecognised. Decades later, when she finally had the time and facility, Mum went through the process of having her psychology degree officially converted at The University of Auckland. She was interviewed by a panel, after which they granted her an equivalent degree. By then, life had moved on so far that she couldn't really face retraining as a clinical practitioner or going back for a Master's degree. Academia had been her dream. She had dreamed of eventually becoming a professor, of teaching and writing. But the language barrier meant she could not interact with her peers in a way that reflected any of this. For many years thereafter, my mother would say the hardest thing for her was that she couldn't make friends by sharing political discourse or having discussions about literature. She would meet people who very likely had read the same books, but for years after we moved, she couldn't convey the complexity of her thoughts well enough in English to form bonds based on any kind of social analysis. She had to resign herself to interacting as a woman with a keen interest in cooking and gardening, at best talking about simple family issues and sharing everyday advice.

Witnessing that change in our parents is probably a central heartbreak of our shared experience as migrant children, at least for those of us old enough at the time of the change to still remember what they were like before. I noticed my mother smiling more. Smiling all the time, in fact, which translated well in the people-pleasing world of retail and hospitality, where she ended up for the rest of her working life. My dad adopted a slightly bewildered wide-eyed expression, which went with perpetually asking people to repeat what they were saying. He began to bow his head a lot. Some instinct told him to appear subservient, to be less of a threat.

When I think about it now, I'm breathless with awe at the memory of my parents adapting to their new position in society, rolling with the punches that hit so hard at the innermost sanctum of their beings. I can't comprehend how they did it. I try to imagine interesting adults my age, engaged in politics and alternative cultural movements, the people I have in my life now, suddenly becoming impoverished migrants far from home. I don't understand how rage didn't overwhelm my parents. It's the first emotion I think of when I imagine that fate, because the situation that forced them there was so deeply unfair. The deliberate cruelty of the regime had tipped their lives upside down, as well as the lives of millions more Iranians for generations. That this great loss was still the best option was not fair. The total lack of control would have driven me to a point of perpetual angst.

But the deeper emotion — the one that might overwhelm any of us similarly batted about — is sorrow. I feel that now, though, if it was happening for my parents, they certainly never let on.

4

Outsider

There's a transition inherent in teendom, where home truths about our place in the world are realised, and the ideas about ourselves that we carried around as children transform. For me, the transition was marked by realising that race exists. That coincided with all the universal doubts we have about our bodies, social hierarchies, and formulating what hopes and dreams we're allowed to have.

My family came to New Zealand from a world that seemed almost devoid of any paradigm where race affected daily life. Later, looking back, I remembered that Mashhad, being on Iran's easternmost border, saw an influx of Afghan refugees when I was a small child. Those who were visible to me were young men working as labourers on roadworks or construction sites. I remembered having an understanding that their country was worse off than ours and they were escaping a war. It didn't occur to me that labouring work was all that was open to them in Iran, that it was what they had to do to survive here. Since they spoke

Farsi, albeit with an accent, and looked more or less like the rest of us, there didn't seem to me to be an issue.

Moving to the West was the first time I had to contemplate race, that I learned I was, in fact, a 'person of colour'. That happened when my parents pushed me into a Pākehā-dominant intermediate school in an affluent suburb of Auckland in a bid to secure my education.

Iranians generally don't see themselves as people of colour in the greater world context the way colonised peoples or those who share direct borders with Western neighbours have been forced to. It's incredible to think about that now, given we seem to be among the most vehemently despised peoples, bearing the brunt of Trump's 'Muslim Ban' and sitting firmly in the 'Axis of Evil'. As a nation, by the late 1980s, we *did* have a sense of shame about our 'backward' religious-based government. We *did* realise that we had suffered imperialism of some sort under our crony Shah, with his deference to the West. We knew that our only democratically elected leader, Mosaddegh, was able to be deposed by an American-funded coup. But we have never necessarily understood ourselves as sitting below European Westerners in terms of race. To the contrary, I think Iranians — at least the vast majority of urbanites — saw themselves largely on par with Europeans. We were an Old-World culture, part of the 'civilised world' who, before the revolution, partook in modern fashion, films, and music. The glitch later was only political.

But race is multi-faceted and doesn't seem contingent on what any group has in fact contributed to civilisation, art, literature, or urbanism. We didn't realise that those parts of our history could be erased in the Western World. Our physical appearance, skin colour, and the preconceptions imposed upon us dictated how we were perceived and what opportunities we were provided. It didn't matter how we saw ourselves. We learned quickly that colour, just like gender and other group identifiers, comes from an external gaze. It's a gaze laden with expectations and misgivings, because we are not white. That means we are not enough, not 'normal' enough. That means we may be despised or feared from birth.

At around eleven years old, this was a tangible realisation for me.

In my interactions with teachers and other adults, I had already noticed that my parents were presumed to be religious and strict, rather than eccentric liberals, which in fact they were. They were also presumed to be uneducated, ignorant, homely, even rural people, rather than urban intellectuals. Who we were was determined by our physical differences. That was not something we had expected or emotionally prepared for. I don't think Westerners realise that in the rest of the world, we interact with foreigners of different races as if they could be like us in terms of education, financial means, and political beliefs. We expect that an African woman could be an ambassador or a doctor, not only a tribeswoman or maybe a small-business owner selling beads (which I later learned is what even the most humanitarian aid organisations often assume African women aspire to). We don't assume 'Asians' are good at maths. In fact, we understand Asia itself to be the most diverse of continents, which covers the vastly divergent cultures from Japan, China, India, South-east Asia, as well as most of the so-called 'Middle East' (which is of course a Western construct that somehow includes North Africa and a diverse group of Asian nations and peoples).

Until just over a year after we settled in New Zealand, I had managed an unscathed existence. I felt different in terms of language and life experience, but I wasn't made to feel lesser. I felt mostly like a kid from a different school who joined the class late in the year.

Then we moved from West Auckland.

Like all good immigrants set on building a better life, my parents asked around about good schools. They were told all about Auckland's public grammar school system and the array of grammar and private schools bunched together in what was known as the 'Grammar Zone', essentially two old central suburbs in Auckland. By then they were working — Dad as a house painter, Mum behind the counter at a local café — and were intensely focused on clawing back some modicum of the life we had had back in Iran, but mostly they were focused on ensuring I had opportunities I couldn't have had back there. We moved from Kelston to a tiny unit on the cusp of Auckland's prestigious suburbs comprising The Zone. My mum remembers I burst into tears when I first saw our new home. It was tiny, weathered, and there was black mould all over the bathroom walls. I said I would never bring friends home again. She promised to fix it up and mostly did. We trooped on. I must have shrugged off that initial shock because I left my friends in West Auckland and began intermediate school in the Grammar Zone with an air of optimism. Again, I looked at the school grounds and thought about how familiar it would all be soon. Starting over isn't such a big deal once you've survived the first round.

The culture shock was pretty immediate for me. This was a far bigger school than Chaucer, but I was one of only three or four 'ethnic' students in my year. That wasn't a deterrent in itself and

I tried to talk to the other kids as I had done in my last school. That didn't work so well here. I started to get a very real feeling of being given the once-over by other children and even teachers. Something about me wasn't quite right.

What drove it home was a girl who ran over to me on the school field as I was walking home one day and asked me if I was a refugee. She was blonde with her hair in a high ponytail. She must have been playing a game on the field, because I remember she was in our school PE uniform and a little flushed.

Based on her tone and the fact that she had a hand on her hip, I instinctively said no.

She replied, 'Good, because I hate refugees.'

I knew even then that she couldn't possibly know what she had just declared. She couldn't possibly mean that she hates people who suffer persecution and war, who have been forced to live outside their country of birth. She must have been repeating hate espoused at home or on TV. Even though I knew it was wrong, I felt ashamed of what I was. I learned not to talk about being a refugee for years to come. Today, I never use the term 'former refugee'. I know many adopt it to denote a life beyond refugee status, but I fear it is also to alleviate the shame that comes with identifying as a refugee, inadvertently reinforcing the prejudice. I don't ever want to feed that.

Thankfully, that bit of overt hatred was a one-off.

One of the main problems for me in terms of being accepted in the social hierarchy at my new school was class. Everyone had expensive sneakers and schoolbags. We had a uniform, so those accessories were the key opportunities to show you were cool. It was the early 1990s, and it was all about Air Jordans, Adidas, and

Stüssy. To my family, $100 seemed like a million. I couldn't even imagine asking my parents for sport shoes that cost about double that. Better clothes wasn't going to be the fix. But, as it turned out, that was just a small part of the problem.

The real stigma seemed to run deeper. From the start, my teacher made a point of refusing to pronounce my name correctly or even attempting my last name. She was a tall, slender woman, maybe a runner, with short platinum-blonde hair and an all-year tan that you could tell she worked at. She was married to a wealthy man who owned some golf courses she often mentioned, probably where the sporty tan was nurtured. Just looking at my name on her roll at the start of the year made her annoyed. She told the whole class she wouldn't 'go there', then giggled. I realised having your name acknowledged and used in the official roll call each morning was a privilege not afforded to people like me.

I noticed there was an immediate presumption that I was 'nerdy'. The teacher gave me thick books, like *The Hobbit*, to read 'at lunchtime'. I silently took the book, but I felt embarrassed. Why did she think I would read a book alone at lunchtime? Of course, I loved books, but I had never been the kind of kid who read during breaks. Like the presumption that Chinese kids will be good at math, I'm sure this wasn't seen as racist by anyone involved. Maybe they saw it as a compliment even. But it certainly didn't come from anything I did or said. Until then, I had always been one of the girls surrounded by friends, making up games and sharing secrets. For some reason that wasn't a role I was seen as capable of occupying here.

*

More front of mind to a preteen girl is that the external gaze of the status quo beholds beauty. Of course almost every person suffers self-doubt and body image challenges at that age, and we know this is doubly difficult for young women in every culture. For me, it meant learning that, while in Iran beauty included our dark hair, broad eyebrows and olive complexions, those features were not part of the standard in the West. At least, they weren't back in 1992 New Zealand. That was news to me at a critical moment in my personal development as a young woman, and a little crushing each day.

A couple of the girls were eventually nice enough to include me in their chats over lunch. When it turned to boys, which it often did, there was a divide. The girls all asked each other which boys they thought were the cutest in our year, starting with the most popular ones. They only ever asked if I liked the Indian boy in another class. They must have assumed either that I couldn't possibly like the cute white boys, or maybe that my traditional family would arrange a marriage for me with some other ethnically ambiguous person, so why even ask. I learned to know my place and just vehemently denied liking the little Indian boy. I even started disliking him for the weird association I had been forced into. That's how people of colour in white-dominated contexts sometimes come to avoid each other, to somehow achieve the desired whiteness. From this constant exclusion, I learned that I wasn't pretty enough for conventionally attractive or socially successful men.

This wasn't just driven home in personal interactions; it came from a complete lack of representation in any forum where beauty or success was portrayed. In fact, the kids at school were obviously not the proponents of this insidious prejudice. Like me, they were merely its passive consumers. Learning that you won't ever be one of the 'pretty girls' because of the texture and colour of your hair and skin, which you cannot change, comes from constantly repeated images of what beauty is, which consistently exclude you. At that age, when every young person is desperately unsure about every aspect of their ever-changing physical appearance, this meant I learned fast about all the ways my body was innately flawed and unworthy. It goes well beyond the usual distress that comes with wearing a female human body.

Most of the media I consumed back then was by way of teen magazines, music videos, and after-school dramas centring on teenagers who lived on beaches with conveniently absent parents. They dated and experienced heartbreak necessitating melodramatic beach runs or staring into sunsets with polite tears running down their faces — the girls' faces, that is. The boys didn't cry, of course. They had cans and chairs to kick at the beach diners they worked at. I was addicted to these shows, but I also remember sometimes quickly switching the TV off with an overwhelming sense of anxiety. In what I saw as the only mature way to go forward, I tried to accept that I was not allowed those sorts of experiences because no one 'normal' or 'pretty' looked like me. I would sternly tell myself that I needed to get over it and focus on other things.

At that age, looking different to most people around me and in mainstream media drove home the challenge of fitting in. Beyond beauty standards, there was also the total vacuum of role models or even acknowledgement that people like you exist in the world. School curriculums have been slow in engaging with books by female authors or with female protagonists, and when you add race, the void is far more gaping. Even up to high school, I don't remember studying books by Māori authors, other than a single encounter with Patricia Grace in Year 12. Māori history is still a battlefield, so to speak, in terms of inclusion in standard New Zealand curriculums. The world I encountered was profoundly Pākehā. There was certainly no space for portrayals of other non-white cultures, given even indigenous peoples of the land were systematically erased.

Relatable role models, moral and aesthetic, have been missing for children of colour growing up in even the most diverse of Western societies, certainly in Aotearoa, for as long as I can remember. That's no small thing. It cuts deep. It affects the way we see ourselves and the way the world treats us later in life. We accept and adapt to the mainstream exclusion, but the point is that young Pākehā boys, and girls to a lesser extent, never have to develop that muscle in their formative years. Having a myriad of images and stories that reflect you in your school curriculum and in mainstream media is a privilege. But it shouldn't be. Without it, those doubts are confirmed: it isn't just the hormones and growing pains; the world really isn't made for you to shine in.

In 2018, *Crazy Rich Asians* became the first Hollywood blockbuster with an Asian leading cast. I saw the film on a flight recently, where I had one of those exit-row seats where you face the flight attendants during take-off and landing. We had chatted and one of them had told me I should watch it, and I was up to a random scene where an Asian male character is being objectified as he emerges from the shower, muscular and handsome. The audience was clearly expected to see him as attractive. But Asian men never get to play those roles — in fact, neither Asian men nor women get to play romantic leads in blockbusters — and that thought meant I sat there desperately trying not to be a person publicly crying during the first twenty minutes of a romantic comedy.

A few months later, during the Golden Globes, the indomitable actress Sandra Oh made a dig at Hollywood for casting two white women as leads in films based on actual Asian stories. I made the mistake of reading the comments online. One commenter, a youngish white man identifying as progressive, said it was clearly fine to cast fictional characters as any race, because if we had to portray their race accurately, the next step would be casting actual murderers as characters who commit murder.

I didn't comment, but I wanted to say: imagine a world where no film or television show you ever watched had a lead character of your ethnicity or gender as its hero, as a romantic lead, as a complex anti-hero even, ever. Maybe there was the odd character that was the butt of 'white-man' jokes here and there in the margins of the story, or once in a decade a film specifically about white men being white men in the most stereotypical way, sometimes as a cliched compliment, sometimes a negative trope — maybe about Vikings, or Nazis — but that was it. So you had never seen yourself as the lead, a hero, or an object of love in a way that reflected your life. But that made sense to everyone, because, they said, none of the films being made were based on 'white-man stories' anyway. The Kafkaesque trap was that you weren't allowed to be reflected in mainstream film or television because stories about you weren't the ones being made into major films or shows. Then suddenly they announce a film adaptation of *The Catcher in the Rye*, the great classic novel about a white, middle-class, sensitive man coming of age that seems to hit home pretty hard with that demographic. You're excited. You finally get to identify with a character; your thoughts and perspective are going to be explored centrally in a film. People are finally investing in one of the stories you grew up obsessing over. It feels like they are finally investing in *you*. Then they cast an Indian woman as Holden Caulfield. But he's fictional, so his experiences aren't based on culture or gender, right? It doesn't matter that you've never been represented in a relatable way. It doesn't matter that you've been erased this whole time. It's fiction. We don't need to be accurate. Not even this once.

The fact is that it does matter.

Film critic and screenwriter Roger Ebert said cinema is about building empathy. That's because it allows us to experience different worlds, to see our world through different eyes. If that's true, exclusion of entire cultures, races and religions from pop culture is deeply problematic. It doesn't just erase those peoples; it actively promotes certain demographics as the only normal, the only complex, the only human way to be. It means that the little game of imagining I wished I could play with that commenter on Sandra Oh's clip is barely possible to members of dominant demographics, because they've never had to exercise that level of empathy. The ability to relate to other people's experiences is built through practice. Is that why this 'progressive' ally missed the point Sandra was making?

It wasn't until I studied the American civil rights movement of the 1950s and '60s in high school when some of what I had personally experienced growing up clicked together. The Black is Beautiful campaign, calling for the acceptance and idealisation of natural hair among African Americans, amalgamated the staunch rise of two equality movements. The fight for civil rights for African Americans was predicated on breaking down white supremacy at every level, just as second-wave feminists campaigned against oppressive beauty standards for women. Oppression by enforced beauty standards was part of the idea that 'The personal is political'. The erasure of men and women of colour from popular culture and beauty standards is part of the fabric of white supremacy. On that spectrum that ends with far worse degradation, even violence, is the step where we learn that the texture of your hair is all wrong.

If you're a Middle Eastern or South Asian woman, it might mean learning there's 'too much' hair on you — your eyebrows, arms, or upper lip — and it all needs to be removed so you look more 'beautiful'. I remember at eleven years old having no idea what to do about this emergency. I tried shaving the soft dark hairs on my upper lip and what I saw as sideburns. To my horror, that just made bald patches. My mother was persuaded to get involved with threading, and disaster was averted by a lengthy, and painful, process of removing the hairs all over my face. But I still hated the soft thicket of upper-lip hair, the impending monobrow, the brows themselves, way too dark and thick for the early 1990s arched style. Now, every time I look at the array of eyebrow-defining products, and images of fair-skinned models with eyebrows groomed to be fashionably thicker, I smile.

The Black is Beautiful campaign was about the rejection of painful chemical straighteners through affirmations that afro hair and dark skin forms part of what beauty is. I know what deep-seated anguish would drive someone to chemically burn their scalp to alter their non-white appearance. I remember as a twelve-year-old feeling like I looked unclean with what I felt was an eternal film of soft dark hairs over my face. I remember feeling like I would do anything to just wash it all away.

Even changing your appearance in all the superficial ways young women do was barely possible to ethnic girls back then. Hair dye only ever worked to make dark hair into various shades of red or orange. A little change meant you could go dark brown with auburn tones. But if you wanted real change, there was a rainbow of peroxide tones from deep rust to light golden brass. All hair dye advertisements and packaging portrayed white women with very different shades of medium to light brown or blonde hair. Only in recent years did they finally make tone control possible for us, no doubt led by the growing financial power of the Asian beauty consumer.

Likewise, make-up was only ever for pink-toned skin. Many of us with darker or yellow undertones will remember when wearing foundation meant looking like we had an alien tone from the neck up, and never remembering to blend properly from the neck down. Of course, the shades were also never dark enough, so most women of colour looked like we were attempting whiteface.

For me, at intermediate school, the messages about beauty also came more directly. The other girls told me from time to time that my hair was gross, because I put oil in it 'like Atika'. A year ahead of us, Atika was of South Asian origin and must have at some point talked about putting oil in her hair. I never had oil in mine, but there was no point arguing facts.

I had developed curves early, as all the women in my mother's family do, so I was also told regularly by the other girls that I must eat 'bad' or 'fatty' food at home because I was fat. In the same breath, those kids would ask if my house smelled like curry. I didn't know what curry really smelled like at that point, since Iranians don't make curries and Indian food wasn't all that widespread in New Zealand. I knew the implication was that the food my family ate was gross and smelled bad. I knew that made me want to cry. I started counting calories and incessantly running after school, desperately trying to lose the 'fat' to put an end to the snide comments. I lost sleep feeling anxious about things I had eaten as far back as years before. I wore baggier clothes and avoided boys, so they didn't have to live with the discomfort of feeling like I was flirting with them. I didn't want them to think I was so clueless as to believe that was a role I could possibly inhabit.

Imagine there was a moment when race suddenly comes to exist and affect your daily experiences of the world. It is made clear that within that arbitrary construct of 'race', you are brown, and that is something you have no control over. That identification carries things with it beyond colour. It carries a myriad of assumptions projected onto you that were never there before. It eventually comes with internalised self-hate, as you react against the projections, try to be less 'brown', downplay it, learn mimicry, or become silent. Otherwise it underpins a reactionary pride, as you begin to 'own' whatever those presumptions are.

I do think it's different for those born into societies where race is an innate part of identity. Processing it later, as I did, comes with the benefit of always knowing that this is a construct to begin with, because you remember life without the barriers. It also comes with the sting of being awake, so to speak, when the knife goes in.

That realisation came around the time I, like most preteens, wished that my parents would just be 'normal'. It was different for me, though, because I started to notice things like how they couldn't really help me manoeuvre the everyday logistics of life or even social decorum, which they themselves were learning. They were even suddenly at a loss when it came to helping with my homework, which they were big on back in Iran. Other than mathematics or science, they were behind me in every subject.

Towards the end of my first year of intermediate, the school held a dance, a Blue Light Disco. It was an annual disco sponsored by the New Zealand Police, which may give an indication of how cool the event was. I was nervous. I wanted to look good, so I convinced my parents to buy me a white denim skirt. I wore the skirt with a bright purple-and-pink cropped top. Both resulted from an arduous and exhilarating expedition at Kmart. That outfit would have been cool in Iran or in some Euro-pop music video, but sadly everyone at the disco was wearing jeans and baggy T-shirts, because Kiwis are nothing if not understated. I did dance a little, but mostly melted into the corners, chatting to the other kids who weren't super into standing out that night.

The real disaster of the night, I realised later, had come before I even walked into the darkened gym. My dad had driven me to the school. As he'd indicated to turn down the driveway of the school, I had become agitated. I told him that he had come too far, to not drop me at the entrance where everyone could see. I asked him to let me out somewhere down the road, so I could walk in alone. He was confused for a second, then seemed to take on my panic and quickly got away from the school. Just before I scurried away from the car, he wished me fun and said he would see me back here at the end of the dance.

The next day, my mum took me for a drive. She stopped the car at a park, turned to me and asked, 'Do you feel like your dad has been a good dad?'

It was an odd, pointed question, and I had no idea what she was getting at. I gave her a simple unassuming 'yes'.

I remember her voice was stern and holding back anger. She said, 'I think so too.' Then she looked straight ahead, away from me. She said, 'I always liked how much time he spends with you, no matter how tired he is.' She raised her voice a touch: 'And he always takes an interest in what you're into. He spent all that time playing the games with your dolls when you were little, taking you and your friends out. You remember? Not all dads do that.'

I was choking back tears by then.

She turned and asked, 'Was it worth your dad, such a good dad, feeling like his daughter is ashamed of him for the sake of what some kids at school think?'

I can still feel the punch to the gut.

'You need to remember that we came here together as a family and we can't lose ourselves,' she said. 'No one's opinion is important out there except the opinion of the people who love you, otherwise you will lose yourself.' Then, more gently: 'Do you understand, dear?'

I nodded.

As we drove home, I sat there, remembering how my dad used to be the 'cool dad' and how proud I was that he was my dad when he agreed to take my friends and me to do things back in Iran. I realise now that what he felt that night went beyond what a normal parent goes through, because, for him, my reaction was part of the fabric of this new world where he was losing himself.

I could see it so clearly in his lack of jokes, in his demeanour when we were out, in the way he struggled to know what people were saying. Now, he wasn't the cool dad anymore, and that was one more thing on top of all the other things he had lost of his old place in the world.

My mother was right, and I still think hard about whose opinion I value and whose feelings I protect when I have a visceral reaction of shame or the need to fit in. It was a real lesson of the regret you will feel later if you don't stand by your people. It applies now to my work. Which communities am I pleasing and whose oppression am I amplifying if I base my decisions on what is popular rather than what is true to my roots?

But, man, was that a harsh truth for an eleven-year-old girl to hear after the school dance.

It was infinitely lucky that before things got hard, and I got busy processing myself as an outsider, my parents made inroads into Auckland's tiny Iranian community. It was a community of families who had been there longer than we had, many of whom had kids my age.

That's how I met Ghazaleh Golbakhsh. We had invited her aunt and uncle over for dinner one night. She had heard a girl her age would be there, so she came along. She walked into our house carrying a bundle of movie magazines, and held them out straight away with a huge grin. Her aunt introduced us and Ghazaleh's first words to me were: 'I'm going to be an actress when I grow up.'

She was darker than I was, tiny, flat-chested, with straight pins for legs and no hips. She showed me her famous Michael Jackson impersonations that night, which were, frankly, totally on point.

We hit it off, and spent much of the night lying on my bedroom floor, analysing whether Christian Slater was cuter than Billy Warlock, one of the guys from *Baywatch*. I was for Billy, but in retrospect Ghaz went with the more iconic of 1990s heartthrobs. I was instantly sold on Ghaz. She inhabited a world where we were allowed to have crushes on cute boys and perv on 25-year-old film and TV stars. A world where we could not only dream about becoming famous actresses, but declare it as truth.

I started to see my social life as a separate world from school. There was a bunch of us Iranian kids who were around eleven or twelve years old, boys and girls, as well as a bunch of older teens who were cooler and came with more drama, which we eleven- and twelve-year-olds could gossip about and aspire to. We spoke on the phone for hours, annoying our parents. In a time when the household only had one phoneline, and dial-up internet was becoming a thing, the phone became a family battleground. We relished these contests with our parents, imagining ourselves as proper stroppy teenagers.

Soon my parents had saved enough to buy a small business, a little liquor shop in Onehunga, which was then a rough neighbourhood in Auckland. They were mildly embarrassed about the type of business they ran, but it was the only thing they could afford. They knew by then that business was the only way they could succeed here, having been thoroughly assured that their qualifications were meaningless. My parents worked in the shop till 10 pm each night, so I was alone at home a lot, and the phone became my world. I would come home from school, heat up whatever elaborate meal Mum had cooked before work and left for my dinner, and basically laugh and chatter with my Iranian friends all night. We would also see each other regularly, at beach trips, or, if we could convince our parents to drop us off, the mall (the dream scenario).

The Iranians in Auckland were a disparate bunch with little in common in terms of personalities, but with a shared commitment to keeping their customs alive. No one was traditional or conservative. They were all people who had fled after the revolution, so wanted to gather together to erase that nightmare. We threw parties like we had in Iran, always with a head-spinning variety of food in volumes to feed twice our number. There was ghormeh sabzi (a slow-cooked lamb dish so rich with herbs it looks dark green, including fenugreek, a particularly pungent herb, which makes it risky served to Westerners), tah chin (a beautiful chicken dish a lot like biryani, where the chicken is cooked golden and a little crisp with saffron, then cooked with the rice as it steams), and, my favourite, khoreshte bademjan (lamb cooked with eggplant and served with rice). Iranian food is high maintenance. Each part is normally lightly fried with cumin and turmeric, so the taste is sealed, then slow-cooked together for hours. We also take rice very seriously, both the type (always aromatic long grain) and the cooking method. It can make or break an entire meal. If the rice is sticking, you've failed as a host, and maybe as a human being. We have a saying that translates to, 'You would start a fight with this rice,' meaning it's not up to standard and, if served, could be taken as an insult.

Dinner was served comically late, but the delicious aroma was always in the air as you came in, mixed with the sounds of high-tempo Iranian dance music on the stereo and boisterous compliments as people greeted each other. The women were always dressed to the nines. The colours and sparkle they toned down for everyday life in New Zealand shone bright in homeland company. People would drink, sing and dance various modern and traditional dances (partly in jest and partly from nostalgia, someone would suddenly start their own folk dance from whatever province they were from and everyone would clap along). These dinners always went into the early hours of the next morning.

As the adults caroused, we kids would peel off into our different age groups and carry on largely unsupervised. For our part, my group held seances, played spin-the-bottle, and flipped through magazines. Sometimes Ghaz would try to teach us the dance moves to pop songs. I remember we dressed up for these gatherings too. The boys were into basketball, so it was Air Jordans if they could get them, basketball singlets over T-shirts, and baggy shorts. The girls would get our mums to sew new outfits, copying the ones in magazines, which we couldn't quite afford to buy. It was all tight, striped, ribbed turtlenecks and long skirts circa the early 1990s. Eventually, I managed to save my pocket money and beg for help from my parents to buy a pair of Converse One Star sneakers to finish the look. They were brown and I loved them. But none of this was for the eyes of my peers at school anymore. We lived in a parallel universe.

I realised later that Ghaz was at an even more monocultural, more isolating suburban school. She was teased because of her dark skin and called 'Speedy Gonzalez'. She was a true drama club geek for all the reasons kids do drama: to escape their reality with others looking to do the same. She and I started writing little comedy skits together and filming them using my parent's camcorder. Somewhere in my mother's garage sits a pile of unwatchable tapes (for both technical and substantive reason) of us performing our in-jokes, barely making it through a take without doubling over in hysterics. We became obsessed with old films, and would bus into the city to sit in the public library reading about James Dean and Marlon Brando for hours. We would also buy old postcards and find posters of them in bargain bins to cover our walls. No one else our age really knew who they were, but that was fine with us.

Ghaz eventually made it into filmmaking. She learned about the lack of roles for girls like us the hard way. After yet another unsuccessful audition, we'd cackle and drink wine, penniless and heartbroken. It was the 'huddle together and laugh' technique for dealing with pain we'd perfected as twelve-year-old Iranian girls, I suppose. She worked in any job that got her on a film set, on films that took her to Cannes, and on theatre stages which seemed more forgiving of differences. In the end, she had a ball, and eventually went on to study screenwriting at the University of Southern California's prestigious School of Film. At the time of writing, in 2019, she teaches film, is making her first feature, and is the founder of Waking Dream Collective, a women's film collective in Auckland, focused on bringing unique marginalised stories and voices to the screen.

Glowing a review as that is of her inexhaustible knack for survival, I can't say she came through with that same air of eternal victory and glint in her eye that she had as a ten-year-old. In the end, having to fight so much harder to be seen every time you walk into a room does wear off the shine.

As we were downing prosecco one summer night recently and laughing about our early monobrows and terrible comedy skits, we dug up her childhood diaries. I brought out mine the next time. It had a worn-out padlock — like anyone was dying to read about how much I hated maths and how I hoped a boy in my class named Ross was looking at me that day.

We discovered something unexpectedly horrifying, if tragically comical. It was about the time, at twelve years old, when we began flirting with some boys on the phone, who we came to know and talk to pretty regularly through our friend Sadra, an Iranian boy our age. We never did meet these boys in person because of the rather huge glitch in our genius idea to describe ourselves as, essentially, white dream girls. There were four of us Iranian girls involved. We told them our names were Anglo names like Erica and Sommer. Ghaz, who always had to stand out, invented hers. It was 'Vanise'. Our diaries detailed our made-up physical features, so we wouldn't slip up on the phone. It seems I had light-brown hair and green eyes. We all had light-coloured eyes and either blonde or light-brown hair.

I remember the totally liberating delight of 'meeting' a boy and being some girl who could be one of the girls in magazines. In fact, I remember literally looking at magazines and smugly feeling like, for that half hour a day I was on the phone talking to Brendon (the boy who ended up liking me most), I could be any of the normal girls in those pages that boys might actually like. We didn't tell the boys we were pretty or skinny. We just changed our race, as if that was enough to imply all the other desirable things. Alarmingly, I didn't see anything strange about this at the time.

After the hearty laughter at our childhood mishaps, Ghaz and I had to stop and admit it was pretty chilling. That not one of us even hesitated to make up these identities, that it was such an unsaid shared fantasy between us, was overwhelmingly sad.

Once we had agreed it would be fun not to tell the boys our real names on that first phone call, none of us considered, even for a second, that we would just be different Iranian girls or that we would at least still have black hair and dark eyes. It was somehow so obvious that, given half a chance, we would of course be white. As we re-read the diary entries over drinks so many years later, another revelation dawned on us. We realised for the first time that the boys we were speaking to were not themselves white. They had names like Brendon or Cameron, but their last names were Sharma and Singh. I can't remember now if they too were pretending to be white, but we certainly had thought they were because we assumed they were attractive and to us that meant white. Just as we assumed they would like us more if we weren't Iranian.

Thankfully there are far more alternatives now. My early '90s experience happened at a time when far less diversity existed in pop culture. Even the blight of being exotic hadn't penetrated the popular consciousness. Now, people invest in and make Hollywood films about normal things like love and laughter with whole Asian casts — I can think of at least two such films off the top of my head. That certainly wasn't so for my generation.

I do believe that the space and community we made for ourselves as Iranian–New Zealanders saved me, and in the end emboldened me to own that outsider status in other less-accepting spaces like my school.

5

Karangahape Road

I don't believe in fate, but sometimes things go wrong in the very best ways.

At some point in 1992, my parents were panicked to learn, way too late, that we weren't actually living in the Grammar Zone for high-school entrance purposes. We were out by a hair's breadth, but it may as well have been a thousand miles. We had no contacts or family links to draw on, so my mother started writing and asking for appointments with local politicians. She felt strongly that meeting with elected officials was something we should embrace as good citizens. Some actually met with her, if only to apologise and tell her there was nothing they could do. One local representative told her it may be my lack of sporting prowess that was holding me back from out-of-zone entry. This was a deficiency we could all easily accept, one which I was thoroughly comfortable with at this point.

Having made no inroads with local politicians, my parents reluctantly decided I would go to the next best school we could manage. Auckland Girls Grammar School (AGGS) had a fancy-sounding name and was the country's oldest high school for girls, but in 1993 it wasn't considered a top school. For one thing, it was in the inner city and smack bang in the middle of the red-light district of Karangahape Road (a detail of which my parents were unaware). The plan was for me to go there for a year while we sorted out the zoning issue. My parents were already moving us into yet another decrepit unit, even worse than the last but more expensive, because this time we would be properly 'in the zone'. But I never went back. I was elated at the thought of a clean break from the fancy kids I had only managed tenuous acquaintanceships with over my two years at intermediate. I could never endure high school with an even bigger horde of haughty rich kids. AGGS saved my soul.

By 1993, I was a thin, ethnically ambiguous thirteen-year-old, with a little bit of a tough exterior and a slightly angst-ridden disdain for anything 'popular', because frankly popularity was none of my business. Not by design, but I was perfect for an inner-city school tucked between the red-light district, the rainbow community, and downtown Auckland.

The story of Auckland's urban poor and Pasifika communities was integral to the school's unique culture and diverse student body. The suburbs around AGGS had once been the centre of state housing and the Pasifika community. But by the time I got there in the 1990s, most of these people had already been pushed out by rising housing prices into the outer suburbs of South and West Auckland.

The student body at AGGS was and still is filled with girls who gained entry by virtue of their grandmothers, mothers, and older sisters having attended the school when their families still lived nearby. Families generationally send their girls to AGGS for a better education than might be available in the far-away suburbs where they now live. This meant that when I first walked through the big towering iron gates at AGGS, the 2000-or-so strong student body was around seventy per cent Māori or Pasifika. That population was peppered with the daughters of a free-spirited Pākehā community, who began gentrifying the neighbouring suburbs in the 1980s. The area wasn't yet solidly fancy or desirable like it is now, though it did boast some of the city's best cuisine and nightlife. The white middle-class families there were either hippies, running organic food stores and wearing hemp, or baby boomers, who at least considered themselves enlightened enough to choose life among student flats and a thriving LGBTQI+ community. Sending their daughters to AGGS was part of that casual rebellion.

But AGGS also has a haughty history of old money — as old as money gets in the youngest of British colonies — that built the nation's first-ever grammar school for girls. That was reflected in the school's name and physical aesthetic.

AGGS is on Howe Street, a leafy oasis lined with towering oak trees and fallen acorns, detached from their polluted urban setting. The school's buildings looked like nothing I had ever seen around Auckland. The first sight as you walk in is the main building, A Block, which stands at the centre of the top lawn, an immaculate English lawn fenced by a surreal thicket of native flax and dense bush. A Block itself could be a small castle or some hall in a Katherine Mansfield story about fancy garden parties in colonial New Zealand. The old manor stands gloating at the end of the winding path into the school. Of course, it has a bell tower and is covered in worn ivy. This is no fresh aspirational wisp. No, this is forever ivy. That alien vegetation tells its lies about culture and prestige so well that the building could, at first sight, be mistaken for one on the grounds of Oxford University, or on a Harry Potter movie set.

All this was in wild contrast with the loud unrestrained manner of the girls walking the halls. Most of the uniforms were worn, hinting at hand-me-downs or second-hand purchases. Some wore non-regulation flip-flops. There were constant eruptions of scream-laughing, singing, casual twirling of poi on the way to class. On the lawn, people played kilikiti rather than cricket. Nothing of the life vigorously lived there matched the school's exterior. This was unmistakably a Pacific institution housed in a fancy old English grammar school. This was quintessential Auckland. The contrast was stark but beautiful. I had never even been to a proper big school before and I had certainly never seen a non-white majority population since I left Iran. Walking into AGGS was exhilarating.

Though the suburbs around the school and their cultural history defined the student body, it was Karangahape Road that most defined our experience of attending AGGS in the 1990s. K Road sits in uptown Auckland and, because most bus routes stop there, a sea of navy blue–uniformed AGGS girls walk along it twice daily. That made us inadvertently part of the most eclectic community in New Zealand.

The road is best known as a red-light district to most Kiwis who've heard of it. In the '90s, that meant walking past strip clubs, peep shows, and sex shops optimally named Vegas Girl and The Pink Pussy. If we left school late and darkness was setting in, it might mean walking past sex workers arriving at their spots for the night along the side streets of K Road, including Howe Street. It also meant regularly encountering trans women, who seemed more open to interacting with us girls and were protective of us.

My Iranian friends were always a little perplexed about my school choice, but, at least in my mind, they were also in awe of the adventure I was having. I was in turn very protective of AGGS and K Road. The sex workers were not a threat. The trans women were funny and warm and beautiful. Nothing there was to be stared at or run away from. It was all just misunderstood. It made me feel good to think I got it, that my new schoolmates and I were part of something less ordinary. Mercifully, my parents remained very much in the dark about K Road.

In reality, it wasn't the sex industry that ruled the K Road experience. This was a place of inexhaustible variety. For one thing, it has been home to an established homeless community for some time. This was well before homelessness was a city-wide problem of displacement based on economic inequality and housing shortage. That's not to say the K Road homeless community wasn't there for all sorts of distressing reasons, including poverty, racism, untreated mental illness or addiction. But most were there — as opposed to anywhere else in the city — by choice. The geography worked — it was urban enough not to alarm suburbanites, but far enough out of the soulless, unforgiving financial centre. In fact, the other residents and businesses there were actively open to fringe dwellers. In a sense, they fancied themselves 'vagrants' in one way or another.

The homeless community was still vulnerable to all the things that make them targets of violence and illness. But from what

I saw, physical harm was almost always inflicted by visitors from the 'respectable' side of town. These were people who came to K Road to be depraved for a night, then forget the mess they left behind. They'd come for a 'boys' night out', a debauched corporate do, a trip to the 'Big Smoke'. They'd come from sheltered small towns and the polite decent suburbs. For the visitors, 'having fun' ranged from drunkenness and a touch of nudity to beating trans sex workers and urinating on sleeping homeless folks. That's when K Road became frightening for its residents. As the suburbs and the heartland descended on K Road every weekend, there was blood on the footpath most Sunday mornings. It's a scene I've seen repeated in recent years, as I've ended up living just off this haven of chaos most of my adult life. They smash up the street and the people, then they retreat.

The sense of belonging on K Road had a lot to do with its business community too. By the early 1990s, it was a little gentrified, but still terrifying to most of society: there were dive bars and underground music joints; tattoo studios and piercing salons. The cafes were grungy — needles on the floor and soiled upholstery grungy, not mason jars and ironic tattoos grungy. K Roaders of that era remember Brazil, the café with its rickety iron spiral staircase into the darkness above. There was the Lost Angel at the top of Howe Street with its cheap toasted sandwiches and, well, needles on the floor. That was an easy place to skip to from AGGS during lunchtime. It was also the heyday of Verona, dark, with DJs that spun long into the night, but strangely also filled with delicious homemade counter food. Grunge itself was a bit new but definitely deliberate and on the mainstream radar given Kurt Cobain had hit hard. So while as AGGS girls we couldn't take any credit for being there by choice, K Roaders were proud to be part of the 'original' grunge scene.

Karangahape Road's crowning jewel, and its safest drawcard, was St Kevins Arcade overlooking Myers Park, itself a scary landmark at night. The arcade was filled with second-hand clothing stores and headed by the sprawling Alleluya Café at the far end. All have since been driven out by renovations, though the general vibe is at least still broadly bohemian.

Because Alleluya was so far down the arcade and safely away from street view, it made the perfect hiding place for truants and became central to my life in the K Road ecosystem. A bunch of us spent half our school lives there. Coffee culture had just hit New Zealand, so we would pool our money and order a cappuccino between two or three people and sit there for hours. We felt like serious vagrants and very adult.

Peter, who owned Alleluya for some twenty-one years before the arcade was sold to developers, had created a community hub. In my mind he was a priest-like figure, floating around between the spaced-out tables and chairs that eventually took up half the arcade with a wise half-smile on his face. He was a bit of a father figure who had seen it all and didn't mind the mess that came and went from his domed house of refuge. Alleluya was warm and bright from the sunlight that poured in through the massive ceiling-high windows overlooking the park and washed over the mismatched fading furniture. You could see the glowing promised land as you walked into the darkened arcade. Everything from the carved ceilings to the wooden tables and chairs were covered in washed-out chipped paint, revealing bursts of red or blue or green, jewel tones grounded down to pastels on wood or plaster.

Some of the most intimate secrets shared by my friends and me in high school were whispered in darkened booths in Alleluya or Verona. We went to Verona after one of my best friends came out to me at fifteen years old. It's also where a friend first told me her dad, who I knew and loved, was schizophrenic and she grew up scared of his episodes, which were starting to come back with a change in medication. We talked for hours about going to art school, as I wanted to do with my two best friends, Anna Jackson and Alicia Frankovich.

Those of us who grew up there never stopped going because the serenity of that meeting point between grit and open sunlight is hard to find. Peter left and the space where Alleluya once was became a new café, something freshly painted with uniform furnishings in 2016. The staff are still young and consciously very street. They were born in the mid-1990s, when Alleluya first opened. The spirit has endured a bit, I guess because of the location and who it inherently attracts, and the strength of Peter's own spirit. Most of this book was written from under that domed window, decades after I first started smugly hiding at Alleluya to compare Dr. Martens boots and avoid handing in unfinished homework.

Arguably, what brought true eclecticism to Karangahape Road was that it was also home to businesses from old and new ethnic communities. There was the best Hare Krishna restaurant in Auckland, where you washed your own tin plates and didn't need to pay for food if you couldn't. Today, a few of the other little Indian eateries still stand, including one with windows stacked full of fluoro-coloured geometric sweets. There was the Cambodian food court and the Chinese grocers. There were tiny girls often playing and giggling on the footpath in front of their families' hair-braiding salons, catering to tiny African and West Indian communities around Auckland, as well as anyone tapping into the reggae revival back then.

None of these outlets — from the sex shops to the dive bars to the bourgeoning ethnic eateries and services — had found a home in the sedate suburbs and most hadn't wanted to be there anyway. It brought the community together as equals and it meant we had prominent elders, so to speak, from all walks of life.

I remember Margaret Hoffman was queen. Though few knew her name or story at the time, we all wondered who she was and how she had come to be here each day. An elegant wiry figure who towered over the strip, Margaret was ageless and unapproachable. She was immaculately dressed, sometimes even in furs, in what were likely outfits gifted to her by the many gorgeous vintage stores dotting her home street. I would call her aesthetic 'worn '70s glam'. Her hair was big. It changed between blonde, red and brown, with grey roots and a big protruding fringe that hit just above her brows. The hairdressers must have taken care of her when it got too unkempt. She often held a hip flask–sized bottle of liquor in a paper bag, sometimes a paper coffee cup as well. She was always smoking. The image burned in my mind's eye is of Margaret sitting on her usual bench, her long, statuesque arms folded across her gaunt, slightly hunched torso, cigarette tipped between her fingers. Her incredible, long legs would be crossed and sometimes swinging a little agitatedly. She would watch us AGGS girls as we passed her and sometimes let out a loud, threatening hoick of her throat that made us think she would spit at us at any moment, which she never did.

When Margaret passed away in April 2011, hundreds turned out for her funeral, including politicians and prominent entertainers. That's when most of us who knew her as a K Road icon first learned her full name. We also learned that she had been institutionalised and received electroshock treatment in her youth. We heard her family challenge the government to better support people like Margaret, at a time when funding to mental-health services had long been inadequate. Those in most need of support were either in prison or living on the streets like Margaret, or, as was often the case, trapped between both nightmares. Even today, night shelters still don't exist for Auckland's homeless community, which has ballooned since Margaret's day. Margaret, who even in her staunch demeanour was still so palpably vulnerable, was almost always on K Road alone. She sometimes slept through the night exposed to the elements and drank all day to forget it.

I was glad that, as I went through high school, I got to see the facets of life that were not all picture-perfect, because deep down I had felt so excluded from that picture already. The friends I made at AGGS astound me. We are largely soulmates to this day, though scattered around the world living vastly different careers and lifestyles.

Alicia holds the most defining space in my AGGS circle, with her wild hair always in a forced low bun behind her head. Having since become a successful globetrotting artist, she now has her head shaved, apart from a declarative thicket at the top. She was a perpetual ball of nerves in the way I imagine every true original must be as a teen, smothered by the rest of us plebeians. Her family lived in an old villa in Grey Lynn. Part Samoan and

Croatian, Alicia was raised Catholic, and was the oldest of four. What we shared was a penchant for observing absurdities in the world around us, in our families, in ourselves. We would sit for hours laughing at dark jokes, noticing how everything ordinary was too strange to bear. A lot of it stemmed from a very teenage delusion of grandeur. We probably also overblew our own wit. But it was a great time.

Alicia and I were deeply committed to art and photography. A great side effect of the posh history of our school was that the Old Girls donated lots of money, so our facilities were top notch. We spent hours in the enormous art rooms perfecting our end-of-year boards.

I remember realising I wasn't an artist after the very first project, because it was when I also realised Alicia *was* an artist. We'd been given a simple brief: create a photo series based on something in our environment. Everyone rushed off school grounds, because we were allowed to for the assignment. I embarked on an awkward portraiture project of the people who ran and patronised the hair braiding studios, though I was never skilled enough to get close or use the medium to capture anything more than each person standing in their shop looking directly at my camera. But Alicia stayed. She took photos of the enormous old oak trees on the fringes of the school, angling each shot at the base of the trunk looking up. The tree itself was towering and insurmountable with a bright light at the very top. She said she wanted to show how things can seem distorted sometimes, how everyday life can seem so intimidating. She found everyday life intimidating, I learned a short while later, because she was gay. She felt like everyone around her could tell, like they could basically see the gay in the way she moved and talked and evaded their eyes. She felt like we were all normal and normal was intimidating to her, because it was out of reach. I was in awe of her ability to express this feeling, the anxiety of being different, in her art.

Though we had often talked about going to art school together, it was then I knew this would not be my path. Still, it was heart-wrenching for me to go to university without Alicia and Anna. In the end, I wanted to do something more outwardly focused. I felt like art would be an indulgence I couldn't allow myself full time.

But the art block and its reigning sovereign, the head of department Trixie Illingworth, remained central to my high-school life until the end. Mrs Illingworth must have been in her early sixties, small in build and always in sensible trousers and button-down shirts. Her hair was cut in a short, grey crop and she had light blue eyes and a pierced smoker's mouth.

By turn of fortune, Mrs Illingworth was our class' art teacher from the start. Our opening assignment was to paint a simple landscape scene. Trixie walked around the class with a deep scowl on her face, checking that everyone had their materials ready. She stood in the middle of us all, looking up at her for instruction, and said, 'If any stupid girl paints the sky as a blue strip at the top of her canvas, she will have to leave my classroom.' Then she marched outside for a cigarette.

The scowl was a permanent fixture, but it only thinly veiled a great magnetism that cut through regardless. She had an open hatred for teaching art to the giant hordes of girls who were forced to take it in the early years of high school, because of her own deep love and commitment to both the practice and study of art. It was difficult for her to share it with an indifferent group.

As the classes got smaller and we were interacting with her as fellow artists, the warmth poured out. She remained a harsh critic, but no teacher was as nuanced in their engagement with our work. Trixie told Anna, Alicia and me that she would make sure we were always in her form class, so we were always housed in the beautiful art block, next to the dark room, where we'd often share passing quiet moments with her.

It was also around this time that we learned about the complex injustices behind the hardened chain-smoking woman before us. We found a class photo of her early years of teaching. She was beautiful, with dark long hair and vibrant blue eyes. We asked her when she'd begun teaching. She told us she had been an artist herself, and had been so passionate about art that she had saved to travel to Europe and dropped to her knees weeping when she first got to see the works of the old masters. But in her day, it was hard for women to be taken seriously as artists. The most you could hope for was to be an art teacher and produce your work as a hobby, more or less on the side. She was married to another artist for a time. Later, she said, she watched as he got to be paid to practise his art, as he gained recognition and lived the life she had wanted for herself, while she raised their son on her own.

That was the story of generations of women. I felt the weight of expectation on me when I heard those stories. What would we do, as the generation that could 'have it all'? Would we practise our art? Would we loudly create rather than quietly teach and nurture others behind the scenes? Not that there's not tremendous value in teaching — those who teach often change the world more than those who insist on fronting movements. But Trixie didn't want to teach. It was the weight of expectation bearing down on her generation that had defined her life. Other women had persisted and forged paths. But they were few. Young Trixie, weeping at the foot of the old Madonna, couldn't turn away from motherhood in the suburbs once her husband was gone. She never got the space, the room of one's own, to think and feel and create. Her feet were in wet cement.

I feel the weight of that expectation. The expectation to be visible and unapologetic about my background, to lead the way for others. I've spoken about it to other women of colour in politics when we quietly talk about the incredible barrage of resistance that we each receive daily. It is a perpetual fight to be taken seriously as experts where we have expertise, to have our talents recognised, and even just to face our day without vitriol. The thing is, as much as I want more and more women and minorities in politics, I am hesitant to put that expectation on them knowing what they will face in response. We can't keep telling women to 'lean in'. It isn't safe. It certainly isn't safe for women of colour. We know that because we see the abuse plainly online. We see it in the unequal treatment by the media. We hear about it constantly from women who have opened up briefly only to have to pull shut that iron curtain we've all woven around us. It isn't fair to place the burden of change on individuals. That ignores millennia of systemic oppression. It ignores that culture needs to change, that the systems are prejudiced. Trixie was strong, but she wasn't strong enough to pour herself into her art, then fight against all of society for recognition, while she starved with her baby under one arm. So she cut her hair short, taught art for the rest of her life, and smoked two packs a day.

Of course, she did inspire another talented woman whose salvation lay in her passion for art, who did get to travel the world and have her work celebrated, while being a woman who loves other women. I don't think Alicia would have made it through high school in such high spirits had it not been for that safe space Trixie provided us, a space to create, but also to be angry about the world we couldn't control sometimes, to be passionate and fearful. At the end of it all, Trixie's enduring anger was a testament to her uncompromising passion for her art and the world she wanted to live in. Alicia and I certainly thrived having that as our standard.

There were inspirational antidotes to Trixie's pessimism among my AGGS teachers. Mrs Cotter, the head of history, was a ball of energy, part doting mother, part witty orator. She deliberately included histories that remain untold to many students in New Zealand, like the Palestine/Israel conflict, the American civil rights movement, and apartheid in South Africa. She avoided World War II and almost all English history, but made sure we studied the New Zealand Wars and even forced us to compare accounts between Māori and Pākehā historians. She signed us up to a saving plan in Year 11, so we could go on an overseas history trip in Year 13. She came on the trip to supervise along with a couple of other teachers, all paying their own way. She said she did it to encourage us to save and travel, because she knew most AGGS girls wouldn't think of it otherwise, given our socio-economic backgrounds. My year went on a cross-country tour of the US, which inspired my history degree with a focus on modern American history, gender and consumerism.

There was Michal Denny, the biology teacher. She was tall and slim, with a short brown bob framing her beaming young face, a cross between Miss Honey from *Matilda* and Madame Curie. Ms Denny was as dry and serious as most scientists are about science, but she was also an engaging teacher. She had a commanding presence in the classroom enhanced by a profound joy she took from both her subject matter and being able to convey that subject matter to fresh minds.

I was uncharacteristically good at science. I even got an interview at Auckland Medical School. My goal was to eventually specialise in psychiatry, because I was interested in analysis and in people. I had initially thought about doing psychology, but my mother had talked me out of it. Although at one time that had been her field and her passion, something she had defied her family to study (ironically, they'd pressured her to go with medicine), she said she knew psychologists didn't make good money and she now knew how hard life was without it.

I told Ms Denny this one afternoon, late in my final year of school, as I was acting as her teacher's aide in a Year 9 class. I remember she was standing in the middle of the room, sorting things on a desk. The students had mostly left for their next period. When I told her what my mother had said, she stopped and looked straight at me. Her tone was serious and a little alarmed.

'You can do anything you want to,' she said.

Then she smiled and talked about teaching. It wasn't a money-making profession, but it was what she loved doing. 'I earn enough to take care of myself and that's enough,' she said. Then she added, 'I'm not married either,' though she did live with her partner.

Here was this woman, strong and educated, choosing convention in her choice of profession, and throwing out convention altogether in her personal life. It made me realise that every life choice is worth making consciously. That it's important to challenge the assumptions behind the norms and ideals we're fed at every turn. It made me realise I didn't need to get my life's path from a bank commercial or anyone else's hopes and dreams.

While some teachers were personally defining for me, the formidable force and reigning matriarch of the school was the deputy principal and PE teacher, Di Hatch. At first blush, she made for a peculiar figure walking the halls at AGGS. She looked like a powerful corporate executive, always in perfectly fitted, expensive suits and sky-high pointed stilettos (I guess her athletic prowess helped her manoeuvre the school's steep incline and hundreds of steps in those shoes). In those days she sported a blonde Princess Diana crop. She was beautiful, impeccably put together, and always stood and moved like an athlete or a soldier, shoulders back, feet apart. It was hard to know how she had ended up in this loud, chaotic school, with its working-class, very brown student body, rather than holding court at a posh private school, teaching decorum and posture to wealthy heiresses. But she was nothing if not a paradox once you stuck around long enough to get to know her. She was simultaneously a lofty and feared disciplinarian, and a loving, hands-on teacher.

The lesson I learned from Di Hatch was the power in being a woman. She would constantly make us aware that we were women. She spoke about our health, our different physical needs. She told us to look at our bodies, to explore ourselves, to bend over: 'Have a look at up there, before anyone else does.' She was the first person to make me aware that I was experiencing the world as a woman, and that women could lead as women. It was a powerful lesson.

*

In my final year of high school, already wise to the implications of living in the world as a woman, I began to remember that I was also a refugee. With that came turmoil. It was a prelude to the even bigger eruption of turmoil that would come three years later with the fall of the Twin Towers and the start of the now eighteen-year-long War on Terror.

In about 1997, I started to notice a new bunch of girls at AGGS. Well, I didn't so much notice them as they noticed me. We had all watched them in passing, a little curious about their different fashion sense, haircuts, names and accents. There were only a handful of them, so the commotion wasn't enough to disrupt the order of things — other than for me, because, as it turned out, they were refugees. They had been resettled in New Zealand from the soon-to-be-former Yugoslav republics of Bosnia, Croatia, and Serbia. Their stories were a little different than mine, in that they had had normal lives until the war broke out. They had actually lived under bombardment in refugee camps in Europe. This all meant that although they had experienced trauma that was in many ways more extreme than mine, they didn't have a whole childhood of surreal oppression. They were secure in their culture. Being older at the time that they left, they also knew who they were within that culture. They weren't shy. They were confident and bold in their distinctiveness. They stuck together and invited me to join.

It was a first for me to talk to people my own age about our shared refugee experience. What was even more interesting was that they weren't happy with things in New Zealand. They knew full well that they did not fit in, but their reaction was to reject the culture here as backward. They wanted to go dancing. They wanted to dress up. No one here was interested in glitzy fashion or throwing their kinds of parties. People our age would hang out in someone's backyard and drink. There was music and the odd make-out session, but nothing they would count as fun. They talked about 'our' cultures being warmer, more exuberant, more political. They were bored here.

With this takedown of their new home came a very unabashed mourning for the loss of their birth homes. I had never felt free to openly grieve for the loss of my life in Iran. Among this new group, we could talk candidly about what might have been. I shared the stories my parents told me about their colourful lives in pre-revolutionary Iran, about my cousins, aunts, and uncles, whom I realised I missed. I missed the unknown life of growing up with them. I suddenly missed, as they did, a life that was whole, where I fully belonged. Of course, I would not have felt that sense of belonging had I gone back to Iran then. I had become too Kiwi. But at that moment, it was easy to glorify those lost lands.

In retrospect, I think I knew full well that their defiance came from the rejection they felt, and which I was rediscovering. It was a rejection that comes from being marginalised, that comes from being expected to adapt while no one adapts to us. I had been safe. I had friends in that enormous, diverse school. But I knew that I would one day go out into the real world and back to being some woman with a weird name, never the pretty girl, not 'normal'. The elaborate teenage angst spat out by this group of new arrivals came from that same knowledge. It was akin to saying, 'He didn't dump me. I dumped him.'

Soon, I stopped going to school much. We would sit around talking in Myers Park, go window shopping. At night, we would dress up and talk our way into bars to dance or drink. I was never much of a drinker as a teen, my dad having taken away any rebellion factor long ago. But we did hang out with boys. I had hung out with boys at parties before, but realised I had never considered I would possibly date them. As popular or accepted as I became, I still felt, deep down, that I couldn't have a normal love life, not with a normal Kiwi boy. I couldn't even imagine it.

So it made sense that my first-ever relationship grew from a shared understanding that we were not 'of' this place.

It began the summer before university. I was still confused about what to do with the rest of my life, but going to study was never in question. Both my parents were fairly obsessed with higher education and frankly it felt like I was buying time. I knew I couldn't quite call myself an artist, so art school wasn't a serious consideration anymore. I ticked Medicine to make my parents happy at first and waited nervously for my interview at Auckland Medical School. This was meant as a path to psychiatry, analytical and people-focused enough to feel right for me. In a moment of clarity, I realised I wasn't ever going to make it through all the chemistry and physics, plus the actual medical training it was going to take. My home was in the humanities. I decided to be a historian, to analyse society, all the progress, the prejudice, the movements, and the methods by which we had thus far done that analysis. I did know that an Arts degree on its own would give my parents rather a fright. So, I ticked Law as well. I would study a conjoint degree, then one day they would wake up to a history professor for a daughter. Obviously, my eventual devotion to legal advocacy was a slow burner.

That first summer between school and university felt exciting. It felt like freedom with more of it on the way. I put in a lot of hours for my parents in their new venture selling Mexican food in a cinema food court. We weren't allowed to sell Iranian food since no one had ever heard of it, and there was already a Turkish kebab eatery there, staffed by Jordanians. Apparently we looked right selling Mexican food. We secretly sold a few Iranian classic slow-cooked lamb and chicken dishes on rice among the burritos.

As it turned out, the first few years of university were tumultuous for me and study was not front of mind. He was a bit older, in his twenties, a little bit hostile, a little bit dark, but with a presence that dominated the room. It sounds cliché now, but I felt like he was an enigma to the rest of the world and it made me feel special to solve him. We started a whirlwind romance at the beginning of my first year at university, and this tumult became a defining feature of my life at law school. It went on for three years, on and off, and finally ended when I secretly moved and didn't give him the address.

Last year, I suddenly found myself for the first time identifying publicly as an abuse victim, with all the criticism, disbelief, and belittlement that comes with that. Ironically, this happened when I spoke about abuse during the filming of the documentary *Women in the House*, commemorating women's suffrage, by filmmakers Vice New Zealand. Serendipitously, filming covered the day Parliament passed Jan Logie's ground-breaking Domestic Violence — Victims' Protection Bill, which makes it possible for victims and survivors of intimate partner violence to take ten days of annual leave. The reason I felt it was important and safe to speak about my experience of abuse when the filmmakers asked me about it was that I was infinitely excited about Jan's achievement. To me, what we were about to do was the ideal of law-making, for the affected community, by the affected community.

The backlash that came after the film was released has made me very hesitant to talk about it again. In fact, I resolved not to write about it in this account, because I didn't feel ready to face that abuse again. Eventually, I realised the hesitation I now feel was a reason *to* write about it. To write, too, about the hesitation. I realised this fear is quintessential of the post #MeToo experience for women who have shared their accounts of abuse. It seems like a reason to keep speaking, or the silence may set in even more terrifyingly than before.

A moment after I described my experience of abuse on camera, I imagined the headlines and the hateful comments. I knew instantly that I would be accused of seeking undeserved victimhood, of lying; I knew I would be told I deserved what I had got. All that happened. The sad realisation was that the real-life reaction to my public disclosure would answer the central question of the film: how far have we really come in empowering women in 125 years of formal equality?

Countering the misnomers contained in that backlash is key to ending violence against women in all its forms. For one, I know that my story is not exceptional. In fact, it is peppered with the usual tropes of relationship violence. But I know I don't fit the typical profile of 'abuse victim' portrayed in narratives of violence against women. I was a university student, ambitious, independent, a feminist. I appeared by objective estimations to be high functioning. But abuse is a dynamic inside the relationship. The power and control cycles apply no matter what we look like as women out there in the world. We need to accept that abuse is so widespread as to have no externally discernible profile among its victims or perpetrators. New Zealand will always lead the world with our record of granting women the vote in 1893, which I believe is the reason it's so difficult to allow the reality of our harrowing domestic and sexual violence statistics to enter our national psyche. It is indisputable that intimate partner violence takes up forty-one per cent of the work of frontline police here, even though we know only around a quarter of abuse is actually reported. Those statistics speak of mass violence, overwhelmingly against women.

When I think about my personal experience, what's shocking is that I didn't recognise it as abuse until it got physical. I was only eighteen years old when the relationship began, and for most of its course I saw it as intense 'first love'. He would send hundreds of messages each day, turn up to my university and workplace without my asking. I spent every free moment with him, either in person or responding to the deluge of messages. He was moody and I felt responsible for mitigating these moods. If he didn't like one of my friends, he would insult them or storm off. He once left me on the side of the road in the middle of nowhere for talking about someone he didn't want me to hang out with anymore. If I went out without him, the messages turned ugly. It would be a barrage of 'Bitch. Bitch. Bitch,' 'Slut. Slut. Slut.' I justified it as he did: it's normal for men to be jealous when they're in love.

I know that my affinity for this tumultuous relationship was intrinsically linked to the dark realisations about my own place in the world at that age, to my ethnicity, and to my status as a refugee. Feeling inherently less than perfect in every way meant I was attracted to the imperfect. I felt we must have kinship in our rejected imperfection. I believed myself wrong and ugly, so why wouldn't I be with someone else who was to all the world similarly awful? Related to that, in the same way we had glorified our war-torn homelands, I wanted to believe there was something interesting and attractive in being wrong and imperfect.

But in the end, I didn't believe I could do any better. I didn't think I deserved better. The world wasn't built for me to participate in as an equal, so why would I try for what most people would expect in relationships?

Things got physical with shoving. I once went through the sliding door of my wardrobe, which broke off its hinges. Another time I fell backward hard onto some rocks right before we went into a party. I had to explain away the scrapes, the finger marks from being grabbed and squeezed so violently. It got worse when twice he threatened to kill me. That's when he choked me, forcefully enough to leave thumb marks around my neck, so I wore a scarf for a week. The apologies came in the usual way: 'I love you. I need you. I wish you wouldn't make me angry.'

My university grades fell and I couldn't concentrate well. I could only really leave him when my friend Kyla and I got together to form a flat. I found an address he didn't know and changed my phone number. It was a good thing that I did keep up with university and fought hard to keep my friendships going. That isn't always possible for women in controlling relationships, especially when children are involved and financial support doesn't allow for independence from their abuser.

This is why Jan Logie's bill is crucial. Jan knew the importance of this profound measure for survivors, because she has spent her life at the grassroots of that sector. She knows that the time immediately after leaving is the most dangerous for women. We need to change our routine. We also need income in order to leave. Survivors should never have to choose between financial independence and abuse. Even if she isn't ready to leave, she needs time out to seek mental healthcare, to heal.

Passing the new law will always be the moment that we as a society accepted that abuse victims deserve real support. That came though representation. It came because women like Jan were in the House, carrying the voices of the women outside who had been silently bearing this burden alone.

For me, the move to a new flat meant I got to explore all the self-loathing and dysfunction that comes with being a survivor. Kyla had been an AGGS girl with me. We shared our complex relationships with race and abuse. She studied psychology and worked for a women's refuge, devoting her life to helping other women. Now the young woman who helped me escape abuse is the director of Wellington Rape Crisis. She remains the only friend I talk openly to about that part of my life. I've never talked about it much because, to this day, even though I know it's wrong, I feel a deep sense of failure and responsibility for the abuse.

The backdrop to my personal struggle with abuse, juxtaposed with the thrill of university life in those undergraduate years, was the global shift in perceptions of Middle Easterners. Even in remote, peaceful Aotearoa, 2001 saw a shift in the way we were seen as feared outsiders. I was lucky to have been here long enough to have lost my Iranian accent and clocked some social capital, but I could no longer retreat into being an ordinary Kiwi. War was waging in the Middle East. Iran was part of the 'Axis of Evil'. The battle cry rang through the West: you are either with us or against us.

I remember being woken up at some ungodly hour on the morning of 12 September 2001 by the phone ringing. It was my friend Shirin. She said I had to turn on the TV, some huge disaster was happening in America. I grabbed a jumper, ran downstairs to see. Tears streamed down my face in those first minutes of realisation. I kept thinking maybe everyone would be okay. It was clear that at least some people were not. The first images I saw were of the billowing smoke where the planes had hit. The towers hadn't fallen yet in those images; it was unimaginable that they would. Then came the harrowing collapse.

I barely moved for the rest of the day. I didn't go to class. Those images were repeated over again. All of us who are old enough to have a living memory of that tragic day remember some of the victims vividly still. Their human stories, the children, the survivors who missed work that day for some reason, grappling with the gaping wound of guilt and sorrow for their lost friends.

In the background journalists speculated wildly about who did it. They were naming al Qaeda pretty fast. I tried to reserve judgement. How could they know? I kept begging the universe: please don't let it be Middle Easterners. Please, not Iranians. It was clear to us that if the killers were foreigners, vengeance would be war and the human cost would be indiscriminate.

It was.

It's so wretched to know that those innocent lives lost on the day, that sorrow, were used as tools to justify the killing of so many more.

We still live and breathe the toxic remnants of Bush Jr's opportunistic war mongering. We are living with the reality of millions dead and displaced. The original fake news was the lie that 'weapons of mass destruction' sat in Saddam Hussein's arsenal. As a Kurd, I know that man was a mass murderer. But what came with the War on Terror was pop-culture Islamophobia, and an 'us versus them' rhetoric. It is what we, in New Zealand, are only now starting to reckon with. I remember that rhetoric starting just as I was first stepping out into adulthood as a 'Kiwi', and growing through most of my university years. Though I eventually learned to be proud of being a little different, it was clear in the wake of that renewed xenophobia that my kind of difference wasn't going to be celebrated. That maybe some of us were never going to be quite Kiwi enough. I realised it meant working a little harder to dismantle the barriers. It meant I became aware of equality movements, the centuries of analysis and resistance born of the pain of entire populations degraded by similar power structures. It meant realising the beauty of joining forces across communities to affirm each other's struggle, and our shared humanity.

6

Justice at the coalface

For me, being a child refugee was to live very deliberately thereafter. My mother told me growing up that I could be prime minister one day. That annoyed me, because I wanted to be a psychologist like her. What she meant was that I had no limits to my dreams. While the glass ceiling was tangible to us as migrants, she felt that the sacrifice she had made meant her daughter was *that* free. I was the child of an ambitious woman who had been stifled by oppression, who had given up every ounce of comfort in her life to fight one murderous regime after the next, then had fled for good with almost nothing. Being a child refugee is to be the child *of* refugees, knowing that others have given up everything to grant you freedom, and that others still do not have that freedom. I worked single-mindedly to fulfil the promise of that freedom, like someone with not a lot of time left, because in the end I was making up for the lost time of the two lives placed on hold for me. Being a child refugee means taking every opportunity, and even creating opportunities that don't currently exist, no matter how far-flung or challenge-filled. It means thinking carefully about the change I want to make in this world, so other people may have those same opportunities. Fairly or not, I knew that is what was always expected of me.

In a converse way, this also gave me the freedom to think very carefully about what I wanted to do with my life. That's what you're meant to do with freedom, what people who've always had it forget. What my parents worked so hard to give me, was options that they never had. I am acutely aware that not everyone gets that privilege. I had the freedom never to settle for any job I didn't absolutely love or value, because money and security weren't the drivers. Living deliberately gives you that gift too. That is the ethos and urgency with which I walked out of law school.

Of course I'd never wanted to be a lawyer. The whole law degree was tacked onto my Bachelor of Arts to calm my parents about future job prospects and respectability. I came out of law school with still no interest in legal practice. At that time, the University of Auckland prided itself in servicing the giant commercial law firms in 'our nation's financial capital'. The thought of that life mostly gave me hives. Those law firm recruitment events we were all invited to were my nightmare. My friend Nicola, the only AGGS girl from my year who ended up at the same law school, and I went to one for the free wine and canapés, then stood to the side staring at everyone working the room. We were handed brochures with pictures of our entire life laid out in glossy print. Here's the gym you'll go to. Here's your unborn children's creche. This is the chef who'll make all the meals you'll eat at your desk. There's your prized retirement plan. It was the life we were all meant to want. But I didn't relate.

By the time university was winding up, I still didn't know what I wanted to do, other than that I didn't want to go corporate. I knew I wanted to work in human rights and eventually as an academic. Besides law, I was graduating with a much more interesting history degree focused on sex and gender. When I later asked for an academic reference, the head of department, Barry Rae, noted my degree title as 'History (Sex)'. So technically I studied sex history, though that didn't really seem like it would enhance my employability. I asked the career counsellor at law school how I might start a career in human rights law. She said I should look in the *Yellow Pages*. It was hard to know whether to laugh or cry. I left and looked up Amnesty International — not in the phone book, though, because even in the vintage year of 2004 the internet did exist.

One winter afternoon, I walked to the Amnesty office, then in an obscure part of town, hardly signposted and up a steep staircase. I spotted a small woman bent over some campaign material, tugging at her enormous red mane as she explained something to a mesmerised group of volunteers. This was Margaret Taylor, Amnesty New Zealand's long-time, legendary activism coordinator. I told her I was about to finish law school and was looking for work, quickly adding that I could work part time for free since I had a waitressing job. I just wanted a start. About forty minutes later, after hashing out our respective interests in activism and Iranian human rights, I walked out as the brand-new Amnesty International refugee intern. That title sounds hilariously problematic now, but the internship programme was split thematically into 'media' and 'refugees'. Maybe it was fate.

By happy coincidence, my work at Amnesty was mostly about a court case. The Ahmed Zaoui case was about the right to fair process for refugees in the age of War on Terror hysteria. At that time, New Zealand was grappling with the realities of our alliance with the United States post-9/11, with two illegal wars waging in the Middle East. It turned out that Helen Clark's Labour Party government, desperate to build relations with Bush Jr's America after declining to participate in those wars, had passed a law giving our security agency sweeping powers to detain people based on 'national security' allegations. Unbeknown to the general population of rights-loving Kiwis, the law effectively allowed indefinite detention without disclosure of evidence or any semblance of a trial. Our courts, I'm proud to say, did not let that stand.

The Zaoui case revealed this law and all that was wrong with it. It was an awakening for me, a moment when I realised that the world was really changed, and New Zealand was not immune. Our nation woke up one day to the Kafkaesque nightmare of an Algerian refugee being held in solitary confinement, without charge or trial, in one of our maximum-security prisons. Ahmed Zaoui had been an opposition politician democratically elected to office before his political party was abruptly outlawed by the repressive Algerian regime. He was forced into exile. He claimed political asylum at the border in Auckland, and was thoroughly investigated for allegations of militancy by the Refugee Appeals Authority, which declared those allegations politically motivated. But New Zealand's intelligence agency got involved to trigger his detention pursuant to an obscure new law, passed quietly, to make New Zealand amenable to our allies. The allegation against Zaoui wasn't even 'terror' — 'national security' could encompass a threat to New Zealand's economic interests. This, I knew, could happen to any one of us born in the wrong place, at the wrong time. It was personally chilling.

For two years, politicians played political football with Zaoui's life.

National Party member Sir Bill English put out a statement on his website referencing the case, calling refugees 'leftovers from terrorist nations' and calling for a 'red light' at our borders. I guess 'build a wall' isn't a cry for island-nation xenophobes. That statement remained on the website well after Sir Bill was our prime minister, and was only taken down after negative media attention leading up to the 2017 election. At least public and press tolerance had turned. That is not to forget that while Ahmed sat languishing in prison, the office of our then prime minister, Helen Clark, told the public he had links to al Qaeda. That allegation was later withdrawn, the PM saying they 'had probably gone too far in making the link'. That type of casual, unthinking overstep was rife at the time and continues today, locking up hundreds in Guantanamo Bay for a start.

Less offensive but also dangerously misleading were the politicians who claimed Zaoui was in 'a three-walled cell'. The idea was that he could go back to Algeria or Malaysia, where his family were in hiding. He couldn't. It was a callous lie, a version of which is still touted now, particularly when people discuss Australia's offshore detention facilities. If you are a refugee, you have escaped harm akin to torture or death for your political beliefs, race, ethnicity, sexual orientation, or religion. That is why the law does not allow your forcible return. It remains a legal and practical fiction to say that refugees can 'go back to where they came from', or stay in a country like Malaysia, where the Refugee

Convention does not apply — unless what is being suggested is that we can go back and face that torture or be executed.

If you are like the Zaoui family circa 2004, or one of the hundreds of people New Zealand still actively prevents from leaving a place like Indonesia or Malaysia to stop their legitimate asylum claims reaching our shores, you live in an indefinite limbo. 'Go back to Malaysia' equated to telling Zaoui and his family to live a life where at any moment they could be deported to face torture or death.

Zaoui's case was formative for me not just as a lawyer or human rights activist, but as an eventual politician in a world where Muslim New Zealanders are shot to death by white supremacists who believe anti-immigration rhetoric espoused by opportunistic politicians. I knew when I stood in Parliament to deliver my maiden speech, with some of those same politicians sitting across the aisles from me, that I had to remind them of the Zaoui case. Those of us bearing the brunt of their populist politics did not have the luxury to forget.

What I will also never forget is that the Green Party were the only political party who stood up for human rights and spoke of prejudice in the Zaoui case. I remember, so vividly, Keith Locke, then Green spokesperson on immigration and foreign affairs, standing with us at town-hall meetings and protests, speaking softly but with determination, and everyone listening. I feel the urgency to uphold his legacy, to live up to the moral and intellectual integrity of that lone politician, who stood up to Islamophobia against popular politicians in both major parties, against the fear and division among the general population. It meant the world to me as a young activist.

Working at Amnesty on the Zaoui case is when I realised that human rights are made effective by the courts. I needed to learn how to do that. I knew that at Amnesty they thought of me as a lawyer because I had a law degree. The truth is that law graduates know very little about legal advocacy, let alone the machinery of the justice system. I realised that if I cared enough about human rights, if this endeavour was about making those rights effective, rather than about me having my dream job, I needed to learn how to be a lawyer.

So I spent a lunch break scribbling down a plan on bits of printing paper. Everything from 'get courtroom experience' to 'United Nations internships' to 'international Master's degree' was in that plan. I bookmarked the website for the Oxford Masters in International Human Rights Law programme and looked at it often.

I wasn't driven by an ambition to climb any kind of ladder, but rather the deathly fear of waking up eight years into a solid corporate job and realising I was further away from working in human rights than when I started. I had a vague idea of the pressure that would come to measure success by status-quo indicators; to stay in a job for that next promotion, for the next mortgage payment, until I'd spent ten years of being mildly unhappy for things none of us necessarily want to begin with. I didn't want to let my feet sit in that wet cement.

To the outside world, it looked like I took a few detours. I took the winding route of becoming a barrister working in the chaos of courts and prisons with all the frustrations of legal aid. To everyone's amusement, I then gave up my place in a great barristers' chambers to go off, at first to take unpaid jobs or short-term contract work with the United Nations (UN) in Africa and The Hague. Somewhere in between those stints with the UN, I did a Master's at Oxford University, just as I had planned. Not in a practical area like tax or contracts or even criminal justice, but in human rights law. As everyone got ahead on the corporate ladder, fixed mortgages and had big white weddings, I was still taking every adventuring opportunity that came my way.

It was all incredibly rewarding, but sometimes the doubts crept in. Sometimes I wondered if it was time to be more responsible, so to speak. When I was deciding whether to go off one more time to work in yet another UN mission station, this time to prosecute the Khmer Rouge in Cambodia, I shared these doubts with my friend Kate. We knew each other from our time working at different UN courts in The Hague. She had herself dropped out of law to become a political scientist.

After listening calmly to my panicky rant, she put down her drink, and said, 'But can you think of anyone whose work or life you really covet, who you think is really amazing, dead or alive, who took the straight path they were meant to take?' And there was my answer.

To rewind, my path after Amnesty began with a life-changing foray into the criminal law. I was in my mother's little gift shop in Mount Eden village. She sold pretty soaps and candles and acted as the resident psychologist to the community, dishing out advice over the counter as she wrapped gifts. Mum and I were discussing a dilemma I was having. I had just passed the Bar exams and I was putting together the papers for my admission ceremony, but we didn't know any lawyers to move my admission.

Out of nowhere, a voice from behind the greeting card stand called, 'I'm a lawyer.' Jo Wickliffe, tiny with jet-black hair and a bright-red smile, suddenly materialised. 'I would be honoured to move your admission.'

We had never met before, but she was a regular customer. She was Māori, a solo mum, who had put herself through law school while she raised her daughter. Now, she was a criminal defence barrister. Jo gave us that breathless rundown on the spot and I was awestruck.

Then, ever empowering of other women as she is, Jo put the rest of my life right with, 'You should come work in criminal law. My friend Lester needs a junior barrister.'

Knowing people, and having access to mentors and jobs that are rarely advertised is everything in a field with so few openings. My family didn't have enough connections to know a single lawyer in our personal circles, so what Jo did for me meant a great deal.

A week later, I met Lester and my life's work began. He was warm and animated, perpetually on the brink of righteous indignation or boisterous laughter. As it turned out, he was the son of an Italian Jewish mother whose family moved to New Zealand before the Holocaust, but lost their extended family in the genocide. He had grown up working class in Kawerau, a small mining town. This, I learned quickly, is a very rare profile for successful practising lawyers. We spent the hour drinking black coffee and talking fast about justice as a poverty issue, as a race issue, and about the role of defence lawyers in a fair trial. I was sold. We didn't talk about the job for more than a brief minute, but soon we were walking back to his chambers so I could see where I would be working. Lester and I were fast friends and still are today. He said later that he knew I would get the job when he saw Amnesty International on my résumé. He wanted to know the person he worked with was interested in more than just getting through every case and billing it. He wanted us to understand our work as essential to people's rights.

We worked in a beautiful old building in Auckland's legal district, equidistant between the High Court and the District Court. I did a lot of running around between those courts, and almost from my first day started to appear before judges on minor hearings. It began with scheduling cases and attending bail hearings where police weren't opposing the release, then moved quickly to sentencing and opposed bails, the things advocacy could really affect. What was truly wild was preparing trials, and then appearing as junior counsel. Most chambers' juniors didn't get to do that. I was lucky to be able to see the whole process through. It was exhilarating. It was also incredibly stressful. There's nothing more real than justice being administered in real time. Evidence being delivered and changing. Legal challenges won and lost. The booming closing addresses to juries. Then the wait for verdicts. The slow-motion turning of our heads, the nervous breaths, before the words that change lives are uttered into that space: 'guilty' or 'not guilty'.

The front line of any criminal justice system is the most human place in the world. Every day I met people having the worst day of their lives. Every day I met victims who were also perpetrators, met cops who bent the rules, even broke the law, even as they believed themselves the guardians of it. We were wading through the fog of the human condition where there is no black or white. The courts are dirty and chaotic. Prisons are grim places to visit.

There's no air in those meeting rooms, even the nice ones for lawyers. You're sometimes there for hours with a client, writing their account down with pen and paper like it's 1972. Everyone looks perpetually sleep-deprived. Everyone is trying desperately to have her voice heard.

People always ask what you do as a defence lawyer 'when you know your client is guilty'. I always answer with the question, 'How would I know that?' The reality is that once you get up close to any human situation, let alone one where conflict and deviancy is involved, you find doubt. There are a million sides to every story. And the job of counsel is to ensure the accused person has their case heard as fairly as possible. Most cases don't even end up in a trial. Most of the time you're making sure your client hasn't been charged with things they didn't do, or anything more serious than they did do, then arguing for a fair sentence. Either way, something terrible has almost always happened. Even when it's not so bad, it's often part of a continuum of bad things that have happened in a life you only glimpse for a moment.

For the record: when you know your client is guilty, you advise them to plead guilty, while still looking after their rights and their dignity. None of us have rights because we are good, but because we are human.

I started going into prisons to interview clients almost immediately. Lester's practice was mostly relatively senior-level trials: violence, sexual assaults, and Class-A drugs. It wasn't easy work. The subject matter of the evidence was often disturbing.

As lawyers we had to read everything, to go over everything with our clients repeatedly before a trial. From the start, I knew it was important not to let any ounce of judgement show or I would lose my client's trust. Knowing your lawyer doesn't like you could breach a person's right to proper legal assistance, as well as their right to be presumed innocent. So it felt important not to avoid eye contact, not to wince at anything that came out in those meetings. If what came out was criminal, it was still important to work through it, to communicate the legal position and the process clearly, respectfully. More often than not, what came out was trauma, terrible circumstances, a series of awful decisions made in those circumstances, decisions that might breach various moral or social codes. It was important to ask questions and make space for information to be shared safely. The humanity in my work was what I cherished. It's something I realised good barristers prided themselves in understanding — even as our friends and family told us they didn't know why we would help 'those people'.

I was aware that I was interacting in this world as a young woman, most often vastly different in cultural background and life experience from my clients, and likely every lawyer they had ever had. Most of our clients were Māori or Pasifika men. Most of the lawyers were Pākehā men, though the Bar is far more gender-diverse now. This was an environment where at first blush I might be deemed an interloper, not easily trusted or respected. I had to be aware of my demeanour, both to command the respect and authority I needed to do my job well, and to communicate my own respect and empathy. I drew on my own experiences of integrating into the divergent socio-economic and cultural contexts of my schools, and of my parents' language challenges that meant people talked down to them. I would adjust my language and demeanour between client meetings, dealings with cops, the prescribed manner of the court, and the smoky rooms where barristers drank, talked shop and made crude jokes. It was all an education, one with which most women in male-dominated professions will be familiar, except I guess most don't move between male-dominated spaces so vastly different in race and class demographics within their day.

At the time I was also juggling my life with my boyfriend, Nick, a design student. We flatted, went out for dumplings and wine with our friends, had potluck dinner parties, and saved hard to go on a budget trip to Vietnam at the end of my first year of lawyering. Eating fancy dinners with Criminal Bar Association people sat in bold contrast to my own social life. But I felt comfortable among the barristers. I've always been a good drinker — that helped. Those smoky bars and nice restaurants were places to let off steam after the high pressure of our work, where everyone understood the subject matter, and no one flinched when you talked about the gory details of a case.

Most people we represented had trouble reading the documents on their file. It meant always asking, in a casual, passing way, if a client wanted us to read the Police Summary of Facts out loud to them before they took it. Anyone who could read and write would return a puzzled look and take their papers. But many nodded gratefully. The justice system largely deals with people with severe learning disabilities, brain injuries and undiagnosed mental illnesses. That includes many with a lifelong diagnosis of post-traumatic stress disorder. To say these people have gone through life without a lot of opportunities is a truism that barely touches on the enormity of society's failures at every juncture before we lock them up. That's not to say everyone who commits crimes suffers from brain injury or mental illness. Or that everyone who suffers from a severe learning disability or serious trauma commits crime. But the connections between these factors are overwhelmingly clear at the coalface of our justice system. I understood our clients to be socially disconnected, and dealing with intergenerational trauma and criminalisation.

My prison visits were mostly to Mount Eden Prison, a high-security, crowded facility in Auckland. The old prison building is shut down now. The new prison visitation area for lawyers, airless as it still is, has shatterproof glass separating prisoners and lawyers. There's built-in panic buttons on the wall. But when I started, the legal visits in the old medieval-looking stone building took place in a space above the family visitation area. You had to go through a locked door, up winding narrow stairs, and into one of five rooms connected by a balcony corridor overlooking the open space below. The guards stayed downstairs and locked the door at the base of the stairs after you. There was nothing separating lawyers and clients in the little rooms. There was nothing stopping you being thrown off the balcony. In fact, if anything happened, the guard had to first find the key, unlock the door, and run up the staircase before they could intervene. They offered some of us a portable panic button. It was for the female lawyers, I assumed, because Lester was never offered one. I never indulged in a button, because I felt it would undermine a client's trust if they had to stare at a physical embodiment of how dangerous I suspected him to be. In the end, I never once felt unsafe or disrespected with a client. They were grateful and desperate for information. We were their lifelines.

The only clients who ever alluded to my age or gender, either to undermine my expertise or in being too familiar, were white-collar criminals. They were always older, wealthier men who had committed premeditated financial crimes, often against very vulnerable people.

We talk a lot now about the overrepresentation of Māori in our prison systems. We don't talk enough about the causes of offending. We know that Māori have far worse health outcomes and education outcomes, that Māori children are far more likely to be taken into state care. But we don't speak about the systemic marginalisation, the systematic alienation from resources, including public services, which has led to these outcomes across the Pacific since colonial first contact. Mostly, we don't say enough that Māori are disproportionately *targeted* by our system of justice.

The right to a fair trial itself is an acknowledgement that prejudice exists. It is the acknowledgement that unless we legally protect the right to be presumed innocent, to have competent defence counsel, and to have equal time and facilities to present a defence, the justice system could be weaponised against the poor and the marginalised. The admission that human rights law is about securing the safety and welfare of the powerless is at the forefront of the ideal of justice. To me, being able to look past the allegations and put a case forward on behalf of the accused, no matter the charges they face, is about holding power structures to account. The fairness of a trial is about balancing out the unfairness in the world — though that may in the end be impossible to do from the inside of a courtroom built within that world and peopled with juries, judges and lawyers bringing our misplaced prejudices and sympathies to it.

*

I'll never forget the first time I got to see real corruption play out in a courtroom. They say bad cases make bad law. That means where exceptionally horrendous crimes are alleged, judges succumb to the human urge to to punish the crime, even if that means allowing procedural shortcuts and forcing unsafe interpretations of the law. They leave bad precedents.

The case was Williams & Others. It was a big High Court drug operation. There were thirteen accused of allegedly colluding to manufacture and supply meth. The Williams brothers were the leaders of this operation, according to police. We were representing one of them, Shane Williams. At some point during the multi-week trial, the lawyer defending Shane's brother Dale, Kelly Ann Stoikoff, noticed something unusual in her cross-examination of the senior sergeant in charge of the case. She raised a challenge to the police search warrant of the first address. This was a case where a number of searches were conducted as a result of that one search that incriminated her client. We stopped the trial and went into a special hearing with Justice Paul Heath, who was presiding. All the officers connected with that search were cross-examined separately.

It transpired that police were there with a warrant to recover a stolen car — what information this initial warrant was based on was unclear, though, as the police couldn't show the car had even been reported lost. What *was* clear is that the police went to the address and immediately searched every inch of the unit, including his fridge, where they found evidence. Not all of the officers were intentionally overreaching; they were mostly following the sergeant's lead, and their understanding was they were there to find drugs. But without evidence to back his warrant, the sergeant was breaking the law.

(From left to right) My dad and mum, with my dad's cousins Saghi and Sassan, who both became exiled author dissidents after the revolution, in the deep 1970s.

My mum at age 18 (on the right in knee-high boots), her sister Mehri (left) and their friend Nazzi at a routine party in her neighbourhood.

Mum and Dad at a cafe in her neighbourhood in Urmia circa early 1970s.

Me with my auntie Nahid in Mashhad, in mid-1981. As a child in Iran, I would stare at this photo with wonder at the sight of my auntie's bare head in public, during my own lifetime.

Me in my grey primary school uniform in our yard in Mashhad, 1988.

Me on my eighth birthday, with freshly cut bangs and all my friends singing 'Happy Birthday'.

In our yard in Mashhad proudly wearing my traditional Kurdish costume, made by my grandma in Urmia.

Happily missing school on a snow day in Mashhad. Many people don't realise Iran has all four seasons, imagining the Middle East to be an enormous desert.

At Western Springs Park in Auckland soon after our arrival in late 1990. The double-denim outfit was one of my favourites that I made sure I packed when we left Iran.

Iranians, including my mum (centre in silver skirt), all dressed up and dancing to celebrate Nowrooz (Iranian new year) in Auckland, circa 1994.

Me (left) and Ghazaleh at a Nowrooz party circa 1994.

Our citizenship ceremony, 7 June 1994. My parents were giddy with excitement and joy. They both wore their best clothes and had haircuts for the occasion. I, my understated Kiwi style already intact, wore jeans.

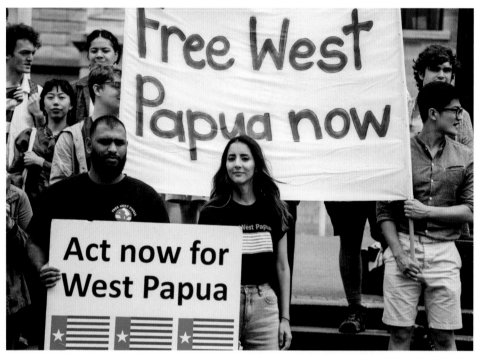

Standing in solidarity with protest movements is vital, while we get the privilege of raising the voices from the frontlines into New Zealand's House of Representatives. The cause of self-determination for indigenous West Papuans is close to my heart. (Photo: Zoë Robinson)

Me and Chlöe Swarbrick the day we were sworn in as Members of Parliament, 7 November 2017. (Photo: Tim Onnes)

Me being sworn in. Dad said he was very moved that I pronounced our last name in true Farsi. (Photo: Tim Onnes)

Family photo right before I gave my maiden speech on 15 November 2017. Back row, from left to right: Mum; Jesse Chalmers, who pushed me to finally stand for parliament; Guy's dad, Gary Williams; and Guy's mum, Roseanne Williams. Front row: Dad, me and Guy. (Photo: Damon Keen)

Having Marama Davidson next to me while I gave my first speech in parliament meant so much, and helped the nerves. Here is the moment of relief and emotion once I made it through.

With Marama (centre in green jacket), my Greens of colour and Left Green Network friends on the day of the co-leader announcement, 8 April 2018. (Photo: Julie Zhu)

At the Foreign Affairs, Trade and Defence Select Committee, 23 May 2019. (Photo: Damon Keen)

Meeting Congresswoman Deb Haaland, who together with Sharice Davids became the first-ever indigenous women elected to the United States House of Representatives in August 2019. We celebrated Māori Language Week by sharing te reo Māori messages of unity and support.

Ilhan Omar and I became the first-ever refugees in our respective nations' House of Representatives months apart. When we finally met in August 2019, we shared the similar challenges we both face, and laughed and hugged.

2019 was my first year of attending the Waitangi Day dawn service as a Member of Parliament. The experience was beyond moving. Here I am, giddy and awake at 4.30 am, with Chlöe Swarbrick, Eugenie Sage, Marama Davidson, James Shaw, and Jan Logie. (Photo: Tim Onnes)

Vigil for the Christchurch terror attack, Aotea Square, 16 March 2019. (Photo: Todd Henry)

Standing on stage at the 16 March vigil. Marama (left) had just delivered her powerful address. I felt ready to speak to and honour the fear and experiences of my communities, which had been poured out in messages to me over the previous day. (Photo: Todd Henry)

Press scrum on Parliament House tiles after my speech on the Christchurch terror attack, 20 March 2019. (Photo: Rick Zwaan)

On 14 November 2019, Behrouz Boochani walked into Auckland Airport and found freedom after six years' imprisonment in an Australian detention camp for being an asylum seeker, as my family had been. It was overwhelming to welcome him as a member of Aotearoa's Iranian community.

The defence case by then was that police lied on the warrant. This was a huge call. It's one thing to walk through an open gate or poke your head inside a car window when questioning the driver. Those types of technically unlawful searches happen all the time. But police dishonestly swearing affidavits in support of search warrants, and lying under oath in a High Court trial, undermines the court's ability to administer justice — which is why we have a system with rules and search warrants and defence lawyers in the first place.

The sergeant's disregard for the law was extraordinary to me as a baby lawyer in that courtroom. I had always assumed we were all essentially on the same side: police, prosecutors, and us. We were doing our jobs to get a fair outcome, not to win at all costs.

We waited a day for Justice Heath to make his decision. He found that the first warrant was obtained in bad faith, legalese for 'they deliberately lied to get the warrant'. It was moving for me to see, at least for a moment, that maybe no one was above the law. The case was ultimately appealed and the Court of Appeal overturned Justice Heath's decision — not based on the facts, but on the notion that police dishonesty did not make the evidence necessarily inadmissible. They found that even the worst police violations in search and seizure are just 'factors' to weigh against the ability of police and prosecutors to get a conviction in any given case. The government soon legislated to make the appeal case law. The moral and legal conflicts in that case have stayed with me.

The reason bad cases make bad law is that they focus on the Williamses of a trial. But if police have the court's blessing to unlawfully shake down the public, those targeted will be the marginalised. This law likely resulted in countless degrading and unlawful searches of anyone police happened to see as a criminal. Where evidence is found, it has a good chance of staying in the case, despite the violation. Where they find nothing, people have no real recourse to complain. So if we know the justice system disproportionately targets Māori and Pasifika men, how many innocent people are enduring this degradation in those communities? How much internalised self-hate is this generating among young people, who are stopped constantly because they look 'bad', 'wrong', 'criminal'? How much justifiable resentment for authority figures and the law is bred?

The most frightening thing I've seen in almost a decade of acting as a criminal lawyer was the sight of a fourteen-year-old boy sitting behind a very large table, awaiting the start of his trial for murder at the Auckland High Court. I was working as Lester's junior in chambers, and we had been called in to defend the boy by youth advocate Claire Bennett, who was fighting to keep him from life imprisonment. He had thrown a piece of concrete over a motorway overbridge at night, which tragically broke through the windscreen of his victim's car, crushed the victim's ribcage and caused his death.

Our client was tried as an adult, because that is what our law requires. I've wondered since then about the origins of what seems like a total lapse of logic in our criminal justice system.

It was a devastating case, given the deeply heartbreaking loss of life. A wonderful 21-year-old man had been killed. His loved ones were in the courtroom each day. His young partner gave evidence that she had lunged from the passenger seat to protect his head from hitting the windscreen before the car finally crashed. She wept uncontrollably throughout her account in that huge, silent courtroom. After that day, our young client said he wanted to write a letter of apology to the victim's loved ones, but needed help writing it. A volunteer youth support person helped him draft a note, for the first time openly expressing his sadness and remorse.

In the years after that trial, I became involved in drafting New Zealand's child rights report to the United Nations. In that process, I came to realise our youth justice breaches are the most overt and long-standing human rights breaches in our system. We bring children into our criminal system far too young, as young as ten years old. Far too often, we treat them as adults rather than allowing for child-appropriate court processes. We openly reserve the right to mix ages in our places of detention, incarcerating children alongside adults, and though in 2018 the government finally committed to ending that, it is a fight we are still fighting.

The case of that fourteen-year-old boy on trial for murder all those years ago is demonstrative of all the grave concerns raised by a value system that prioritises punishment over both the rights of children and the fair administration of justice.

As lawyers entrusted with his defence, the weight of responsibility was crushing. None of us had ever worked harder on a case. But there was nothing we could do to protect our child-client from the untold stress and trauma of the two-week trial (held in the same courtroom as some of New Zealand's most notorious criminal trials), from the intense media attention, from the police cells where adult offenders were also held, or from the nightmare of a lost future at fourteen.

In practical terms, we had trouble communicating with our young client to ensure that he understood his rights and that we had all the information we needed to formulate his defence. This difficulty was worsened by the fact that we no longer had Claire's expertise in youth advocacy — not all cases involving children have a youth advocate involved once they go up to the adult courts. Like most children entering the criminal justice system, he suffered from mental health issues and learning difficulties, exacerbated by regular school changes as his family struggled to find affordable housing. He and his siblings were known to Child Youth and Family Services, for all the kinds of concerns that usually lead teachers and neighbours to alert authorities about the welfare of children. Those files made for grim reading.

Our youth justice system provides specialised lawyers, judges, and police teams, and tries to divert children from formal criminal justice systems, because the science of cognition says that's appropriate. But when the accusations are more serious, we legally strip young people of their status and rights as children. So while brain development continues to attach to the child's age rather than the consequences of their actions, children are suddenly presumed capable of assessing risks when they swing a bat or act as a lookout for older mates, and of knowing the permanence of death. That was very much at issue in our trial. Young Crown witnesses came along to our trial and talked of all the nights spent throwing rocks over that bridge onto the motorway. On this one tragic night, in a show of dumb bravado, one of them had thrown a much heavier 'rock' into the darkness below. It all happened in a matter of seconds. There's no way an adult would miss the incredible risk to life, but did a fourteen-year-old child think about that risk and deliberately take it? In light of the science that says our brains don't fully develop risk assessment mechanisms until years later, why would we put that question to a jury in a trial applying adult rules and standards?

The second problem is that the trial itself is unlikely to be fair without processes that effectively meet the needs of children. While in the youth justice context we admit that trained professionals and different processes are needed to ensure children are able to engage with information and communicate according to their developmental needs, we routinely rely on verdicts against children resulting from an adult process where these safeguards are missing. If our client can't concentrate on the witness evidence because of the language and setting of the court, which research tells us is probable, did he exercise his right to instruct counsel? This might be the only instance in our justice system where standards designed to produce fair and reliable verdicts are actually lowered when an accused faces more serious charges.

That we are so willing to set aside science and procedural safeguards suggests that deeper socio-political or cultural forces are at play. It seems to reflect an almost vengeful need to punish these children, even by the act of stripping them of their status as young people. We seem to revert to the basic principle of 'an eye for an eye'. In the case of the young murder-accused I assisted, the Crown had repeatedly refused to accept a guilty plea for manslaughter, which Claire had tried to enter from the offset. That means the young person accepted that he had committed an unlawful act resulting in a death. But the Crown felt he should go to trial for a more serious, more intentionally harmful crime, one that would result in him being held in prison well into his adult life. High Court trials are very expensive gambles, one the Crown lost in that case.

This reaction seems to signal our wilful blindness to the context in which serious child offending takes place, disproportionately involving children from a background of poverty, mental illness, and family upheaval or abuse. Added to those indicators are the ethnic demographics, which I think are telling. Children who are arrested and charged with serious crimes are disproportionately Māori or Pasifika.

In that context, it is interesting to note that in another area of our justice system we apply evidence of child cognition very differently. The law deems children incapable of consenting to sexual activity if they are below sixteen years old, so we accept that even fifteen-year-olds lack the necessary mental development to knowingly and intentionally engage in sexual acts. The suggestion that a ten-year-old could be anything but a victim in those circumstances is morally and legally obscene. But a ten-year-old can be held responsible as an adult for his actions as a perpetrator of violent crime or murder. This inconsistency requires a leap of logic. It raises questions about who we choose to protect and who we are happy to demonise, based on the demographics of the youth offending.

Lester made a moving closing address on the final day of that trial. He began by talking at length about the irreversible, tormenting, loss of a beloved young man. He spoke as a dad about a son lost to his family forever. Then he spoke about the other, young life, on the line in many ways. We were never asking for an acquittal. The whole trial was about the difference between doing an unlawful act that caused death, a thing accepted from the start by the young accused, and doing it with deliberate understanding that would make it murder. The verdict was what we asked for, manslaughter. It meant avoiding a sentence of life in imprisonment with at least a ten-year minimum sentence. We won, so to speak, and it was a relief, though no joy could come of it in the circumstances.

Working on that case forced me to answer some hard questions about the system I was servicing. Are children who are serious criminal offenders victims of institutional biases that see one group as inherent victims and another as perpetrators? Who see one group as deserving of protection and another as one that society needs to be protected against? Or worse, a lost cause? The answers to these questions are complex and should shake our understanding of our institutions and ourselves as fair and free from prejudice.

The focus can't simply be on the harm done, even in the worst cases, because the way a society deals with deviancy is a reflection of the strength and goodness of its value system.

During the years I spent standing at the coalface of the criminal justice system, it was glaringly obvious that certain sectors of our society are stuck in cycles of victimhood and crime because they are excluded from mainstream pathways to success. It resonated with me, knowing what it was like to have my family assumed backward, unlikely to be educated or interested in things like politics or art or equality. It reminded me of the more marginalised outsider communities like the one on Karangahape Road, many of whom were constantly in and out of this justice system. Failure or crime was all that was expected of them, and most of what is provided for by the state is court and prison. Except it is clear and proven that prisons don't mitigate crime all that effectively. If that is the core work of our system, then we need change.

We need to invest in all the other things that make society fair, which actually prevent crime. We have to invest in ending wealth inequality, in treating addiction, in providing mental healthcare. We need to end gender inequality before we can end gender-based violence. The justice system *is* necessary, as a form of just conflict resolution when the worst happens, but we know it can't solve the underlying causes of crime or recidivism. In fact, unless we address all the other things that make our communities unsafe, unequal, and unstable, the justice system itself may only act as a contributing factor to inequality and instability, and in the end cause more harm.

What kept me committed as a lawyer is the fact that criminal law is one of the most pure areas of human rights law, precisely because of how flawed our system is. I couldn't disengage, because, rightly or wrongly, people were coming through that system, and we needed to make it as fair as possible. Every day we applied the Bill of Rights Act, the Human Rights Act. We argued against unlawful detention, discrimination, and abuses of power. The courts stand between us as individuals and the mighty force of the state, so while we need to transform that system, to decolonise it, I couldn't pretend there wasn't a need every day for us to make it at least incrementally more fair.

It was a steep learning curve. It meant facing what was a deeply unsettling side of the world every single day. I found it felt better to acknowledge those terrible truths and engage with them, because, having seen what I had seen in my life before then, I couldn't pretend the world was perfect anyway.

7

My global experiment

One day, after two and a half years working in a job that allowed me to both gain profound work experience and reflect some of the values I held most dear into the world, I gave notice. I was moving to Africa for a three-month unpaid internship at the United Nations International Criminal Tribunal for Rwanda (ICTR), with no promise of paid work at the end. This was a move forward, in line with the plan I had jotted on bits of paper years ago, and something I felt I had to do: to keep making opportunities, seeking them out ravenously; to live without limits to my dreams, as I was meant to do. But it was also a move toward my past, as a victim of displacement caused by regime brutality. I was diving back into a world where atrocity existed, where all was not peaceful. I needed to remember that my comfortable life in Auckland was not all that real in the context of global realities. I couldn't forgive myself that comfort.

What compelled me to go was a need to dig deeper, not just into what justice means, but what horror humanity is capable of and how it can be atoned for. Over the years that I worked for the UN, I got to dip in and out of normalcy on my trips home, but always with the acute awareness that harrowing injustice existed and my work was to face that. People would ask me how I coped with the stress of dealing with mass crimes every day. I'd tell them I felt better at least trying to resolve those conflicts, as complex and unresolvable as genocide and war may be, than living a life removed from them.

The truth was that I needed to feel connected to something of the horrors I had so luckily escaped in Iran. I had personally witnessed the devastating effects of mass oppression, torture and war. Because of that experience, there was no closure for me. Yes, we had been lucky. We had got out. But while I had been taken away from the violence and oppression experienced by other Iranians, the regime continued, and while it continued, it managed to harm even the escapees. Our families were scattered around the world. We were stripped of our homes, our language, our culture. I had since replaced all that, but there was grief in what I had lost too. I also grieved for my parents' loss. I grieved knowing they could not so easily replace their identities, their ability to make friends, their ability to work as professionals in their field. That is what Iran lost, too: generations of human resource, innovation and activism that might have moved our country forward. The trauma on both sides of the border is continuous. For me, the state-sponsored atrocity that shaped my life was ongoing. Helping build accountability for state crimes was part of the reparation I felt I owed for escaping.

My entrée into the UN justice system came about because of my work in the courts back in New Zealand. The path technically began with an act of casual boredom, when I opened the latest issue of Auckland Law School's alumni magazine, one of those subscriptions that mysteriously arrive and follow you around for life. In this particular issue, published sometime in 2006, there was an article about an exciting new appointment in the school's academic ranks. Kevin Heller was going to teach International Criminal Law, a subject never offered while I had studied there. I asked Lester if I could leave work early two afternoons a week so I could take the course. He heartily agreed.

Because I was turning up to class in suits and with court files, I attracted Kevin's attention, and soon we formed a sort of camaraderie borne of the fact that I was, like him, a battle-worn practitioner rather than an idealistic intellectual, which I guess was who international law academics mostly encounter in their classes. He liked me straight away on that basis alone. Kevin was a classic 1990s American West Coast liberal professor type, complete with goatee and vintage-looking bowling shirts. But he defined himself as a defence lawyer through and through (as most defence lawyers do).

In the winter of 2007, toward the end of the semester, when a senior defence lawyer from the ICTR contacted Kevin to set up a meeting during his trip to Auckland, Kevin invited me along. Peter Robinson was in New Zealand interviewing witnesses, Rwandan refugees who had been resettled here after the genocide. I drove all three of us in my tiny two-door Toyota to a fish restaurant, because New Zealand seafood was what these Americans were excited about. I learned later just what a formidable force Peter presents in the courtroom, but in person he was soft-spoken and a little fatherly. We shared stories about our trials and complained about the resourcing issues for defendants. By the end of the evening, he had asked me to come intern at the ICTR. There was no job guarantee, he said, but he liked my chances because they didn't get a lot of real practitioners at the tribunal. He said the UN was realising that hiring people with PhDs and human rights lawyers who had only written UN reports wasn't the best way to run trials. I put in my application that week and was accepted into the next internship cohort as a defence intern.

The Rwandan Genocide had taken place between April and July 1994. It was billed by international press as a one-hundred-day genocide. The simplified narrative is that colonisation began in the late 1800s, under German then Belgian rule, favouring the Tutsi ethnic minority, who were granted higher status and power than the Hutu majority, which created or deepened ethnic divisions that eventually erupted into genocide. The truth of Rwanda's ancient and modern socio-political history has a lot more to it than that. The cycles of persecution and violence after the Belgians left continued under the first Hutu-led regime, which displaced Tutsi communities, many of whom fled to Uganda where they lived as refugees for decades. In 1994, Rwanda was to have its first multi-party elections. Tensions between the Rwandan Patriotic Front (RPF), a Ugandan-based Tutsi-led group, who had already invaded Rwanda back in 1990, and the dominant Hutu-led government were high enough to warrant a UN peacekeeping force. But on 6 April 1994, before the election could take place, the assassination of Rwandan president Juvénal Habyarimana, triggered war and violent genocide of the Tutsi. The RPF invaded and eventually won the war. In the end, evidence of mass crimes existed against both sides, and the violence ripped apart the lives of Rwandans across the nation.

It was Lieutenant-General Roméo Dallaire, the head of the UN peacekeeping force in Rwanda, that first turned my attention to the work of the UN tribunal built after that overt failure. I read Dallaire's dark and seething memoir *Shake Hands with the Devil* in Queenstown on a jovial conference of New Zealand's Criminal Bar Association. He recounted how the UN ignored his pleas for resources to stop the violence before, and even while the genocide took hold. I wondered how the justice process underway in Arusha, Tanzania, would ever redeem the international community's apathy. I wondered too how a justice process could ever heal the kind of engrained and fresh wounds encompassed in Dallaire's account.

The job of the ICTR was to determine which leaders were or were not criminally responsible for the atrocities, to what extent they had been planned, and who had had control. In the end, though ordinary people of both ethnic groups suffered great violence, the UN court never prosecuted indictments against the invading, liberating forces of the RPF, against Hutu civilians. They had won the war and the leading Tutsi general, Paul Kagame, was and remains in power today. The functioning of that tribunal depended on the cooperation of that Rwandan government, so it could not well investigate its sitting members. This was a bitter pill of real politics that the institution swallowed early on, and was marred by thereafter.

In the 1990s, the United Nations international courts stood, for the first time since Nuremberg, as an experiment in holding governments and armies to account. It was something I needed to be a part of. I felt like I needed to know that the rule of law, the human-rights-based system I had committed myself to, could end impunity for even the most powerful criminals. That we could send a message to the oppressors that our values were stronger than theirs. That we could call them criminals and murders, but not until we had brought them into the banal world of courtrooms and afforded them the right to defend themselves. It was about building a world where no one was above the law, even as we gave those oppressors the rights they themselves had taken away from others. I imagined what a gift that would be for the people of Iran.

I flew to Arusha in June 2008. Arusha sits between Mount Kilimanjaro, Mount Meru, and the vast plains of the Serengeti. The ICTR was housed there because it was deemed secure and stable. Walking into the tribunal that first day was surreal and exhilarating. But it would surprise most people to know just how pedestrian it all was. The buildings were run down and defence teams in particular were crammed in narrow, barely lit offices with little access to UN resources. We even had to buy our own printing paper. The proceedings were slow, as everything was simultaneously interpreted into three languages (English, French, and Kinyarwanda), and lawyers from different jurisdictions argued from vastly different evidential rules and advocacy styles. Still, the subject matter was incredibly complex and fascinating. The law we made was novel in the field. I felt incomprehensibly lucky.

Then there were the UN interns. The first cohort of interns I encountered were my ICTR group. They were all smart and, mostly, loud, wealthy, and American. Although certainly driven, they weren't necessarily there to start a career in human rights or humanitarian law. There for the summer from their fancy universities, they were mostly padding their résumés and collecting exotic anecdotes. On our first night out, one of our group ruined her Manolo Blahnik stilettos and we heard complaints about the gravel back roads of Arusha for the rest of the night. My decision to only pack a pair of weathered sneakers and two pairs of flat work shoes for this stint felt validated.

That night, we went to a party for the launch of a mixed-media art exhibition, held in a sprawling abandoned property down one of the offending dirt roads. I was mesmerised to see how modern African art would be received by this nomadic UN crowd, which was a little cool, a little gaudy, and mostly there to get profoundly drunk like it was any night out. It turned out that, to most of the interns, international justice, like cross-cultural art collabs, was just another excuse to make out. They did 'self-care' between weeks at the court by leaving for the beaches of North Africa or Zanzibar. I had budgeted carefully to afford one safari and one trip to Zanzibar; flying to other regions or going on these trips every other weekend would have meant missing rent.

I made fast friends with my roommate, Amy. To save money, we shared a room and a double bed from the first night we met. We were in an ad-hoc flat group with two other guys, Henry and Matt, who shared the other bedroom in the house we rented. Theirs was equipped with single beds. My housemates were all Americans and we were all interns to different departments of the court. Amy was a prosecution intern. We lived on a winding village path, ten minutes' walk off the main road, which was itself about half an hour's drive out of Arusha's town centre. We drank giant bottles of beer and ate hot chips and skewers of tough, charred goat meat that had been barbecued outside, with the locals in our hamlet pub. The tribunal was one thing, but there were even better moments when you realised, 'I'm in Africa.'

Amy somehow befriended some Americans working to build a conservation camping facility, and on weekends they would take us into the Serengeti to camp on the savannah. It wasn't the same as the safari tours that try to tick off the Big Five (lions, leopards, elephants, buffalos and rhinos). It was quiet and far away from the crowds and most of the animal herds. But it was still incredible. We didn't see anyone other than local Maasai living on the land, the flashes of their red-striped cloth brazenly clashing with, yet complementing, the burnt tones of the savannah grasslands. We also spotted the odd giraffe or zebra family, moving languidly in herds like in a weird dream.

I was assigned to the Government One trial, which tried the top-level government leaders accused of orchestrating the violence. Our client was Joseph Nzirorera, the Secretary General of the *Mouvement républicain national pour la démocratie et le développement* (the National Republican Movement for Democracy and Development, or MRND), the political party in power at the time of the Rwandan Genocide. I decided I would interact with him like I would with any other client. There was no other appropriate way to be. Of course, that meant forcing a disconnect between the subject matter of the trial and the daily work of assisting the defence team as a professional. I kept thinking about the Iranian leaders, their rise, and possible fall. Jewish political theorist Hannah Arendt called it the 'banality of evil', and that is right, because the people accused of genocide and torture are always, in the end, just people. There's no magical mark of evil, nor good.

Nzirorera always appeared to me as a politician. He wanted to talk to the interns and tell us about Rwandan history. He was charismatic and eloquent. It was chilling to think how those attributes may have helped him benefit in a climate of ethnic division. I think about what charisma can mean in politics in my own work now. We hear about the cult of personality, and what politicians may get away with, inspire, or suppress, because we trust them or are dazzled by them. Sitting across from this man, affable and intent on winning my favour, I tried not to think about the cynical possibilities. He was innocent until proven guilty.

I realised later that retelling history was an obsession for the accused at every international tribunal. History was what they felt was at stake. The narrative of who had enslaved whom, when, and why was retold by the victors back home and the inmates in UN cells. It was a surreal experience to hear from someone in that position. It was heart-wrenching, whichever way you looked at it. I sat there in that sterile little room with the grim yellowing light, my notebook open, yet writing nothing down. No matter how much it mattered to the inmates, millennia-old history was not what we were adjudicating at these trials. Whichever version of history came closer to the truth, we were concerned with accountability for the specific crimes before the court, which nothing would excuse if proved. I knew that this kind of rhetoric, bought and sold by politicians on all sides of so many ethnic struggles, had led to hate so ferocious that it ended in a genocide trial.

What I got in those sessions with Nzirorera was a glimpse into the deep-seated and complex causes of ethnic violence, not because his perspective was accurate but the compulsion to tell it reflected those partisan wounds. These stories had clearly been passed down through generations, and had at one point turned into powerful political propaganda. Both Hutu and Tutsi had suffered great injustices based on their ethnicities in Rwanda's ancient and recent history. I realised that, on its own, our process in Arusha was never going to restore equality between the groups. That was my first point of disillusionment with a parachuted-in UN-style process. That brand of justice was slow and inherently one-sided in the context of the very fresh wounds of war.

The question of how society moves forward after large-scale, systematic abuses of human rights is deeply personal for me because it is directly related to whether my parents and I would ever see our birthland again. If ever there was to be safety for Iranians, regime change must come with a return to the rule of law and human rights. There must be no room for vigilante mass vengeance, as there had been after the revolution. That kind of victor's justice had grown from institutional killings of old regime officials to the wholesale torture and execution of any dissident, with carte blanche authority for the new regime to define its 'enemies'. Now, the victim groups are even more vast. The regime has targeted women with particular zeal. Entire ethnic and religious communities, including Bahá'ís, Kurds, and Jews, have suffered disproportionately. Then there is widespread political persecution, the mass graves of Communists, Socialists, and Mojahedin. But change cannot risk violence against regime supporters, which could mean targeting mostly poor, Shi'a communities, likely with war-martyred sons and brothers. Given the numbers this would affect, it could mean civil war.

What I want for Iran is a fair system of justice to adjudicate mass crimes. The promise of the UN courts was important, because they individualised blame and adopted a transparent process to set the facts straight. This meant groups wouldn't continue in cycles of violence and blame. It was clear to me that if we got it right, my mother might one day live on her family's vineyards in her old age, speaking her local dialect. My dad might drink whiskey and listen to Pink Floyd with his cousins, tell jokes to old friends and hear belly laughs in response again.

That's not to say we were looking to move back. Our lives are in New Zealand. New Zealand is our home. But there's a difference between being happy immigrants and being permanently displaced for fear of persecution.

After my first internship, I did another two stints with defence teams. I was in The Hague working on the Yugoslavia Tribunal, when I was offered a paying contract job back in Arusha, this time to work on the appeal of Simon Bikindi.

Bikindi had been one of the most famous pop singers in Rwanda at the time of the genocide. His case had been novel in law because he had been charged with inciting ethnic violence through his nationalistic songs. It was argued that the songs were either overtly provoking ethnic conflict or that, in the context of high tensions, singing songs promoting Hutu nationalist politicians amounted to incitement. He was acquitted of all but one count of direct and public incitement. Bikindi refuted that allegation vehemently, and I was on his appeal team.

Years later back in New Zealand, I was questioned about having acted in Bikindi's defence and been in a photograph taken within a series of our team members with Bikindi before the hearing. I understood the uproar. It is difficult to look past accusations of inciting genocide. Most people view the work of human rights lawyers as fighting for a clearly oppressed group, when it is in fact to uphold a system of justice based in human rights. That will always involve applying the law equally to those accused of any crime. It is hard to communicate that ideal to those outside of the bubble of rights-engaged professionals and activists, but I think when faced with the choice — to either empower defence lawyers in the same way we do prosecutors and judges, or the alternative, presumably to take people out back to disappear into dungeons without trials — almost all of us do see the point.

But I was surprised by the way one reporter opened my Facebook page in an interview and went through every photo I had taken with a black person to ask if he or she was a criminal. These were lawyers, tour guides, other interns, and people studying with me at Oxford. I realised the articles were all printing the full indictment of charges against Bikindi, all the charges he had been acquitted of. You would never get away with that in the context of a Western defendant. What makes a journalist set aside those objective rules? What makes them look at one of those photos and see anything but an accused person and their lawyer? What would make them then look at photos of other persons of colour with a UN lawyer, and seek confirmation that they too were not criminals?

The Bikindi case is also fascinating in the context of the conversations happening right now about free speech. Everyone who has studied atrocity has come up against the kind of language that inspires mass hate and violence. It starts early, with political opportunism in peacetime. Terms like 'vampires' and 'ragdolls' that Hitler used to describe the Jewish community are well known. In Rwanda, it was 'cockroaches'. The Khmer Rouge called their victims 'enemies of the people'. Since the start of the War on Terror, and now with Trump's war on migrants, we've heard terms like 'enemies of freedom', 'animals', and 'criminals' used to describe migrant and Muslim communities. If history has taught us anything, it is that, at a certain point, among certain groups, dehumanising language becomes very deliberate code for other groups to be targeted, oppressed, and ultimately murdered.

Bikindi's role in singing songs wasn't found to have crossed the line to incitement in and of itself. But he was there at political rallies, singing next to politicians who benefited from the hatred of the Tutsi and a Hutu-dominant vision of Rwandan nationalism that his songs espoused.

I have remembered Bikindi's case often recently, since it is all about interpreting language and the harm it may cause in a certain socio-political context. I thought about the language of atrocity when there were news reports of white supremacists talking about lynching me in secret chatrooms because of my race. Days later, a fellow politician called me 'a threat to freedom in New Zealand' on a national radio programme. This happened only twelve weeks after the Christchurch terror attacks. It was, in fact, his response to my call for a review of our hate speech laws to protect minorities against extremism — the same extremism growing in those chatrooms talking about killing me for my race, the same chatrooms that praised the Christchurch terrorist.

Context is important.

Just as singing nationalist songs isn't always going to incite genocide, calling someone 'a threat to freedom' isn't necessarily going to feed extremism or put that person in very real danger unless these things are done in the context of existing marginalisation, in both cases already causing violence against members of that group with reference to that very rhetoric. To my mind, the concern in this case wasn't about me, but the fact that people from refugee backgrounds, from the Muslim world (whether we are Muslim or presumed Muslim, as I am), and from non-white ethnic groups are experiencing increasing hostility and violence. It is that context in which we must assess the public-safety aspect of language.

One thing I learned from my work with UN atrocity trials is that atrocity is begot of ordinary hate and prejudice. I think about that when I think about the Christchurch terror attacks. I think about the voices of Māori coming together to support and to amplify those of our migrants of colour in the wake of that atrocity. They said in a chorus, 'This is white supremacy and it has existed in New Zealand for a long while because this is a colony.' Acknowledging that history, those lived experiences, was important. I think about the concentration camps filled with migrant children along the US border right now, and the fight for indigenous Hawaiians to preserve Mauna Kea. I think about Ihumātao — sacred, disputed land occupied by protectors, who were stood over by cops. Words matter. The way we tell stories, and record and teach — or don't teach — history matters. What we see happening today, in all these places I have mentioned, is frightening, in part because it has happened before and the world has said repeatedly, 'Never again.' That is why we have to name hate, and stop it in its tracks, in all its forms, even close at home.

From 2008 to 2012, in a whirlwind of exhilaration and touch of self-imposed pressure to 'do it all', I worked between Auckland, Arusha, The Hague, and Phnom Penh, Cambodia. I worked as a member of defence and prosecution teams, starting at the bottom and eventually settling into the UN system proper. A contrast to all of this, to those very real experiences of courtrooms and mission stations, was Oxford. That beautiful, aloof English institution gave me space to finally research and write about Iran, about the way my people persecute minorities in the most abhorrent way through the justice system itself.

I applied to go while I was packing for that first internship to Arusha. The website for the Master of Studies in International Human Rights Law was still bookmarked on my work computer. I had been silently taunting myself to set a deadline and apply. But practical forward-moving steps aren't easy to take. I was a little paralysed every time I began to click through. It was an arduous and daunting process, asking for references, writing that admission essay, pressing send. For me, it felt deeply surreal to be an Oxford applicant, surprising, I thought, how I could even muster the confidence to ask for that consideration. But the thing that spurred me on was that this course was for practitioners. They only accepted around thirty people from around the world every year, and fancy grades alone weren't going to make it. They wanted you to establish a working record of human rights practice.

The wait for that acceptance, or rejection, was a maddening one. I told no one about it to avoid periodic questions about how it went and of course the dreaded announcement that I didn't make the cut. No one but Ghazaleh, ever the safe space with whom I could share outlandish dreams and failures, with no raised eyebrows or pity in return.

When the acceptance email came in, I wrote a deprecating response rejecting it to send on to Ghaz, a lame insider joke that I thought was exceptionally witty. Of course I hadn't pressed 'Forward'. I sent it as a reply. My inconsolable shriek a moment later shook the office. Thankfully, I don't think anyone really receives those reply emails.

When I told Lester about my acceptance, his response was, 'We're taking the afternoon off,' and we went straight to my mum's shop to tell her the news. She took a good minute to read the short acceptance letter, looked around and burst into tears on the side of Mount Eden Road.

I deferred the start of the course to go to Arusha, thinking the internship would only be for three months, but as it turned out I was in and out of Africa and the grassy knolls of England. Oxford was all cricket fields, duckponds, and grand dining halls. Hogwarts was partly filmed where I stayed on and off over those two years, where I ate meals sitting on ancient wooden benches along enormous slab tables, under dark stern oil portraits of the men who sat at those slabs before me.

But Oxford was also where I got the time and space to write about Iran. To distil what thoughts I had gathered on justice from the institutions where I had worked, and analyse the way that regimes used justice institutions to persecute and abuse its perceived enemies. I wanted to know I could prove it. I researched Iran's 'Revolutionary Courts' and the way oppressive regimes often use pseudo-judicial means to criminalise, marginalise, and kill minorities or their political opponents. These are the courts that regularly execute dissidents, religious and ethnic minorities, and women for seeking to access equality. I wanted to see whether those courts had legitimacy by any standard of human rights law or justice. I wanted particularly to include Islamic standards of fair process. It was important to ask whether the regime's appeal to Islam was valid or false. It is so easy to say that Sharia requires brutality, but brutality can be derived from any ideology or religion to achieve the ends of a brutal ruler.

It was a subject matter I carried close to my heart and followed because of my family's close friendships with people who disappeared into that system or felt the imminent threat of its reach at any given moment. That was especially felt among my mother's Bahá'í friendship group. But in Oxford I also found my own uncanny, life-changing friendship and connection with persecution in Iran. One of the core faculty, teaching among other things the Minority Rights elective course, was a Bahá'í, Iranian-descended lecturer called Nazila Ghanea.

During my first week in Oxford, Naz asked me to go for a walk along the river. We ate a picnic of strawberries as people punted gently past us on those long, ethereal gliding boats, avoiding Her Majesty's alarmingly large swans along the way. Soon we broke into Farsi, and laughed aloud at ourselves when we tripped up on the words. There we were, a couple of long-displaced Iranians, finding each other in the English countryside. We talked about our people's history and our own families' broken-up lives, our love of the rich food and customs we kept alive with that older generation. Naz's work focuses on religious freedom. As the course developed and we talked more, it was always a wonder to me that she fought as zealously and with as much care for the rights of Muslims there in the United Kingdom as she did to end the persecution of Bahá'í in Iran. If religious discrimination is allowed anywhere, against any faith group, then the gross rhetoric of oppressors like the Islamic Republic wins.

Once I came to publish my dissertation, I converted into a test for the trial of the 'Yaran', the case of the seven Iranian Bahá'í leaders in Iran's Revolutionary Courts. The Revolutionary Court in Tehran convicted the seven Bahá'í of crimes including 'espionage for Israel', 'insulting religious sanctities' and 'propaganda against the system', and sentenced them to twenty years imprisonment. Not only were the Yaran criminalised for peaceful practice of their religion, but my interest ran deeper, into the legitimacy of an institution when it was in fact inseparable from the executive government and its security agency, and held processes without the right to robust defence. This wasn't just an Iranian problem; we now lived in a world where military action in Iraq and Afghanistan justified a parallel weaponised system of 'justice' in Guantanamo Bay. It was time to reclaim that word.

Later, my publication was translated to Farsi. I can barely read its title in that language anymore, but it means so much to have contributed something to legal scholarship there, where that test and that case study could not have been written about without dire repercussion. It does mean, of course, that I have my own fresh grounds to fear political persecution if ever I was tempted to go back.

That space to be Iranian as a human rights lawyer, or give some small measure back, was what had taken me to Oxford, though I remember my time there mostly for my fellow Oxonians. To be among them was a respite from the mostly jaded and disconnected UN types I had thus far encountered. My class included Gemma, based in Gaza via Sydney, Australia, to this day, one of my true soulmates. We laughed till we cried some nights in our dorm room or out in the gardens, noticing the absurdities of where we were. I also remember Robert Pitman, from the great state of Texas, who became the first openly gay judge to sit on the federal bench. He had had to leave briefly to be sworn in by Barack Obama as the first openly gay state attorney. People were flying in from war zones and humanitarian disasters to talk human rights and drink together at centuries-old pubs, with honestly the most ominous winding stone staircases to the women's loos. This was a self-selecting group among human rights lawyers, who were interested enough in their field to study it but dedicated firstly to its frontlines.

With the distance of time, it's curious, even to me, that I went to these places alone, stood in those courtrooms, sat in those exam rooms, as a twenty-something-year-old Iranian Kiwi refugee, far away from everything familiar. I realise now that having refugees for parents means that nothing ever looks as hard as fleeing your home. Stepping out of my own comfort zone to face a challenge was always a privilege rather than a hardship to me. Saying yes to each move was less of a risk to me than missing an adventure someone had risked their life for me to have one day.

Where I felt most at home was Cambodia. I woke up that first morning in Phnom Penh, walked out into the golden light, already potent at 7 am, and felt happy. It was August 2011. I was staying near a Buddhist temple, a wat, on a narrow lane. The footpath was full of people already busy cooking and selling things at stalls, welding, and driving tuk tuks. I didn't know anyone in the city. I remember the erratic sounds and smells, and the calm I felt among that chaos. Under that yellowest Cambodian sun, every colour looks more earthen. Something about those greens and browns reminded me of a place I had been before, a place in my childhood. I felt a kinship with the tumultuous history of the Cambodians and with their optimistic joy.

The community of internationals was far bigger and more diverse than in Arusha. It was safer and easier to make friends, find my people. They had built a society more committed to living in Phnom Penh, rather than with one foot out the door. The nights were warm and free, and people were always out and up for company.

I was now in a secure UN job, as an intermediate-level prosecutor, rather than an intern or contracted lawyer, like on the Bikindi appeal. It was a coveted position. You could become a proper 'lifer', and with that came responsibility, autonomy, money. This was a space I felt less at home. I couldn't shake the feeling that they had made a mistake in choosing me. That I wasn't good enough.

Women and people of marginalised groups often talk about imposter syndrome. As success and praise come, we feel like our fraud is irrefutable. That is in part because we have not seen people like us commonly navigate that world. We dare ourselves to push through, but every success comes with the terror of being 'found out', or at least the unshakable feeling that we're acting a part. I felt like that. Deep down, I was sure there wasn't meant to be a little refugee girl in the life I was living.

This was a feeling that had been steadily growing since I completed my Master's with Distinction. At the time, it didn't seem real. I started thinking about how the standards at Oxford had clearly dropped and researched university rankings to prove it to myself. I didn't go to my graduation ceremony and looked through the photos of my classmates in their caps and gowns with longing. I hadn't felt right celebrating an accomplishment I was sure I didn't deserve. I kept thinking about how rushed my dissertation had been, because I was working so much at the time. I felt ashamed.

That inkling of undeserved success intensified with all the security and relative prestige of my job in Phnom Penh. The further I climbed this new ladder, the more that feeling of terror permeated. The affirmations felt unsettling. Being praised and looked up to didn't feel natural. It felt like a lie. This wasn't borne of a deference to authority or class hierarchy. I was raised never to assume righteousness, even competence, based on any title, whether professionally bestowed or hereditary — my mother never let my dad's side of the family forget how little regard she had for their royal claims. I was raised to show everyone the same respect, but never assume they were better than anyone else unless that was proven in substance. Where I come from, authority is often self-appointed, misplaced, and deserving of challenge. Neither of my parents ever let me forget that the greatest gift in moving away from all that was that we get to talk back.

That's helpful when you're standing up to judges, or trying to reform a system. Back at Oxford, I got together with a bunch of other gung ho secularists in my class to challenge the college practice of having prayers before meals. The professor we first spoke with assumed I might like a rotation of different denominational prayers, including a Muslim version that I would lead. That wasn't the point. The indignity was the fusion of academia with religion, any religion, especially in a human rights programme. And frankly, I had already had to flee one place where that wasn't well understood, so I wasn't for leading formal prayers.

It's because of how I was raised, and what I had seen of Iranians challenging systems sold to them as millennia-old tradition, that I wasn't intimidated by Oxford's institutional prestige. After all, deference to tradition at Oxford had, for 800-odd years, included a ban on the admission of women. But it's one thing to band together with other nonconformists to poke at the status quo, then to celebrate by having pints in the old stone pubs where for so long only well-bred Englishmen were allowed to clink glasses. To be given status and security in that same system, to pull back the curtain and take a seat on the inside — that has not been comfortable for me. My time in the UN, interwoven with my Master's studies at Oxford, tested my sense of myself as someone who was allowed to achieve that type of success.

The anxiety began with a kind of paralysis at work. Small things like opening the mountain of emails in my inbox felt impossible. Emailing submissions I had drafted became difficult. I avoided reading over them, certain I had made a hash of every task. I needed deadlines to be imminent before I could finally press send.

Then I stopped sleeping. I would lie in bed with my eyes open, thinking about all the things I had done wrong that day, all the things I had ever done wrong or differently than I should have, all the ways I wasn't and couldn't possibly be enough. I wondered when they would all realise and I would finally fail the way I knew I deserved to fail. I would wonder that all night and all day. But things kept going on and I kept doing the job to everyone's satisfaction. That was only more unsettling.

Then something happened that made me realise that the way I was feeling wasn't right and that I should get help. I agreed to give an informal talk to our interns about my career path. It should all have been very routine. Back in New Zealand I had been a practising barrister, so speaking in court was something I did every day. I had been giving presentations to victim groups and regional gatherings the whole time I was in Phnom Penh, though I had begun to avoid them as the self-doubt set in. I justified that as an issue of time: the trips were often overnight in far-flung Cambodian provinces or in Bangkok.

Suddenly, I was nervous. I sat there frozen in anxiety, as my colleague, Salim, introduced me. Then I stood up and looked around the room. I knew everyone there by name. They were sitting with snacks, casually smiling up at me. I began by telling them I completed my first law degree at Auckland, then worked as a criminal barrister. I had a lot I wanted to say about the importance of learning advocacy and of starting at the bottom in order to become a good lawyer, rather than idealising these fancy UN jobs. But the next thing I said in the casual retelling of my credentials was that I had a Master's degree in international human rights law from Oxford. I could barely get the words out. I noticed my breathing had become shallow. I wanted to flee the room. My mind went blank. I sat down and looked over at poor Salim, who had so eagerly brought us all together. He looked perplexed for an instant, then suggested we go into a discussion format. People began talking among themselves while I calmed enough to engage and answer questions.

I came home and recounted the experience to my friend Kate, who was in Phnom Penh to observe our trial as part of her research. I had had a lot of strange secret misgivings bottled up by now, but this felt like something I needed to tell someone about. I was scared.

She listened to my disjointed account, then said, 'You know you're describing a panic attack.' I didn't know that. I had no real language to recognise or describe anxiety or its symptoms.

I told her about the insomnia, and something else I had noticed that I hadn't wanted to accept. My hair was falling out. At first, I had told myself it was the normal amount of shedding, but then the clumps pouring down the shower drain seemed to get distinctly larger. My hair parting widened and I had started flipping my hair to the side or pulling it back in a ponytail to hide the patches.

As we talked things through, I realised my imposter syndrome was getting the better of me, and it would probably take more than sheer willpower to get over it. But our talk revealed another insidious truth about the source of my anxiety: the work environment I had entered was hostile and unhealthy.

The United Nations, for its vast and glaring flaws, is the only institution with the mandate of ensuring international peace and security. To me, that mandate and the dream of carrying it out together as a global community will always be worth honouring. But, although the notion of justice is universal, its application through the terms of a UN institution felt limited and imposed, probably because the UN's inception and design was always led by Westerners partnered with whichever leaders looked like the affected community and happened to have power at the time. There was a void of voices from victims and survivors of atrocity, oppression, or violence, not just as witnesses but as lawyers and judges, with equal respect and say. That certainly was not how the Cambodian members of that court were treated or talked of by the international team I was in. They were treated as tokens, bypassed and stepped over in decision-making, presumed to know less and work less hard than the international team. It was unsettling for me to know that truth, to hear the things I always knew Westerners said about us.

There was also a lack of support for women's involvement. We know the failure to engage women in international justice historically meant that gender-based crimes were excluded from prosecutions. Now, the definition of genocide rightly includes rape or enforced pregnancy. While these precedents arose from the ad hoc UN tribunals, women were still not mainstreamed in the courts themselves. The truth is that women are affected by the full range of crimes committed in war or by oppressive regimes. We are affected differently as we flee, often unarmed and with children in tow. We have fewer means to flee at all. We are affected differently when conscripted as child soldiers. If catering to the female experience is limited to charging sex crimes, our input is ghettoised. So, women, too, must be prioritised as witnesses of crimes, as lawyers, as interpreters, and as judges.

For much of my time as prosecutor, I was one of two women, and the only woman of colour, in the international team of about fourteen lawyers and analysts. Every person in a senior or management role was a white man. My office mate was idealistic and whip-smart Sarah. She had thrown in a senior partner–tracked job at a Sydney law firm to follow her dream of working in international justice. At one point, a senior female lawyer joined our team from Canada. The toxic and firmly male-dominated environment burnt her out within two months. She told us that, and to get out, too. Sarah and I began to cling to one another, to whisper about the ways we were undermined, the ways we were overlooked and marginalised in decision-making, the expectation that we work all the time, through the night and on weekends, with no say in how our work was directed. For me, there was persistent sexual overtures. I felt like I should be better at managing that than the younger women in the office, the interns, until I realised we were all in the same boat. At least they could leave at the end of their internships. There were two senior international lawyers at the Khmer Rouge court, one on a defence team, the other in our own prosecution team, who were universally referred to as 'Internimator' and 'Internimator Two', because of their prolific bedding of interns. Sarah and I did talk about the strategies we could use to protect the female interns that came through our office from the vast army of men, but when their complaints were raised by us, they appeared to have no value. We were told to talk directly to the men being complained about. Once when we did raise a complaint, the result was that the intern's extension of time with the office was cancelled and she was asked to leave.

Sarah left as soon as she could.

Left the sole woman in our team, I represented the Office of the Prosecutor in local and regional forums on gender equity. I felt compelled to tell the truth that the court itself was falling short. In response came cordial nodding and enduring apathy.

I only felt ready to raise a complaint on my own behalf in my exit interview with only two weeks left at the court. Until then, I had tried to manage the middling waves of harassment on my own, told myself that as an adult professional woman I should be able to set boundaries and cope with the hostility that came after. Making a complaint had felt risky too, because I wasn't in a position of power. I would still have to go to work every day and face whatever worsened dynamic could come after. But as I was leaving, I couldn't let it be. I felt responsible for the women who would come afterward. I thought maybe a complaint would be taken more seriously if a staff lawyer made it, someone on her way out with nothing to lose or gain. I was told that, given strict processes around workplace harassment, my disclosure would be advanced to the UN human resources office back at headquarters and they would be in touch once the process was underway. I never heard back.

Limits were hard to set against that entrenched work culture. Living in that climate, as well as the devastating subject matter of our work, had worn people down. One lawyer, at the tender age of 36, had developed a nervous tic. Another never left his office during the workday, and sometimes well into the night. He had every meal delivered to his desk and sat surrounded by piles of paper and trays of dirty dishes yet to be picked up by the cafeteria staff.

It felt good to tell Kate all this and have the magnitude of my reaction affirmed. I started taking time off to travel the local region with friends. I spent my weekends really living in Phnom Penh, among the chaos and noise, riding on the back of motorbikes. It felt good to experience a life in Asia, as an Asian, of sorts. But mostly, I realised, I wanted to come home and put down roots. I felt like jumping from place to place and between jobs had helped the imposter syndrome set in.

I also knew I needed to come home because I felt if I was away for much longer, I would cease to have a home. I had been in New Zealand only fleetingly for four years. Living overseas, when people asked me where I was from, I had a split second to decide if they were asking about my accent or my complexion. I could either say New Zealand or Iran, unless I felt like delving into the more complicated truth. When I got the subtext of the question wrong, and it was followed with, 'But where did you learn English?' or 'But where are you from *really*?' (the question that tells us we aren't allowed to identify as Westerners unless we are white), I felt bad for seeming like I might be denying a part of my origin story. I didn't want to morph into a true nomad, one of those expats with indistinguishable accents who couldn't really say where they were from or relate to any culture as their own. I did need a true homeland.

So, for the second time in my life, I quit a great job, dropped off a safe path and moved.

The anxiety didn't stop with that. I came home with a deep sense of insecurity about my work prospects. I felt inadequate to everyone who had done the mature thing and stayed to build a legal career. They were all in their stride. People had bought homes, scattered across the suburbs. They were planning their weddings. Showing off their beautiful babies. I felt like I was coming last in a race I hadn't entered. I woke up every morning to search the listings for any kind of job in international law or human rights. They were few and far between. At first it was nice to have space and time to think and walk, drink coffee in familiar haunts. But I began to feel disconnected. The sleeplessness set in again. Leaving the house took effort.

The turning point was an offer to act as co-counsel in a case before the Supreme Court. Having never turned down a terrifying opportunity, I said yes.

They sit very close to the lectern where you stand to address them, the Supreme Court justices. In a half circle, much like what Judgement Day might look like in some post-apocalyptic nightmare for lawyers. You speak from notes, but they regularly interrupt with questions.

Standing up to speak after my co-counsel was harrowing. But I was proud of our work; I had wanted to speak my part. Our case was about police misconduct and what constitutes an abuse of process in New Zealand law. It was a case about the integrity and independence of our institutions. I began to speak, looking directly at the Chief Justice, Dame Sian Elias. My voice croaked out quietly into the silence of the courtroom.

Think-on-your-feet advocacy has always been more my strength than anything else. As I went on, it became apparent which justices were for us (Dame Elias, for one) and which were more set on challenging us. The interruptions soared. I knew I had hit a stride when I looked one of the legends of the bench in the eye and, with all the appropriate airs and graces, told him I could answer his question, but that its basis was a misrepresentation of my argument. 'This,' I said to myself throughout, 'is one time you'll keep breathing, thinking fast, and talking in the face of the fear.' There was no second shot at this hearing. It was all a bit of an out-of-body experience. I couldn't settle my heart rate for a long time afterwards. I could barely read the transcript for corrections when it came. Nor could I read the judgement for a couple of days after it was issued, though I knew we had won.

As validating as the experience was, the stress of it pushed me over the line to seek treatment. With the help of a friend who I knew had had similar experiences, I started seeing a psychologist.

There were some difficult sessions dismantling the dense web of my childhood trauma and the defences my mind had built up to survive. The things I saw in Iran, the move, and growing up with parents intensely affected by stress and trauma of their own had gifted me some unhealthy coping mechanisms. It was and is frightening to face all that. I see the same psychologist to treat the anxiety when it returns now, whether to process the success and praise that comes with public office or the hate and vitriol I receive as the representative of marginalised groups. It is something that affects my life in phases, and comes with a score of symptoms: sleeplessness, a need to retreat, a constant knot in the stomach, a worry about being undeserving. But now I know what it is. I know whatever is causing my anxiety won't kill me. If the Supreme Court didn't, nothing will.

Today, presenting as a proud woman of colour, being unapologetic about my achievements, and behaving like I belong in every meeting room or on every stage I'm invited to walk upon is still a struggle from time to time. But I do it deliberately. I don't apologise for taking up a seat at the decision-making table. I don't downplay the achievements that took me to Oxford, or the United Nations, or the New Zealand Supreme Court, though I feel the knot of anxiety and shame appear even as I list those things now.

I know that other women and young people, particularly within marginalised groups, also suffer from doubt. The trick is to allow that doubt, to acknowledge just how difficult it is to live with it, to see its causes, and to celebrate each other for standing in spite of it. For me, admitting the struggle is part of representing that experience. It has taken therapy. I have come from a place of experiencing physical panic from speaking to a small group of interns, to speaking into megaphones at mass rallies and speaking at parliament with strength and conviction. The doubt has never completely dissipated. But I know deep down that I belong, that *we* belong. We beat on, because the more of us there are, the less we look like imposters.

8

Why politics? Why Green?

My decision to run for political office was driven by the need to protect the values that I hold so dear, the values that colour my first memories of Aotearoa. Because from the moment we fled Iran we had a sense that we were going toward a set of values — freedom, equality, democracy, which our own revolution had hoped to achieve — rather than just a different place. From first landing at the base of that escalator in Auckland Airport, holding my parents' trembling hands, to the drive into town, what I remember is the feeling that here we had rights and dignity. Now, I wanted to bring what I had learned around the world — about holding governments and power to account — home.

I felt an urgency to protect democracy itself, as someone who has seen the world without it. To me, it seemed like a global brand of mob-rules politics was getting too close to us for comfort. My platforms from the start were human rights, representative democracy, and the battle against prejudice. It felt like these were becoming part of the global zeitgeist, as other women from marginalised backgrounds — migrants, indigenous women, women of colour — also rose to power, forming a counterpart to populist politics. In the United States, the antidotes to Trump were the elections of the first-ever indigenous American women to Congress, Deb Haaland and Sharice Davids; Muslim women; 29-year-old Alexandria Ocasio-Cortez, a woman of colour from a working-class migrant background; and Ilhan Omar, the first-ever refugee elected to Congress, around a year after me. What is extraordinary is seeing the rise of the most marginalised of people, not only being elected but behaving as if election is our right.

For the first time, there are politicians speaking from real, lived experiences to issues never before given a national, let alone global, platform. Our issues aren't only race and gender — we also speak about poverty, healthcare, education, housing, and the climate crisis from perspectives that were, until now, perilously ignored. If revolution is a taking of power by the powerless to change government, then ours is a revolution. To have a voice in leadership has never been a reality for our communities. Our rise comes at a time when once again our very humanity is openly questioned and our lives are threatened by extremism and hate. This time, we're fighting back from positions of power.

It felt important, and thrilling, to lend my voice to this fight. Yet for every joyous interaction, there was a hateful tirade. For every person who supported me in my candidacy, who proudly took a stake in helping bring about my win, there was a troll behind a computer screen. I found out almost immediately on becoming visible in politics that, to some, my presence was a source of fear and outrage. For me, that hate is a strand woven through the narrative of my life in politics as New Zealand's 'first refugee MP'. Writing about the hate and analysing its roots is in itself critical — that's why I have set aside an entire chapter (see chapter ten) for it. But to allow the abuse to eclipse my work and my story is to surrender. If racism's aim is in part to distract us from our work, then I can't allow that. Instead, the people I have come to represent — my Green whānau and every community whose issues my work addresses — deserve better. I wanted to write about my politics, my works, my drive, as separate from the experience of prejudice, because I refuse to let the hate define me or my story as a parliamentarian.

The decision to enter politics was never a choice between political parties for me. The Green Party had been my natural home and whānau in politics for more than a decade. Ever since I got to stand side by side with Keith Locke at those Zaoui protests, I was grateful for a movement that saw the world as an interconnected whole. We have always been 'outsider politicians', so to speak, and it was an infinite relief to find that community when I first moved back from Cambodia. I joined the Green Party again, and began going to meetings. Immediately, as it is Green custom, I was asked to stand for roles, and I did. I became the co-convenor of Auckland Province. The Green Party is a giant internal democracy, so decisions are made at local branch level, then fed up to the province, and in turn to the party's executive, where I also served for two years after the 2014 election. So policy and governance decisions are made, not by the members of parliament, but members all around the country, by consensus. That connectedness was a big deal to me, to be part of a movement of engaged, energised equals.

James Shaw, now co-leader of the Party, was the first person to tell me I should stand for parliament. This was in 2013, at the party AGM in Christchurch, before James was an MP himself. It was the meeting where Russel Norman delivered an angst-ridden speech about 'crony capitalism' and John Key selling our democracy to 'his corporate mates'. He said, 'This matters because democracy and human rights matter. But it also matters because democracy is at the heart of every other economic, environmental and social debate we face as a nation.' We were all abuzz.

That night, a bunch of us out-of-towners stayed up drinking Waiheke wines or feijoa home brew or whatever typically Green lubricant was generously supplied by the old-timers. I remember James and I both excitedly argued for the need for a written constitution. By then I was practising public law, and doing a bit of judicial review, which is as close as New Zealand practice gets to constitutional law proper. I was happy and probably loud, jumping between chatter about different models of human rights, obscure points of constitutional democracy, and the courts. James was hotly engaged in conversations with other international lawyers about the concept of ecocide and constitutional protections for the environment. We talked about holding the biggest corporate polluters to account and what that might look like in law. Would personhood of nature be enshrined in the same way that corporate personhood is? (Personally, I've always felt like corporate accountability is the answer. In giving personhood to imaginary business entities, we mostly pretend there are no real people making harmful decisions for profit behind it all. We need the law to hold corporations accountable far more readily, whether it is nature or humans who suffer.)

James's argument was that I should stop talking about what needs to be done and become an MP myself. I hadn't considered it, and it would take another three years before I could muster the guts to stand. James had always been sure he wanted to be in parliament. Thinking about it now, it was exceptionally generous of someone vying for a place in the small Green Party caucus to actively, excitedly, encourage others to do the same. That's good leadership.

Over the next few years, my work in human rights law helped crystallise in my mind the need for constitution reform and system transformation. I had been helping on the latest of the 'Family Carers' cases. We were fighting for fair pay for families caring for their profoundly disabled loved ones. This was a case about pay equity, but also the fundamental rights of disabled persons to remain in their homes, in their communities, with their families. The government wouldn't pay family members full-time pay at around minimum wage, while it would pay corporate agencies about $70,000 per year per person in care. The families had brought two previous cases claiming discrimination based on family relationship, which is unlawful under our Human Rights Act. They had won. The government forked out millions to appeal these cases all the way to the Court of Appeal. The carers kept winning.

Faced with the choice to continue breaching the law or change, the government did the unthinkable: it passed law to cut them off from the Human Rights Act remedies regime altogether. With a bare majority in parliament, under urgency, they cut an entire class of persons off from their human rights. In a move I had never heard of, they named the two cases in the new section of the

Health and Disabilities Act, saying they would have no precedent value in future cases.

The case I worked on came after the law change. Nothing drives home the necessity of protecting human rights in a superior law more clearly than sitting with elderly mum Diane, trying to help her care for her severely disabled adult son, Shane, without access to the Human Rights Act. In fact, Crown counsel stood in the High Court and said that the rights of disabled persons to care were not true human rights, like the right to free speech. Arguing the archaic line that only civil and political rights, rather than social, economic or cultural rights, count is to ignore the inequities that prevent marginalised persons from accessing their political rights to begin with. Shane and Diane sat in the back of the courtroom, along with many other tireless disabilities activists and families anxiously waiting for justice. I was incensed and ready to change that government. In September 2018 with the help of my friend Julie Anne Genter, as Green Associate Minister of Health, our government announced that the law cutting family carers off from the Human Rights Act would change, as would the unfair payment regime itself be reviewed. Such a relief.

Still, the decision to stand as a candidate, to really do it, was a tortured road. Jesse Chalmers, my flatmate and friend who had anchored me back home and in the Party for years, was another staunch advocate. She is a descendant of Greens so committed they were founding members of the Earth Song eco-community. She's also a successful businesswoman, whose company manufactures organic soy products (obviously). Jesse has a no-nonsense manner and unshakable ethics. A tiny woman with long auburn waves streaming down her back, she knows a bit about interacting in a world where she is in her way a minority, and authority is hard won. She does not suffer fools or mince words or shy away from challenges. She believes in pushing through and staring down the doubters. Being told, over wines, for several years, to go fix the world from parliament by that impressive force helped give me another little push towards my candidacy.

Then there was Guy Williams. We met at a charity event to fund the work of Michelle Kidd in 2016. Enormously tall and loud, he was at that point a comedian on TV and commercial radio, and he was the event's 'celebrity host'.

Whaea Michelle is a woman who begins her day at dawn to check on Auckland's homeless community, before heading to the District Court to help the hundreds of distressed and confused folk forced to navigate the dehumanising process. I had known Michelle from my first days in court. She made sure she knew every one of us barristers. She was one of the first people I came across in that system that spoke openly about mental health and addiction underpinning our imprisonment rates, and of the need for compassion as we herded people through these traumatising proceedings. I've seen her cry with devastated young mums as they are given prison sentences, hold up collapsing addicts in the dock. I've accepted the warmest of hugs on days that would have been otherwise crushing. So that day in 2016, I knew I had to drag myself to the ritzy Northern Club, where Michelle's fundraiser was being held.

A little late and flustered, I checked in with the organisers in the otherwise empty back room. The rest of the guests — mostly lawyers and judges — were already seated. Guy was back there too, waiting to go on stage. He introduced himself and asked what he should know about the crowd. I told him he could make fun of this crowd for probably voting ACT or National, which is why practically every public service is defunded, but then holding fancy charity functions to make up for it. Of course, a lot of barristers are incredibly focused on social justice because of what we see in the courts — that's probably what got most of us to the charity event to begin with. Still, it was true enough.

He put that in his stand-up routine and the room fell mostly silent. He bombed. My table, though, found it hilarious, both to hear the joke and to see the tense reaction of the room.

Guy and I talked briefly afterward, but I was mostly focused on talking shop with old colleagues. In the end, he saw me drop my name badge somewhere, picked it up, found me online, and asked me out on a date.

We later realised we had met three years before, when he helped campaign for the Green Party and I was the Auckland party co-convener. He has a political science degree and had helped the 'Double the Refugee Quota' campaign. I had seen his stand-up, which is very different from his work on radio or TV at that time (which frankly I had never seen before we met). His stand-up is far more political, and tends to focus on race and privilege, which can be a bit confronting to those audience members who wander in expecting to see gags from TV. He jokes about having the confidence of a mediocre white man, though there's truth to having the abandon of someone with status quo privilege. Guy became a firm advocate for my candidacy whenever I wavered. He, as my sounding board, became the well-spring of my confidence some days.

One of the moments that cemented my resolve was a conversation when I was lamenting the loss of some of my favourite Green MPs, like Catherine Delahunty, Jeanette Fitzsimons and Keith Locke. I said something like, 'Who will be the next Keith Locke?' and Guy said, 'You. You'll have to be.'

That stayed with me, not as confirmation that I could ever be as good, or frankly as iconic, as my heroes, but as a call to arms. What are convictions without the courage to act, or to at least try?

We went through that tumultuous 2017 election together. Guy has a passion for the mechanics of and the people in New Zealand politics, so I never have to explain things from the ground up. My work has been sustained by having the space at home to vent and strategise with a partner equally invested in its outcomes.

Being a Middle Eastern woman has proven an overburdened birth right in politics, but my identity was not a driving force for my candidacy. No, my decision to engage more and more actively with politics was first driven by the state of New Zealand politics from the moment I moved home. After three terms of a fiscally conservative National Party government, inequality was at record highs, there were constant threats of coal mining in our national reserves, and human rights were, increasingly, blatantly trampled. Theirs was not the Aotearoa I knew and loved.

It is also undeniable that my political roots began with my parents' generation of Iranian revolutionaries. They were not afraid to demand transformation. Instead of incremental reform of a broken system, they asked for nothing less than participatory democracy and a redistribution of their nation's natural resource. What is profoundly inspiring about that revolution to me is that

Iranians had never experienced politics free from repression, nor public control of their oil. But they knew their nation, at her best, deserved that reality. Iranians were fighting for a world they had never seen before, but knew was possible.

That will always be the source of my political impulse.

The sometimes-harrowing experience in human rights and justice was another driver for my shift in focus from working on a case-by-case basis to instilling systemic change via parliament. My drive was to set goals that the human rights framework — the human rights dream — was built on. That means we aim to eliminate poverty, not just reduce it or push it from sight. We decolonise our systems by restoring self-determination to indigenous peoples, not just 'settle' some land claims. We divest from an economic system that is destroying our planet.

Like a good activist law-nerd, my vision was rooted in constitutional reform. I wanted Aotearoa to begin that constitutional conversation. What would be the values we would enshrine in law? Are we comfortable in a system where our Bill of Rights Act can be explicitly breached by any bare-majority government? Can we be a post-colonial society while our founding constitutional document is continuously ignored, and treated as impotent against modern lawmaking? Are we all that 'green' as a nation while our climate commitments are not even binding on the government that signed them, let alone corporate polluters?

I went into politics with that burning desire to champion rights-based constitutional reform, with all my experience in justice and in child rights advocacy, and ideas about how my expertise could help shape democracy. I thought hard about what I might bring to the table, what made me worthy as a legislator. But it was my identity, my face and my story that shaped my first experiences in politics.

I announced my candidacy in January 2017, which by dark coincidence was right around the time that Donald Trump signed his so-called 'Muslim ban'. People emanating from my part of the world were being refused entry into the United States by the 'Leader of the Free World', based on our actual and perceived religion. Six months earlier, Brexit had won a catastrophic victory after a hate-filled campaign that villainised migrants and saw one lawmaker, a mother of young children, shot and stabbed to death for standing with us. I think about that lawmaker, Jo Cox, almost every day in my life as a politician.

I received an outpouring of love from around the globe when the announcement was made. It was unexpected and overwhelming. It came from Trump's America, Britain under Brexit, and every corner of Aotearoa. People I interacted with daily smiled a little more broadly, took a breath and said, 'Kia kaha.' They told me about their children, second- or third-generation migrants, and how they now knew that those children could one day be prime minister. It was heartbreaking to hear they hadn't thought that possible before. I heard from young women of colour, who told me on the bus about their activism on university campuses. They saw me as part of a continuum of their movement that encompassed my place in national politics and their work arranging vigils, setting up feminist groups, reporting harassment.

All this attention was, to my mind, not one bit earned. I hadn't actually done anything but stand. Something essential had been missing for so many of us in politics, and in public life, for so long. We had been trained all our lives not to think it possible, or to think ourselves deserving enough. But we were starved for representation.

I never for a minute expected to get in the first time I ran. Campaigning as a candidate was such a new and alien world that it barely felt real as a daily experience. It was a gauntlet of debates and media interviews, where every emotion from pride to fear, to my own deep, reoccurring imposter syndrome was exaggerated. It was a revelation to find I could speak, out loud, on a stage or under studio lights. Speech-making was more daunting than responding to questions, maybe because I was used being in court, which is such a think-on-your-feet affair. I began to improvise my speeches. It worked better to speak in the moment to each audience rather than prepare and perfect a static stump speech. It was a blessing to have very little time to think about any of this in the moment.

In that new world, I formed some of the most unexpected and enduring bonds with other first-time candidates. The Greens attracted a talented and diverse candidate pool in 2017. This was a gift to me, to each of us, in that we got to share the surreal and often hostile context of minority candidacy. I have to name them, because I miss them and their invaluable credentials in parliament every day. There was Rebekah Jaung, a medical doctor, researcher, and campaigner for victims of sexual slavery and for inter-Korean peace. Teanau Tuiono is an international environmental lawyer, indigenous rights advocate, and community organiser. There were Julie Zhu, award-winning theatre producer, filmmaker, and founding member of Asians Supporting Tino Rangatiratanga; Ricardo Menéndez March, now the outspoken advocacy coordinator at Auckland Action Against Poverty; and Leilani Tamu, ex-Pacific diplomat and author. None were elected save for me. All experienced pushback based on their race, and based on minority issues they raised. The issues themselves were ignored, or deemed too emotionally driven — or perhaps they were too emotionally delivered, since our tone was also perpetually policed.

We formed chat groups where we could post about the abuse we had received, both online and in public meetings, and the constant battle we faced for resources and platforms as we campaigned. These are people who bring far more than the essential representation that their communities lack. They bring substantive expertise, abilities, and analysis about the issues that matter to every community we serve. But the struggle to be seen and heard was very real. It was a struggle in different ways, in both conservative and progressive contexts.

Seeing the value in diversity does not mean progressive political institutions will amplify or resource minority politicians as true equals. Diversity in politics, as in any institution, can't be fixed from the top down. A diverse bunch of candidates, the face of any political party, doesn't solve the problem that politics itself is very mono-gendered and monocultural. We learned during the campaign, from event to event, from one media interview to the next, that unless the campaign team, media advisors, volunteers, and staff are as diverse as the people expected to front political issues, we can't truly do our work as representatives. That is the level of support that majority groups get when they stand as candidates — their issues and perspectives are well understood, their communities have received years of attention from politicians, and they themselves don't have to work to achieve acceptance from constituents or TV audiences. We had to make all that happen from the ground up.

Talking about these ordeals over dumplings on Dominion Road, or comforting home-baked treats, was a lesson in how much more minorities have to bring to the table. We all knew first-hand how much harder minorities have to try in job interviews. Being ranked on a party list is like a daunting, extended job interview. Being from a migrant background generally means you are the first in your family and probably your broader social circles to take the step. Our names, our faces, our lack of institutional connections mean we have to work extra hard to prove ourselves or be noticed.

That election, however, was a little turning point. We forged a little winding path for other minority politicians to follow, and we can see it being trodden more confidently already in local elections.

In 2017, the Green movement in Aotearoa had lived a devastating, heart-stopping election with a happy ending. It had been a rollercoaster — for each of us personally, as well as for the nation. It was hard to catch our breaths.

The Green Party almost halved the number of MPs we had in parliament. We lost a co-leader and two senior MPs just six weeks before the election. At around the same time, we dipped briefly below the five per cent threshold needed to enter parliament. We nearly disappeared.

By election night, we did make it comfortably back to parliament. The win was hard-won and extraordinary in many ways. We elected a government with a progressive promise, that spoke to inequality, that named climate action as a key focus, and was itself comprised of the most representative members our

House of Representatives had ever seen. We got more women, more Māori, more rainbow community representatives. We got a young, first-time mum for Prime Minister. We got Chlöe Swarbrick, at twenty-three years old, our youngest member of parliament in almost forty years, since Marilyn Waring was also elected at twenty-three years old. I got to wear the label of 'New Zealand's first refugee MP'. This set us apart from the politics of hate and division rising in other Western democracies.

That is not to say for a moment that we didn't bring far more than those labels, both in expertise and experience, to our work. But the process of standing for office has made me acutely aware of the significance of lived experience as integral to true representation. I know it because people tell me every day. To be reflected in leadership roles means something in and of itself; it's proof of equality and inclusion. But lived experience is also invaluable expertise. It means so much to those underrepresented communities to have someone who knows a little of their particular challenges active in the decisions that shape our world. Chlöe's current experience of youth counts as much as age, because navigating the mental health system, getting a job, or finding a home works differently for young people, differently even than it did for young people of another generation. Interacting with any of those systems and the people who run them is different, again, for Māori. We know women have needs and vulnerabilities that have been overlooked for centuries. Decision-making without diverse representation is not only hurtful, it is weak and ineffective.

The message of hope and change is never as powerfully expressed than by those who embody a group less represented in leadership. This was true of Barack Obama, and it was true — in different ways — for Jacinda Ardern. I had known Jacinda from her Auckland Central campaigns — I was in the Green Party's Auckland Central branch alongside our candidate, Denise Roche, so we campaigned for the Green vote while cheering on Jacinda's team for the electorate seat. We also crossed paths a bit after hours in local pasta joints on K Road. She is a social person by nature; that much has always been an obvious and maybe even defining aspect of her work as a politician. She was warm, and would lean slightly into every conversation in the bustle. She was always calling to other women in local politics in the room — it was like a little squad bound together by the passing nods and check-ins months apart in these safe spaces. As a woman far younger than the average politician, her leadership already came with the rightful fervour of a change of guard. To me, her election was met with so much joy, because she embodied and spoke to so much that we, as New Zealanders, hoped — at our best — to convey. From the start, her image as a leader evoked a recollection of our past as we wanted it remembered: caring, egalitarian, and, uniquely, empowering of women. Simultaneously, her message set us into the future. We got to be the nation open to transformation and to innovation, as we had imagined ourselves, but had not been for some time. In reality, we had drifted far from those values, with John Key hurling us into an American-style culture of every-man-for-himself individualism and aspirational wealth worship. It wasn't working, as it never works. From archaic trickle-down economics, to the smiling face of a man making fun of 'gay pink shirts'. The last government made it hard for us to recognise the nation that first gave women the vote and prided itself on providing universal healthcare.

Whether the government that resulted from that election delivers on enough of its progressive promise in all the other ways, the promise of representation was largely delivered, at least broadly for women, and that means a lot. We became a nation led by an unmarried woman having a child during her term in office, with her partner co-parenting. It was notable that the only other elected head of government to give birth in office was the leader of a Muslim nation, Pakistani prime minister Benazir Bhutto, in 1988. As feminists, we got to share in that tradition, and bring it into the twenty-first century. This point of representation has a tangible impact on our lives as women. For the first time in our nation's history, we can point to a real-life example that proves we can do any job *and* have children at the same time, if parenting gender roles and the institutions of work adapt to accommodate us.

It is undeniable that her win also played into that global hunger for a change in the politics that guarded an old-world order, which many of us were ready to tear down. In the end, the change had to be embodied by its leader.

The Green Party has always been the party of transformation in Aotearoa. In 2017, we campaigned hard for systemic change. We said success in government must be measured differently than by narrow economic metrics that ignore record poverty and a climate crisis — in 2019, a year into government, we operate under the framework of a 'wellbeing budget', first championed by Greens years ago. We said the word 'crisis' a lot, because we knew that Aotearoa, human and whenua, could not afford another three years under the politics of regression.

Our government is still young, and whether it delivers change commensurate with the hope that delivered its win is unclear in many ways. We support the changing of guard as it stands because we know that many of our most vulnerable would not survive the alternative. But we know, too, that what we promised was not incremental reform. It was revolution. Making our society fair and combatting the environmental crisis we have inherited will take courage from us as politicians. It will mean redistributing power and resource, not just changing the front-facing image of government. That is the promise of our Green movement.

The night the election was announced, we partied, elated and exhausted. We still knew little of the election result other than that we were in, and we had a brand-new MP in Chlöe. It was bittersweet. I know that, like me, she has felt the weight of the loss of stellar Green stalwarts like Mojo Mathers and Denise Roche.

I had to wait another two weeks for the special votes to be counted to know my fate. With two weeks of advanced voting, a total of 446,287 people voted outside their electorates in 2017, including 61,524 people from overseas. It very much felt like it could go either way.

The day the results finally came in was also the day Guy and I moved into our little apartment together. All the boxes and furniture were still sprawled around us when the call came. Suddenly, I had to get dressed and go to a press conference. It was an exceptionally odd thing to process: a press conference, for me. It was a life-changing moment, but I honestly can't say I knew what it all meant. I'm still not sure when I will ever say out loud, 'I'm a Member of Parliament,' without the jolt of disbelief and embarrassment.

I slapped together an outfit from the only clothes I could find that weren't boxed and crumpled, failed to find stockings, and drove to two dairies trying to buy some before we made it to the Stamford Plaza, where the conference was being held. Why hadn't I thought to do this frantic dance yesterday, or last week? All eight Green MPs had flown to Auckland for the announcement. These people, whom I had admired and campaigned for over the years, my role models and inspirations, were now somehow my peers. We were all giddy. I had a moment trying to imagine work next week and couldn't. That was the other wild thing: I was to start work in two days.

In a few minutes, with no media training and no lines prepared, I was at the lectern. I don't remember what else happened, but I do remember Lloyd Burr, of Newshub, asking me a question that sounded like a jab about our caucus of six women and two men: how did I explain it?

'This is what meritocracy looks like,' I said.

Being completely unprepared as I was for the win, I had no plans that night. I told any friends specifically asking that I might get a drink at a diner called Peach Pit on K Road. Karen, my first-ever Kiwi friend and my best friend from Chaucer School, came. Though we hadn't seen each other for years, she found a babysitter on the fly so she could celebrate with me. It meant so much to me. I kept introducing her as my first-ever friend in New Zealand.

A young woman had booked half the diner for her birthday party, replete with cake and streamers. She recognised me late into the night and we joined parties. We ate birthday cake and drank prosecco from mismatched glasses. It was perfect.

Chlöe and I came into parliament a couple of weeks apart. Different as we are in our backgrounds and life experiences, we will always be shaped and united by our shared moment as the two new Greens of 2017. Coming through that chaotic, heartbreaking, exuberant, celebratory election that threw us in the deep end together isn't something we'll ever be able to communicate to anyone else. We were new, figuring out these unknown parts of ourselves that came about in the unknown world of politics. It would have been even more daunting alone, without another Green learning the art of being an 'outsider politician'. What keeps you going in this place some days are the shared glances of confusion or alarm, the smirks between two people who still remember that things can be done differently outside of this archaic machine. Being trapped in the debating chamber late into the night without a hope of changing anyone's mind on a vote because party battle lines have been drawn can be crushing. Sometimes you need to barge into the office next door with a glass of wine and vent with someone whose brow is as furrowed as yours.

It's a difficult ask, distilling the operative parts of your past, together with the drivers of your future, into a fifteen-minute speech. It's daunting to put all that on the record. But by the time I came to write my maiden speech to parliament, in October 2017, I knew what I wanted to say. I wanted to talk about the common values of democracy and equality that my parents had fought for as Iranians, a fight that had almost crushed their lives. I wanted it noted that these values are common values, uniting us across borders, though they are sometimes violently suppressed. I wanted to talk about my work before I entered politics and my aims for the future. But I knew also that the public gallery would be filled with former refugees. A number of organisations were in touch to help bring our people to Wellington and to parliament, most for the very first time, to see me deliver that speech. It was important to tell the story of Iran as it was, the oppression and torture, the war, and the profiteering Western collusion in the tyranny we suffered. That is a common refugee story.

For myself, as much as for all those across the nation, listening for their voice in that House, I also had to acknowledge the hate and abuse. I had to say that racism and threats of violence are part of the experience of the 'refugee MP'. As uncomfortable as it would be, I had to say that those in the House with me had sometimes been responsible for fanning those flames. I would look across the debating chamber and give examples, because scapegoating migrants is a choice that politicians make and we do feel that out on the street.

I had to say these things in my speech, because my job is to bring those voices, those experiences into the House. To shy away from that would have been to abscond on the responsibility to represent. It would be a dishonour to the memory of a welcoming nation that first gave my family and me freedom. Aotearoa is a place where a nine-year-old refugee can grow up to sit in parliament, so it is worth holding our leaders to the high standard of equality that, at its best, our nation can represent.

I'm glad I did that, even as people shuffled in their seats and one opposition member tried for a heckle in the silence. After my speech, I looked up into the public gallery and saw my own feelings of relief, validation, pride, and gratitude reflected back at me. Later, we embraced and cried a little, and laughed at our common histories, our foods, and insecurities. The House of Representatives felt a little like a safe space for us, and that was an incredible thing.

Here is that speech:

*E ngā mana, e ngā reo, e ngā karangatanga maha, tēnā
    koutou katoa.*
Te mana whenua o tēnei wāhi, Te Āti awa, tēnā koutou.
Otirā ngā iwi whānui tēnā koutou katoa.

Mr Speaker, I congratulate you on your election and look forward to your guidance in this house.

I begin by acknowledging what a breathtaking honour it is to sit among this Green caucus.

I acknowledge also those who sat here before now, especially Catherine Delahunty and Keith Locke — you spoke to injustice wherever it happened. That meant a lot to someone like me. Mojo Mathers, for proving to me, and us all, that we all exist beyond our labels. And Metiria Turei for baring her scars bravely to highlight the pain of others.

But today, I want to acknowledge also, those who tell me every day that I don't belong here. That I should go home where I came from. That I have no right to criticise governments here and I should just be grateful I wasn't left to die. Hundreds of messages, comments. Mr Speaker, some call for rifles being loaded. I'm numb to it, because this is reality for those of us from minority backgrounds.

But I want it noted that this happens every time we scapegoat migrants in this House, every time a TV presenter asks a PM when the Governor-General is going to look like a Kiwi and sound like a Kiwi — and that PM laughs. Every time we call refugees 'leftovers from terrorist nations' for political gain.

We feel the effect of that out on the streets. We can't shed our skin.

Patriotism that represses dissent — or creates second-class citizens — is archaic and dangerous. It's antithetical to our culture.

So this day I stand, proud and determined. This day is about democracy and equality, values which New Zealand holds so dear, embodies and stands up for so boldly.

I love this country, but patriotism — a love of this country — means expecting the absolute best for her. Standing up for the country that we know is possible.

I protest, fight for equality, and fairness because justice is what love looks like in public (that's Dr Cornel West).

Mr Speaker, I am the child of revolutionaries. My parents faced tanks for democracy. At gunpoint, fought for human rights. Risked torture to take back their country's resource, back from dictators, corrupt corporate interests, and imperialists — to put it back in the hands of the people.

The Iranian Revolution was one of the biggest popular revolutions in modern history. Iranians poured onto the streets to fight inequality. But their revolution was hijacked, and my life was ultimately shaped by one of the most repressive regimes in the modern world.

Everyone knew someone who disappeared into a torture chamber; everyone knew women flogged for disregarding

Islamic dress. Everyone worried about their phone being tapped.

This was just the backdrop to a bloody war we fought against Saddam Hussein's Iraq. I remember the bombs, the sirens, running to the basement. Waiting.

Mostly I remember the kids my age, who stopped speaking because of shellshock. Then scarcity set in as America backed Saddam. We had to use coupons for food. Later, we found out that the West had backed both sides in that war. For profit.

Mr Speaker — *that* is what refugees are made of.

So, I feel a kinship with First Nations peoples, with tangata whenua. Because we too have been alienated from our land and resources by war and imperialism. We face the same prejudice and degradation. That is why I want Te Tiriti o Waitangi to be a living constitutional document in this county, shaping policy, including on immigration. We need to work together — migrants, refugees, Pasifika peoples and tangata whenua — for we have far more that unites us than that which divides us.

Mr Speaker, my mum was a child psychologist. She never worked because she refused to sit Islamic religious exams — she didn't believe religion should influence mental health services.

My father was an agricultural engineer who worked on developing plant-based renewable energies — green to the core.

So, let's remember that our values exist in all cultures — the Middle East, just like the West, has fierce environmentalists, feminists, governments selling us off to multinationals, but also religious fundamentalism.

Let's amplify the voices in all cultures who stand for tolerance and equality — above those who would silence them.

Mr Speaker, we fled that repression when it got too dangerous for us. We landed at Auckland Airport — the fear was palpable. I can still remember it. I was nine years old. I knew the unthinkable was awaiting us if we were returned. But we weren't. We were welcomed here.

My two most vivid first impressions of this incredible country were the warmth of that welcome — I didn't realise it then but that was our rights, our humanity being recognised.

And that it was so Green.

That is what New Zealand is to me.

My work in this House will be committed to upholding those incredible first impressions.

Mr Speaker, I became a lawyer because I wanted to enforce human rights. The criminal law is the purest form of human rights law in our system.

The most frightening thing I've seen in almost a decade of acting as a criminal lawyer all over the world was the sight of a thirteen-year-old boy sitting behind a very large table awaiting his trial for murder at the Auckland High Court. I acted as part of the defence team fighting to keep him from life imprisonment. He was tried as an adult, because that is what our law requires. He had thrown a rock over an overbridge, which tragically took another young life.

He suffered from mental-health issues — as do most in our criminal justice system. He was brown. He was from South Auckland. His family couldn't afford electricity, so they moved from house to house until it was cut off. He didn't have a lot of schooling. His CYFS file was the stuff of nightmares. Our most vulnerable.

The frontlines of our criminal justice system is where I learned about unchecked prejudice. It turned me into a human rights lawyer — and my focus turned to child rights.

It was living in Africa working on genocide trials where I then learned how prejudice turns to atrocity. Politicians scapegoating groups, as a group, for any social ills; dehumanising language in the media used for political gain — every time I see that, I think, 'That is how it starts.'

I saw that at the Rwanda Tribunal, at The Hague and when I prosecuted the Khmer Rouge in Cambodia.

Holding politicians and armies to account for breaching their powers. Giving voice to women and minorities who are most viciously targeted by abusers. These experiences have instilled in me a commitment to human rights and democracy that I first had for having seen the world without them.

Human rights are universal. We don't have fewer rights based on our religion, where we were born, or who we love. We don't have fewer rights for having children out of wedlock, or being charged with a crime.

There is no such thing as the 'deserving poor', or the 'good refugee' — we have rights not because we are good, but because we are human.

Human rights are indivisible — we have a bundle of rights. You can't have one without the others — you can't say we have democracy or free speech unless we also have the right to education. We don't have the right to education if the kids we are educating are hungry or live in cars. No right is realised without all rights being realised. And over the past decade in New Zealand, our democracy has been undermined because too many of our economic, social and cultural rights were breached. I want to entrench them.

Finally, human rights create enforceable obligations of this and every government — this isn't charity; the people don't have to beg. We can't privatise them away. We have a mandate to govern only if we can provide those rights to everyone. I want New Zealand to get back to a culture of expecting this.

None of that is separate from the environment — protection of human rights is intrinsically linked with protecting nature. Just ask the people of the Pacific, whose homelands are being drowned out because of unrestrained growth, waste, pollution, and consumption that they did not benefit from or participate in.

One of the greatest threats to both human and nature's rights is the subjugation of democracy to corporate interest. A rampant market on a finite planet.

New Zealand must lead by example on these global issues. We've stood against status quo interests when it was the right thing to do. We will be that righteous little nation on the global stage again.

I never meant to run as the first-ever refugee MP. But I quickly realised that my face, my story, means so much to so many people. So my fear of tokenism is dissipated.

I remembered getting notes and emails from my female interns, especially of minority backgrounds, telling me over and over again how much it meant to see someone like them forge that path. Some of them are carrying that mantle today. I realised then that it was important for that process to have victims of governance by repression and mass murder stand up in those courtrooms, mostly dominated by Western men. Representation matters.

So this is a victory for a nine-year-old asylum seeker, but also for every person who's ever felt excluded, out of place, been told she has limits on her dreams.

For getting me here, I want to thank the voters — you have humbled me forever. You voted for diversity, for fairness, and for nature when you voted Green this election.

To our Green activists and staff, especially in Auckland — you worked harder and harder as things got harder this election. You inspire me.

My campaign team, especially Ron and Daniel, and my second, political family, all of you Chalmerses — your support is life-affirming.

My parents, both strong, Iranian-Kiwi feminists — you gave up everything when you stood up for freedom. You gave up everything — your friends, your family, your professions, your language — because you weren't willing to raise a little girl in oppression. I thank you.

And to maybe the most political person I know. Though a very large, loud white boy, my partner, who at some point (it feels like a lifetime ago) stopped me mid-rant, when I was lamenting the lack of activism in politics, losing some of my favourite MPs. I was saying: which candidate will stand up against the GCSB [Government Communications Security Bureau]? Who'll be the new Keith Locke? You stopped me and said, 'You will be that candidate' — and I was. We're both political, we are both adventurers. But you are also patient. I thank you for that. And for love. But mostly: courage. On that day. And every day.

Mr Speaker, I stand here today as the child of revolutionaries, as a child asylum seeker, an international human rights lawyer, an activist — as a Green.

My standing here proves New Zealand is a place where a nine-year-old refugee, a girl from the Middle East, can grow up to one day enter parliament. It proves the strength and goodness of New Zealand's values.

He oranga whenua
He oranga tangata
Ka ora tātou katoa
Nō reira e te whare, tēnā koutou, tēnā koutou, tēnā koutou
  katoa.

9

The work of democracy

The work of an MP in a small party in government is such that on any given day you cover a head-spinning range of topics in an inexhaustible variety of contexts. From school halls, to ministerial meetings, to mass media — you have to be 'on' every minute. I hold thirteen portfolios. They are grouped in my mind as the 'international stuff': Foreign Affairs, Trade, Defence, Disarmament, Overseas Development Aid, and Customs; the 'justice stuff': Justice, Courts, Police, Corrections, and Electoral Reform; and the 'minority issues': Disabilities and Immigration/Refugees. Human Rights is the fourteenth portfolio, one that only Green Party recognises, but I believe should exist in and of itself in government. In reality it should underpin every other portfolio.

I chose to be on the Foreign Affairs, Trade, and Defence committee, because I knew those were issues where the big parties agreed. Without the Greens, there would be no one asking the hard questions. At first, it was a space where I was unwelcome. National Party member Gerry Brownlee told me

I was in the wrong room on the first session. 'This is a *senior* committee,' he told me. Eventually we formed a committee friendship, in part because I laughed off every 'loony Green' joke. The committee came to accept the minority view among them. We have formed a collegial union, and I can get things over the line, like an inquiry into New Zealand's development aid policy — a rewarding win.

My first daunting political hurdle, and the biggest disagreement between the Greens and the government's coalition parties, came the very month I was elected. It was about trade, a portfolio that had just been handed to a brand-new backbench MP, still catching her breath.

The government suddenly announced its intention to sign the infamous Trans-Pacific Partnership Agreement (TPPA), a trade deal we had all protested en masse as opposition parties. It was promptly renamed by the addition of the words 'Comprehensive and Progressive', and, with that, the CPTPPA was heralded as a new deal. I had the job of reading the 6000-page agreement, acquiring enough information from the still top-secret trade talks, and ascertaining whether the key issues for our constituents had in fact been addressed. This is a deal that isn't all that much about trade. It mostly outlines the special rights and privileges of the globally trading corporates, as against our elected governments and our non-internationally trading constituents. Everything from their special exemptions from our privacy laws to deregulating online technologies from which they profit is in there. I had an advantage, having been part of the protest movement from back in 2015 when the protests were constant and mounting in Auckland at least, and being relatively adept at deciphering international legal texts. It was clear to me that this may be an improved deal, but our core concerns still remained.

For one thing, the actual text of the new deal was never put to consultation. Our people, the people who had protested the deal and voted for any one of the three parties who opposed it before the election, were devastated. Once it was done, we found out — all too late — that the most egregious threat to democracy — the clauses that give foreign corporates and investors special rights to sue our government — remained. The threat of billion-dollar lawsuits will hang over the heads of us all, and over future governments, influencing policy decisions on health, education, and environmental protection. It was an archaic and frightening reminder of how the world was now ordered. It was something I had learned a lot about during my Master's studies, because human rights compliance now rests more so with the power of multinational corporations rather than democratically elected governments. Our one-vote-per-person democracy is a feeble enforcement mechanism in the face of lawsuits that are designed to prioritise the interests of foreign trade above all else.

What was particularly chilling to me as a Green is that where corporate investors had accessed their new rights under similar agreements, in eighty-five per cent of cases it was to stop environmental protections. In 2002, when Indonesia tried to ban particularly damaging mining practices in its native forests, the mere threat by multinational mining companies to sue pursuant to clauses much like the ones we signed onto in the CPTPPA forced it to exclude foreign corporations from that ban. The Indonesian Environment State Minister Nabiel Makarim openly admitted, 'If shut down, investors demand and Indonesia cannot pay.'

In a place like Iran, democracy is scant, so we know the oil trade trumps our rights and degrades our environment with impunity. But now, even in otherwise healthy democracies like New Zealand, international traders dictate all sorts of policy in a far more polite and insidious world order.

We, the Green Party, opposed the deal. That should have been uncontroversial since our position had long been on record. This was how mixed-member representation was supposed to work in government. Still, it was the first time that a government party was dissenting this term. The issue was huge and a marker of our core differences on both the economy and democracy. It was scary and uncomfortable for us all as government parties. That was the pressure to back down, or at least to do it quietly, silently. That wasn't an option in my mind. Public discourse about dissent is as important as the votes in the House. Giving voice to that dissent was important to me.

Sitting in the select committee meeting that heard public submissions was particularly difficult for me. The overwhelming majority of submitters opposed the CPTPPA. But it had already been signed by the government. Every parliamentarian on the committee — government and opposition — had to support it.

Maybe it was the defence lawyer in me, but I felt strongly that a point of principle, based on truth, must be made loudly. It felt like a fork in the road, a defining moment in what kind of government we would be and what kind of Green Party. For me personally, as a politician, it was a moment to take a deep breath and find my voice. I studied and dissected the text, the criticism, the Minister of Trade's explanations, spoke to everyone I could. It was clear what I had to do.

When I stood to speak in the House at the CPTPPA hearing as the lone voice of dissent, I didn't hold back:

> Instead of installing the transition to an innovative and sustainable economy that New Zealanders voted for, this deal will make it far harder and more expensive to implement the Zero Carbon Act, to combat child poverty, to be responsive to future challenges facing our little nation.
>
> … Our hope and intention is that the TPP is the last of its kind. I have been working to introduce change that will require us to make trade fair. To require deals like this to be made democratically. Transparently. That they should be contingent on our ability to protect human rights, combat climate change and do right by tangata whenua.
>
> We need to make trade fair. Fit to serve our twenty-first century concerns, with all the lessons of failed neoliberal ideology.
>
> Instead on March 8, we are not signing on to a free-trade agreement, we are ceding sovereignty to foreign investors.

In that hearing, I tried to hold the despair of every submitter, to amplify it. I wanted to apologise to them. Many of them hugged me afterward. I hoped only that having a dissenting voice was some consolation in itself.

My work in that dense and unruly portfolio of Trade has since focused on how we might join together with other progressive nations to drive a new model of fair international trade. We are a small nation. We need trade. International trade, at its best, builds relationships that encourage a rules-based order, exchanges of ideas, even empathy between nations. But what I see from the inside, as a lawyer, is that even the term 'trade deal' is a misnomer. These agreements create obligations and restrictions on how governments regulate and make policy in every area of our lives. They are an important aspect of international law, but they are designed to wildly favour the interests of Big Money corporations — from Facebook and Google, to Big Oil, to pharmaceutical companies. We can turn that around, and use the binding nature of trading contracts to give teeth to our climate obligations and human rights law — to really honour Te Tiriti o Waitangi.

My work on the trade portfolio has given me the platform in government to help restore the balance of power. The meetings with trade negotiators and officials are hazed with secrecy and coded wordplay. It's handy to have a handle on international law, to know the language and effect of those instruments. There is an expectation that I will know nothing, but being underestimated is a fun advantage. It's sometimes hard to get an answer, but, calmly, I persist.

Around the same time as that first rumble over the CPTPPA, news came that Australia was shutting off amenities, including water, to its Manus Island offshore immigration detention centre in a bid to force the detainees to move out of the facility and settle in the local community. With nowhere for them to go, though, and after years of deliberate propaganda driving suspicion and hatred against them, the detainees rightly feared for their lives and refused to leave. The United Nations and Amnesty International had long called the conditions in Australia's offshore detention centres — effectively prison camps — torture. Now, the trapped refugees and asylum-seekers were being exposed to far worse. The detainees included an award-winning journalist, environmentalists, political activists, and members of the rainbow community from Iran and places like Iran, where they had been forced to flee unthinkable persecution or war. Some had already reached out to me with their stories. But now they, their families, Australian activists, and refugee communities here began reaching out with urgency. Australian Green senator Nick McKim flew to Manus Island and kept me updated from the ground. I remember he first called me a couple of times while I was in a caucus meeting. I missed his calls. Then came this message:

> I'm on Manus Island and hoping we can have a chat about what's happening here and whether you can ask NZ PM to increase the numbers of refugees NZ is offering to take. People are going to start dying here soon. Thanks, hope to hear from you.

I had to stop and read those devastating words aloud between tears. People were at risk because sanitation and healthcare were cut off, and because those conditions pushed their mental health to breaking point. Indefinite detention is considered torture in human rights law. This was an atrocity.

I began saying that overtly. I interviewed with Australian media, with the BBC, and continuously with local media. I also said, because I felt it to be true, that New Zealand's own silence till then had amounted to complicity. It was the first time I realised what this voice was that I had, not just as a politician, but as a refugee. It felt like it meant something. Sometimes after those interviews,

I would collapse to the floor in floods of tears. A voice for 'those people' seemed very important then. The victims trapped in those prison camps were the ones whose voices were silenced. This was the most essential advocacy I had ever done.

Thankfully, our new government did rise to the occasion with a renewed offer to take 150 people from the prison camp. When Jacinda was in Australia for her first visit as Prime Minister, I know she raised this offer immediately. Behind the scenes, apart from the frantic work of finding a solution to the crisis on Manus Island, I was finding out the number of families with children on Nauru. We could potentially rehome everyone with a child, but we didn't have enough mental health resources to support them during resettlement. Australian charities communicated a confidential proposal to fly counsellors and healthcare workers over to help with this. But senseless cruelty prevailed as the Australian Government refused our offer. It was devastating to be powerless from a position of relative power.

I could barely comprehend how lucky my family had been to escape that fate. I know that some of the children in those prison camps stop speaking, just like the little shellshocked girls and boys I knew in Iran. These children had escaped oppression, war and persecution with less trauma than that inflicted upon them on Manus Island. For those of us who have been through the refugee experience, who know the anxiety and visceral fear of that flight for safety, the fate of the Nauru and Manus detainees is incomprehensible. We also know that the misconception that travelled down the line to justify their torture is the same prejudice that fuels racial slurs against us online, the one that justifies the bombs that fall on our nations, the one that leads to white nationalists shooting up our community gatherings. It is the lie that says some people are less deserving of security and dignity based on the colour of our skin and our displacement. The lie that we are less human,

I turned my energies to advocating against the National Government's ban on refugees in Africa and the Middle East, euphemistically called the 'family link' requirement. People in those regions were required to prove not only that they were escaping war or persecution but also that they had a close family link to a New Zealander before we would allow them in our refugee quota. It was a policy not unlike Trump's brutish 'Muslim ban'. This was couched in vague appeals to distance — that is to say, those places are so far away, and we should take closer refugees, though we continued to take refugees from central America, and refugee policy is by definition based on needs, not convenience. Worse, it included a blanket, unspecified reference to 'security risks'. The policy was clearly borne of the War on Terror prejudice that marked entire, diverse and vibrant nations, including victim communities themselves.

Sitting in ministerial meetings, talking to media, and accepting petitions, it was hard to ignore the fact that, had circumstances been different, this policy would have excluded me and my family. It meant so much to stand for the only political party that allowed me to campaign against it at the election and to fight against it in government. In October 2019, after two years of sustained negotiation, of raising the issue countless times with the Minister for Immigration, of rehashing all the political issues, we overturned the policy. In a world after the Christchurch terror attacks, it was much-needed reassurance to refugee communities from the Middle East and Africa, whatever their faith — and I include myself in that group — that we are considered equals, at least in this formal way, again.

Defence, the portfolio about war, is the other to which I brought a lifetime of personal grief and dense professional knowledge. I began my work on Defence with the clear aim of challenging defence spending and ending our military deployments in the Middle East. It's what Keith Locke would have done. In fact, I try to sit down with Keith as often as possible, usually over scones and home-brewed coffee, to share our experiences. He is still exceedingly well-informed about global politics and the details of military policy. Peace is core Green business — for one thing, there is no climate action while war wages on for profit and access to non-renewable fossil fuels. The wars and sanctions and power dynamics that destabilised the Middle East and displaced my family are intrinsically linked with the climate crisis — they are about oil.

My challenge was going to be Ron Mark, ex-military man and New Zealand First Minister of Defence. I knew that our positions on defence were diametrically opposed and he had all the power. I also knew that I would have to go into my work with Ron, as in my work in every realm before then, without prejudice about him, or preconceptions about his views or political affiliations. That is the only fair and effective basis for persuasion.

Parliament is the most adversarial context I've ever worked in. Rather than consensus-building or true debate, we are expected to hold our party lines and either ignore the opposing view or fight, almost with actual hatred, what our political opponents stand for.

People heckle, tease, and jeer loudly as speeches are delivered. We rarely, if ever, sit together with anyone from the opposition to break bread or sip wine, even though we are all trapped in the complex together late into the night. But surely our job, our democratic duty, is to listen, actively find solutions, and persuade others of those solutions.

The one hope-filled example of this was the time, in May 2019, women parliamentarians from across the House, across the political divide, came together to stand with me, against what they saw as bullying and abuse: 'We, as women MPs, consider your behaviour towards a colleague, who has been under attack with death threats and is already in a vulnerable position, unacceptable.'

So I went into my meetings with Ron Mark with no expectations. I found that he was pleased to be working with someone who had experience of both war and war-crime prosecutions. The first interaction we had was when he walked over to say that he had acted as a defence lawyer in military tribunals and he was glad I understood that soldiers had a right to be presumed innocent. This was at a moment when I was being criticised in the media for my work as a defence lawyer at the international tribunals. I was heartened.

The Defence meetings were warm and almost jovial from the start. The minister was like a proud dad. He would invite senior members of the military to join us, especially high-ranking women, who he knew had not been celebrated sufficiently to date. We had difficult conversations. I was concerned about the processes of justice when gender-based crimes were reported within the military system. The independent report on this remains highly redacted. I am still deeply concerned about the NZDF's alleged involvement in war crimes in Afghanistan and have raised this persistently. I am obstinately opposed to the billions of dollars we spend on war-making machines, feeding an immoral industry. But I'm proud that we have been able to agree, the minister and I, on two essential issues: ending our deployment in Iraq and Afghanistan, and making climate change a key priority for Defence.

This came about through dialogue. It also came about through human understanding. I realised Ron Mark's history with the military is deeply personal. He was a foster child, one of countless Māori children removed by the state and placed in care. He joined the military as a teenager and that became his most enduring home, his family. He went on to be deployed in war zones, including the Middle East. His vision of war is not one that relates to profit or diplomacy in the sense of pleasing our Western allies. It comes from the frontlines. I firmly and openly disagreed with his position on almost everything from the start, but it was important to allow for the human experiences that had brought him there. In turn, he regularly told me that he was glad I understood war, and respected my opinions based on that. I believe that trust created a space for change. We've come to a place where we can even laugh at ourselves, to the discomfort of the officials and uniformed officers in those meetings.

In one meeting, we discussed the need for better access to mental health services for a particular veteran whose cause I had taken up. Ron told the officials to prioritise this, they duly took notes, and we were about to end the meeting when the Minister turned to me and said, 'You know, Golriz, I think about what you and I have been through in our lives and I wonder how we've come out of it okay, we've ended up normal.'

I looked at him and said, 'We're not normal! You're obsessed with war planes and I've been in therapy for three years.'

We laughed far too much given the dark humour, and stood up to shake hands, still chuckling. A room full of soldiers and parliamentary advisors stood horrified, unsure whether to laugh or shuffle papers awkwardly until they could usher the meeting to a close.

In early June 2019, we got there. We have an end date to the Iraq deployment, a transformed deployment of only three civilians in Afghanistan, and climate change acknowledged for the first time as the key focus of our defence force. Of course, I can't take credit for all that, but I do think a constructive debate helped. I also think we have a ton more to do to transform our Defence policy into something truly green. But at least I know that is something I could actually contribute to in my position.

As time goes on, I see the undeniable value of setting the agenda, even from a place of a relative lack of formal power, which is what it is to be a backbench MP with no pre-agreed portfolio wins. Activists know this so well. My job has been to bring those voices into the meeting rooms with ministers, knowing that no matter our political background, we get to face each other as equals of a sort in those meeting rooms where the public has no access, and that can be a powerful thing. Now, two years in, as I see the change mounting a little, I know my job a lot better. I know it comes with real possibility to affect change, with real responsibility. Raising a voice for prisoner voting and for political funding reform have been as important to me as the big oppositional campaigns like the TPPA and for peace. I know that my expending political capital on issues our partners in government broadly agree with but would not prioritise, that were not popular per se, and bringing those conversations to the public arena has shifted the paradigms. This has seen us restore voting rights to thousands of prisoners, seen the ban on foreign donations, seen funding of youth courts so that seventeen-year-olds can escape the brutality of adult courts and prisons. Those are issues that needed concerted and coordinated work by movements of activists, academics, commissioners, and me as a backbench MP. The job of the Green Party as I have always seen it is to keep asking for what is right, not wavering, not assuming the firm 'no's' in those first meetings were ever permanent or ever needed to define our relationships in government. It will be a basis to keep pushing until the change is Green enough.

In politics, as in any field, we bring the whole of ourselves to our work. My first term in politics will always be a little defined by my health. 2018 was the year I was diagnosed with multiple sclerosis (MS). That wasn't something I had spoken about publicly before, because, to be honest, it was an experience I could barely process for myself for a long while. Telling people you have MS means being met with terrified silence, or a truckload of questions you don't have the answers to, or an outpouring of grief and love, which in its own way is overwhelming at times. It means reassuring people that you're still the same person.

The other reason I was reluctant to talk about it was I didn't feel all that entitled to speak about the MS experience until I had lived with it for a while. Do you get to talk about this illness after one attack, after two? Do you get to talk to it if your symptoms on the daily are mostly 'just' fatigue? Until recently, my approach was to silently push through.

In February 2018, as I was finding my feet, living between two cities and processing life as an MP, I started to lose sight in my left eye. I thought it was a fleeting annoyance and left it for a few days. By Waitangi weekend, I realised the eye ache and sight loss were becoming more acute. Guy and I were at a friend's wedding in a remote beach town that weekend, and I didn't think it was serious enough to leave. When the holiday was over, I saw my doctor, who told me to go immediately to hospital. I had optic neuritis — damage to my optic nerve — which the ophthalmologist gently told me was often the first symptom of MS. It was a fifty-fifty chance I had the disease.

'Not me,' I thought. 'I'll be okay.'

And so began a months-long process of tests, waiting lists, and trying hard not to google an illness I was not diagnosed with.

The diagnosis felt like a relief. The limbo had been torture. It took another six months to gain access to medication. I have learned over the year or so since then that chronic illness comes with constant battles for access to information, treatment, testing, and re-testing, as well as constant battles to be heard. There is a huge power imbalance. As a patient who knows nothing about your condition, something happening within your own body, you are reliant on professionals who are often immune to the stress you are experiencing. Another thing I learned is that nurses, unique among medics, are gods and goddesses who walk among us and should be paid their weight in gold.

For me, MS comes with fatigue, sight impairment (now fully recovered), and numbness and tingling of my feet and legs, a constant reminder that my spinal nerves bear scars — in turn a reminder that my brain does too. It means being less able to travel and sometimes less able to put in the late hours I would like to — stress and fatigue increase the risk of attacks, and hasten the permanent nerve damage.

I've been told from the moment of my diagnosis, by all the medical professionals involved, that this is not the illness it once was. 'No one ends up in a wheelchair,' they say ad nauseam. They mean to be reassuring, but it's hard to have that much faith in medicine when it's your brain and your spine that are affected. I wish they had told me instead, 'It's okay to end up in a wheelchair. You'll still be you, and we'll help you live better by making the world accessible, as it should be.'

I realise now that there was extraordinary stress in my life around the time of my first attack. My grandma had fallen ill in Mashhad and, over a few months, deteriorated to a point where we knew she would pass away imminently. I was closer with her than any of my other relatives in Iran, because we called her on the phone every time I was at my dad's. She would tell me how much she loved that I travelled the world instead of having babies too young, throwing shade at my cousins. She would speak about her life with my grandad, a much older man who had died many years before. She would laugh at our family antics, at herself.

My dad was exceptionally close with his mum and deeply distressed by his separation from her at a time when she needed him. He began considering a trip home. Talking him out of this risky endeavour was difficult, especially from afar, while I was working in Wellington, but eventually I succeeded. When my grandma was finally gone, I flew home to find him in front of a small shrine made of photos, candles, and fresh flowers from his garden, trying to grieve alone. He and his sister, who was also in exile in Austria, talked through their guilt and sadness. That is a side of refugee life no one speaks much about. The fact that we can never go home has meant we have missed saying goodbye to both my grandmothers, and my mum's older sister, who died a slow death from a brain tumour. I never knew how to fill that void for my parents, how to be for them the big close-knit families they missed.

So, we as people bring the whole of ourselves to parliament. Humanising that experience may be the key to making it effective and — for me — surviving. Having the warmth of Green Party co-leader Marama Davidson in the office next door through all this has often been my lifeline. We both have protesters for parents, and we are both from backgrounds that make us unlikely parliamentarians. Our regular MP/co-leader check-ins would often turn into late dinners at her little meeting desk, shoes kicked off, periodically bursting into laughter at the situation in which we'd found ourselves.

Leadership comes easily to Marama, because she has a genuine love for people. She connects with rooms full of people and massive crowds from behind a loudspeaker with the same unaffected warmth as she does with every baby she spots across a crowded room and runs to cradle. With that affinity for human connection comes a fierce intelligence that I think is commonly underestimated. She has an innate understanding of political issues and their broader contexts. There is little more I could ask for than to have another woman of colour sit me down and talk me through the decades of microaggressions we have both experienced and tell me straight that people like us have to work harder than anyone else in politics, be more prepared, be stronger. We have to, because we are unconsciously assumed less able, less qualified, irrational, angry, and easy to tear down. We can see the same patterns of attack and challenge experienced by our sort in politics around the world, and we learn from it.

'But,' she said to me, 'it is worth it. We have to give our people what they deserve. The ones who do want us here.'

It was something to have the hard truths laid out with love. It takes the edge off the self-doubt.

The other most sustaining part of the MP experience will always be connecting with communities at the grassroots. Those who reach out most often and bring me in as their own are women, from schools and universities to the Women's Centre with its seasoned, unshakable feminists. I also work closely with refugees and ethnic communities: Asians, Africans, and of course all manner of Middle Easterners. Walking into a room where people know who you are, or relate to something you've said or done, is surreal. I will never ever not feel profoundly undeserving and grateful that I get to do and say things that affect even a single stranger to the point of them giving me thanks when I first meet them. I will never not get butterflies in my stomach when that happens. It feels simultaneously like a flight response, the one that makes us turn down compliments down and flee from praise, and a warm, deep sense of gratitude.

I learned a lot about the essence of minority representation and solidarity between marginalised groups from my fellow minority Green candidates and activists during the election. Once we knew our experiences were shared, we spoke openly about the hurt and alienation, and asked questions about the origins of these experiences. Why were we, who were so different from one another as individuals, dismissed in the same ways?

Korean New Zealander Rebekah and I talked about how difficult it was to watch our parents process the abuse, mocking and derision directed at us based on our race. It was painful to see the look of utter humiliation and heartbreak on their faces at candidate meetings and when they had seen online comments, as they gently asked questions about it. They were of course proud and supportive of their children, so they tried to hide their sadness. Eventually, we tried to shield them from the abuse.

I can only really imagine space for us and our political perspectives existing within the Green movement. Although there was no one else like me when I first became active, I remembered the first time I felt seen in New Zealand politics was when this party stood against popular prejudice with wrongfully detained refugee Ahmed Zaoui. I remembered Keith Locke.

Through all the calls for Greens to 'stick to the environment', it is also a constant relief to know that our Charter firmly recognises the connectedness of ecological sustainability with the 'just distribution of social and natural resources, both locally and globally', non-violence, and appropriate decision-making. This is a movement where I have thrived precisely because the emancipation of historically marginalised groups is essential to ecological and social justice. The Charter directs that decision-making take place 'directly at the appropriate level by those affected'. Making space for Māori, women, gender minorities, and the disabilities community has always been a commitment within our movement. We know that governance at any level is only weakened by exclusion.

In July 2019, that meant we were the only party whose MPs joined the occupation of the sacred Māori whenua Ihumātao. We joined together with land protectors against the commercial development of the land, land that had been confiscated and continued to be colonised despite its special status. We knew that this was our job, that it was what we would always do with the strong and loud support of our party because our Charter specifically upholds Te Tiriti o Waitangi and Māori as tangata whenua of our nation. Walking into the peaceful, beautiful gathering of mana whenua and so many others from around Aotearoa at Ihumātao was not the first for any of us, nor for Green MPs past. I will never forget the aesthetic juxtaposition of protectors preparing food and singing on the whenua with the endless line of uniformed officers. It looked like a photograph from a time past. This was the moment that the movement needed us most. It meant something to me, as a refugee to this land, to stand with tangata whenua.

What brought me here, and to the Green movement, was the thought of what my parents fought for and lost. I want to protect the free, equal, democratic ideal I found in Aotearoa, my homeland. I want to get Big Money out of politics because I was raised on stories of how governments and people are bought and sold for oil money, how the news serves those sponsored interests, and how everything we hold dear as a people can be yanked away if the institutions of democracy are weak.

Then there is the constitution. I hold myself to my maiden speech and the belief that our rights, including our economic and social rights, must be entrenched to protect democracy, and to finally honour the promise of Te Tiriti.

I'm often screamed down as 'unpatriotic' or 'hateful' of the nation that took me in. But to me, talking about the faults in our system and trying to fix our safety nets is my way of paying this country back for its generosity, as well honouring what so many have fought for and lost in Iran. Justice, to slightly paraphrase Dr Cornel West, is what love looks like in politics.

These are conversations I hope we can have as a nation. They are conversations that we as a government owe our people.

You are not us

A need all humans share is to be accepted and wanted by our communities. We are pack animals, so we need to belong. Most of us know what it's like to be bullied, to be made to feel out of place. Those moments stay with us. There's a twinge, even years later, an ache in your heart far more enduring than any ordinary failure.

Belonging to a marginalised group is a lot about being excluded, less popular, less accepted, less wanted, especially if we dare become visible, if we dare to be ourselves. As women of colour, we have been told to know our place. We have been villainised, criminalised and forced into closets for so long. Now, at this moment in human history, as more women of colour claim positions of power in establishment institutions and take our platforms, we face abuse and violence with our wins.

The hardest lesson of my political life was learning that I was not always among friends, that I was unwelcome — not in any personal sense, but as a politician. I realised that my face and my story, quite apart from my politics, inspired different things in different people. Sometimes, that thing was hate. For most of my life as a refugee Kiwi, I had been interacting with the world more or less as an assimilated, raceless 'individual', not a member of a marginalised group. That wasn't how I understood my place in the world on a daily basis, not as a point of solidarity or degradation. Coping with and addressing abuse wasn't what I had envisaged as part of my job when I stood as a candidate, but it eventually morphed into a constant backdrop of my experience as a parliamentarian.

The decision to stand, with the idea of fronting as a lawyer with expertise on human rights and the constitution, was a huge achievement in my journey grappling with anxiety. But the lesson came quickly: for people like me, who bear the brunt of populist rhetoric, identity and democracy are inseparable. In entering politics as a refugee and a woman of colour, my identity became the battleground.

The reality is that marginalised identities are both ours and imposed. We live our lives, interacting with the systems out there in the world, from the prism of our races, our genders, our manifested religions, and our sexualities, whether we want to or not. The healthcare system, the courts, our employers, state and commercial media — they all treat us differently based on these indicators. Our needs are both objectively different and made different by the disparate treatment we receive from the world. We need representation. We need to be true equals in our big human tribe, for protection against very real harm. We've seen that as women when choices about our reproductive health are whipped away by the likes of US state governments. Māori have seen it as a justice system antithetical to tikanga Māori, which targets and incarcerates them en masse, as generations of babies are removed from their homes, as their sacred places are sold as commodities. We need participatory representation, or the very system that gave us the vote will swallow us whole in a majority-rule system of democracy.

That lived experience of prejudice is a big part of what makes me a representative. When you have known any kind of oppression or exclusion, you have an appreciation for other forms of oppression. My experience of hate was particular to my race and background as a refugee, as well as living in this world as a woman. But knowing systemic marginalisation exists makes it far easier to understand and acknowledge its different forms. The parallels exist in the plight of indigenous peoples, other peoples of colour, the rainbow community, people living with disability. We are forced again and again to prove prejudice exists, that our experiences are not a one-off. We see that with the endless denial of the gender pay gap, which is both gendered and racialised, in the face of reams of research. To have this privileged platform comes with the responsibility to speak loudly to systemic prejudice. We have to build solidarity across our movements, so we can help end the societal gaslighting that tells us each as individuals that our oppression does not exist.

I announced my candidacy for parliament via a short press release on 17 January 2017. I had good relationships with a few journalists, having done interviews as a lawyer on various rights issues over the years. But I had never been one to reach out for publicity. I had never drafted a media release. There was no media support for candidates, because our communications staff were all employed by the New Zealand Parliament and legally bound to help the MPs only.

My friend Murdoch Stephens — who was a bit more adept at media communications, having run the 'Double the Refugee Quota' campaign — helped. In fact, he was the one who had, some time before, figured out that I would be the first-ever refugee MP. He was determined that fact should be in the media release. It took some convincing for me.

I thought carefully about how that would affect the way I related to my ethnicity and background as a refugee. I asked myself if I would represent those diverse groups, and why that might be problematic. I was wary that as women of the so-called 'Muslim world', our identity is pitched as 'victims' of the eternally archaic and frightening abyss of our culture and (if we make it out) as reborn symbols of Western triumph.

Murdoch's argument was a valid one: it matters for people to see refugees, and for refugees to see ourselves being visible participants in New Zealand life. It was meaningful for me to celebrate my background, because that would help humanise a community in need of affirmation. These were arguments I had heard before. I had already worked to become comfortable with representing the face of Middle Eastern refugees during the latest humanitarian crisis, when activist communities had reached out. I realised the need was bigger than my fear of tokenism.

But tokenism was still an issue I knew I had to guard against. I had grappled with being the 'good refugee', as I agreed to have my image included in various campaigns to raise New Zealand's refugee quota and to support refugees here. I had been in videos giving soundbites about how Kiwi I felt and what hell my family had escaped. I had been, you could say, identified as one of the 'model refugees' because of my Oxford education and career with the United Nations. That was problematic. Tokenism is one thing, but the 'good refugee' narrative has always troubled me for the unfair burden it places on people to somehow earn the safety to which they have a right. That would be a narrative I would try to debunk. I identified openly as a refugee for that reason. The truth, I realised, is that unless we tell our own stories, unless we take on roles in public life, the misnomers persist.

The media pick-up was pretty impressive for a new candidate. Almost instantly, I was regularly on the evening news talking about my past as well as other rights issues. At least some of that attention came from the zeitgeist, the eagerness for 2017 New Zealand to stand as the counterpoint to 2016 global populism. It was, I thought, a combination of my human rights work and the refugee story that got me covered.

As the campaign began, I spoke at Rotary Clubs, schools, and gatherings of Green and not-so-Green communities. Inevitably, variations of a certain question dressed as a compliment always arose: 'How do we help other immigrants assimilate to our culture as well as you have?'

I would respond first with my own question: 'What about me makes you think I have assimilated to "your" culture?'

The answers were a wonderful list of prized feminist attributes: 'You're an independent woman,' 'You've forged your own path,' 'You're outspoken,' 'You're educated,' 'You have a good job and you travel and you dress Western.'

In response, I would explain that I am the daughter of feminists so staunch that they were willing to lose everything rather than raise a little girl in oppression. I learned feminism from men and women who faced torture for their rights. I would tell the story of my mother wearing lipstick in Iran as a daily protest against the patriarchy that told her to be colourless and desexualised. Our feminism does look different sometimes because our patriarchy is different. But she knew subjugation was wrong long before she was forced out of her culture. She fought as an Iranian woman against her own culture, and against a religion she was raised in, just as Western feminists had to do. So I felt the responsibility to be free, independent, and outspoken, *because* I'm an Iranian refugee, not in spite of it.

It really is an important lesson, accepting that our values exist authentically in every culture. Dominant voices — the ones with platforms or those we are fed by media — may not represent that. We need to look harder, find and amplify the voices that do speak to equality, or environmentalism or human rights, if we value those ideals in our own culture. That has to come into policy-making. Whether it's criminal justice or development aid, I've found this a nuance that needs to be repeated. We can't assume any community needs us to impose things like fairness or feminism. We need to look for those voices within that community and support their leadership, because only culturally authentic solutions will last.

From the start, the reactions to my candidacy made it clear that there was something special in it, for different reasons. It's important to acknowledge the unexpected, endlessly touching flood of support that came immediately, and still does, particularly in response to spikes in abuse. It is, on the hard days, an essential emotional respite for me. It is infinitely moving to put something of yourself out into the world and receive any positive feedback at all, to be supported by strangers with a shared worldview. All this for the opportunity to speak from lived experience that happens to be my own, but also belongs to millions — an experience that should have never been so marginalised that people feel grateful for a single parliamentary representative.

But with the love came the hate. Becoming visible as a politician meant receiving the latent wrath on behalf of all those communities I represent. We all receive it in increments daily, but it came in an overwhelming torrent in the public eye when I stood for office. It became so defining of my work, even as a candidate, that when I eventually stood to speak for the very first time in the New Zealand Parliament, I included it as an opening theme of my maiden speech. It was, I had realised by then, not only an important part of the experience of those I had come to represent, but demonstrative of a threat to our democracy. Racism is offensive and harmful in any context, but I couldn't ignore that its aim in my context was to drive me out of politics, to silence my voice. It was representative of people's discomfort with migrant participation in public life and in democracy.

It came in the form of comments on articles, on my own social media page, and in 'hit-job' opinion pieces published by mainstream media. The comments included not only vile diatribes, but more than a few calls for actual violence. One of a few relatively well-known commentators would attack, and hordes would follow. The hordes might have been fake accounts, even generated elsewhere in the world, but haven't we learned that can rile enough hysteria to win elections, even in the 'world's greatest democracy'?

The first broad criticism was that I was too foreign to sit in parliament. That a person like me entering parliament demonstrated the need for a ban on all immigrants from running for office. There was an air of reason to this line of attack — protecting New Zealand's interests and so forth. Of course, Russel Norman, the co-leader of the Green Party at the last election, was a far more recent migrant than I, having moved here from Brisbane, Australia, as an adult. Our caucus already includes my very American friend Julie-Anne Genter. Both received passing remarks about their accents, but nothing of the vitriol I experienced.

The second criticism — shrieking more loudly over the generalised xenophobia and racism of the 'foreigner' attacks — are the specific attacks against me as 'a Muslim'. This 'accusation' generally takes one of two more developed lines of reasoning, both bigoted and Islamophobic. The first is that as a Muslim, I can't be trusted not to impose Sharia law and so must be disqualified as a politician. Never mind that at the time of my candidacy, our prime minister was openly, devoutly Catholic and had admitted that his faith determines his political position on women's health. I watched the same hysterical calls against Ilhan Omar as she entered United States Congress a year or so later, as the first-ever refugee to sit in that very publicly, if not officially, Christian-dominated House of Representatives. I knew just how Kafkaesque those attacks felt.

The second 'reasoning' for the anti-Muslim attacks is the obvious declaration, 'She's a terrorist.' I'm not sure why I needed to be elected to office to do what it is terrorists do. Another somewhat baffling accusation was that I was a 'terrorist spy'. Apparently, my well-laid plan was to move to New Zealand as a child, and wait to one day bring down Western civilisation from the backbenches of parliament via the Green Party. It was slow work. There were decades of what may look to the untrained eye to be complete divergences from the terrorist spy pathway. I had to study law and focus on human rights to throw them all off. I had to go to Oxford University, work for the United Nations (presumably also as a spy), drink alcohol, and live in sin with atheistical white men, just waiting for this golden opportunity.

In this scenario, any fears of my purported plans to terrorise the West must be thoroughly laid to rest by my demonstrated incompetence. But the word 'terrorist' still comes to mind any time a Middle Easterner becomes visible.

To correct the factual basis of the 'Muslim terrorist' attacks was never an option. I remembered the persistent accusations that Barack Obama was secretly Muslim back in the 2008 American election. Whenever this was raised with his opponent, John McCain, he would graciously point out that the Obama family were church-going Christians. Of course, this implicitly reinforced the offensive suggestion that had Obama been Muslim, he should not become president. Only a church-going Christian was acceptable. It was an answer that casually fed the hysteria and perpetuated the rumour. Deliberately failing to condemn the underlying prejudice allowed the damage to continue against Obama and all Muslim-Americans. I wasn't going to satiate the bigots by denying what no one should have to deny in a free and equal society.

Besides, I know the prejudice against me as 'a Muslim' is far more about my ethnicity. The same assumption is made about Sikh men who wear turbans, and other South Asian and Middle Eastern peoples. The point isn't that Islam is bad or dangerous, because people can calmly debate Christianity or any other religion, particularly in the context of separating church from state. Even on issues where prejudice is high, like systemic child abuse in the Catholic Church, people are easily able to criticise and prosecute the Church to protect children against paedophile priests without suggesting Catholic lawmakers are themselves paedophiles, or that the Bible encourages child sex crimes. Christians are not shouted at to 'go back where they came from', though New Zealand is not indigenously Christian.

Meanwhile, ANZAC services were cancelled in Auckland in 2019, because there was a suggestion that they would include a Muslim call to prayer in memory of fifty-one Muslims who had been murdered just a month before. So many threats of violence were made against the organisers by anti-Muslim community members that the gatherings were made unsafe. I don't accept that the issue is about religious hymns being sung at a secular public event — Christian holidays, hymns, and traditions are accepted in public culture without protest. The point is that we look different, we are dark-skinned, we are foreign, and the discomfort and hate we inspire is only justified with ex-post-facto War on Terror reasoning. Other migrants of colour are feared and isolated with any raft of other stereotypes: as criminals, as misogynists, as legal proprietors of desirable Auckland housing. Some of those points of villainisation regularly encompass indigenous peoples, marginalising them as outsiders within their very own land, implicitly justifying the historic and very current colonial violence they experience.

The final all-encompassing attack is that I carry that dirty, scary label shared with those faceless hordes breaching pristine Western borders. The problem with me is that I am a refugee. Not just a woman, not just a foreigner, not just suspected of being Muslim and with it a terrorist, but also a refugee. People fear us because they've seen our vast numbers. They fear us because we are dark and Muslim-looking.

But they are also, in my experience, exhausted from all the sympathy we garner. They tolerate us while we are grateful and humble. Of course, we *are* grateful. But the ask is that we remain nothing *but* grateful. That we manifest no signs of feeling equal once we settle in our new homelands. That we never seek equality — through, say, activism for our communities — never seek leadership roles, never speak a word about ourselves unless grateful is the beginning and end of it. We are to be grateful we escaped torture or death because of our race, religion, ethnicity, sexual orientation, or political views. We should be eternally grateful for having accessed our right to seek and be granted asylum from violence. Though it is a legal universal right, we must beg for it with our faces pressed against the dirt, holding our babies tight (single men and women don't count, right? They never seem included in the good refugee pictures) because we failed to be born safe and free. Then, we must remain quietly smiling, eyes down, always happy just to be here breathing air and contributing to the economy.

Interestingly, there is a breed of online abuser who is angry about the unfair political advantage I have via the refugee victim narrative. Those same people at some point decided I wasn't even a real refugee. This line was much like the Obama 'birther' movement, demanding he produce his American birth certificate. The attack against me arose when I opposed far-right Canadian speakers Lauren Southern and Stefan Molyneux. Southern re-posted my video explaining the damage her ilk did to ours. It felt necessary to explain that the rights of marginalised groups who are targeted and degraded by far-right white supremacist rhetoric must always be balanced against their right to spread hate, and certainly their right to a public platform like the council venues they were attempting to use for their gigs in Auckland. Human rights are always necessarily balanced against one another when there is a conflict, and certainly against public safety. It was a moment when we called on the city to come together and stand with those being made unsafe by hate speech, and the call was met with overwhelming support. It makes me shudder, though, to realise I posted the video and we turned up in protest about six months before the Christchurch terror attack. At the time, Southern went on the offensive and supporters around the globe, but especially in Australia, flocked to tear me down.

Again, the attacks were largely along the same bigoted lines. One thread that came through was the very laboured argument that based on general knowledge information about Iran in the 1980s, my family couldn't have been persecuted. It doesn't make an ounce of difference to say that the appropriate legal agency in New Zealand has investigated our specific claim, heard evidence, and confirmed our refugee status. Refugee cases are confidential for many reasons. They contain information that may place others in danger back home, may put entire freedom movements at risk, and most often they contain accounts of pain and injury that is both intimate and humiliating. Besides, no amount of disclosure kills a birther myth. Facts don't matter when the accusation comes in bad faith. Responding legitimises the demand, the belief that minorities owe any old online angst warrior proof of our right to exist, or a personal rundown of our family's trauma.

*

The hate hurled at me in all its forms would not have been all that surprising for minorities. My presence in public life only amplified what we experience already, made it more visible, at a more torrential level. We've always known we are feared and reviled, because people tell us that in daily life. I knew to hide my refugee background at school because an eleven-year-old girl told me how much she hated us. We all have our stories of being told to go back where we came from, of being asked gently about our backward families or our weird-smelling food. We know we don't get jobs because our strange names mean we're knocked out at the CV-vetting stage without a look-in. There are studies that have proven that now, but we didn't need data. That's why migrants work hard and start small businesses. We do that with the hope that a generation or two later, having shed the foreign accent, we might be able to find a little hole and gently put our elbow through until we are allowed to walk all the way into mainstream society. Maybe we'll even be allowed onto the standard paths to success and respectability. So we work around the clock, change our names, and straighten our hair. We don't do these things because we are born hating ourselves or our cultures; we do them because we realise we are despised for being different.

What I experienced when I first popped my head over the barrier was the hatred for us as leaders. Imagine a woman of colour acting as an unapologetic equal participant at the decision-making table itself! My audacity in even announcing that intention garnered a special kind of hostility — it felt like a visceral, hysterical panic.

What was also clear from the start was the overt and implicit misogyny running through the attack lines against me. It covered the spectrum of abuse women of all walks of life get online. It went from ongoing comments about the way I look, both positive and negative, including crude sexual overtures. But they also escalated to suggestions of sexual violence, either direct or in the forms of public incitement, like many other threats of violence I receive. It would go something like, 'She deserves to be ...' or 'About time someone ...' — insert suggestion of gun violence, rape, or anything else vile and unsettling.

Leaving aside the violence and objectification, the implicit misogyny was an experience all women will recognise. Its relentless aim is to undermine. It was clear to me, and all us as women, that a male politician in my lowly first-term small-party position wouldn't get the volume of personal attacks I was receiving. Most of it was race-based, but a large part was also based on the assumption that I was not qualified for my job. Chlöe and I both had to respond to questions like, 'Do you think you're ready for this job? Do you think you can do it?' as the opening question of interviews after being elected. It continues to this day. There's the classic correction that begins with 'Well, actually ...' and goes on to provide an incorrect or self-evident piece of information. The need to correct or explain things to us is apparently overwhelming for some reason. We constantly get comments like, 'But is she qualified?' or 'She's naïve.' Of course, there is no requisite qualification for elected officials other than being duly elected.

A comment on a video the Green Party posted in which I spoke about ending military deployments in Afghanistan and Iraq read:

239

'Why didn't the Greens have a guy present that speech?? Sex appeal and sex sells. Couple of minutes of my life I'll never get back.'

The peace campaign was of course close to my heart for personal and professional reasons. I broke the rule against looking at the comments or responding to them. In fact, I bit back. I told him my qualifications, as women have to do again and again, as if we owe this proof to the endless challengers unaccustomed to hearing our voices coming from a place of authority. I have a Master's degree focused on international human rights law and experience working for the UN in post-atrocity contexts. Then I attacked. I was tired of the tirade and I wanted it turned around. He was the one in the wrong. He was out there doing this to other women online, and likely in life, who couldn't retaliate. I said: 'The fact you can't look at a human being without objectifying them, and the fact you can't see women as professionals or experts, is vile.'

It never feels good to post something like that. I imagine it feels like punch well swung in a fight you didn't start. Confrontation and conflict about your own personal right to exist is deflating, humiliating, even when you are in a position of relative power. Plus, to me, lashing out at another person doesn't feel right even if it feels provoked. I always regret coming out swinging. I feel ashamed. In the beginning I was calmer, much more open, even, to debating my own humanity. Then it became obvious most of the attacks weren't meant to open a conversation. They made me angry and sad, and I thought about those same people out in the world bullying other people with less of a voice than I have. I felt like I had to strike back.

Then James said to me, ever so gently, one day as we were chatting: 'I've thought about whether to tell you this because I know

I don't have any measure for understanding what you go through. I know I'm a straight Pākehā man and things are different for me. But I thought I would tell you that your responses online are getting angry. I know that's understandable. But it's not like you.'

Of course, anger is valid. I say that to young activists who find the world of politics and protest infuriating. Even within our own progressive movements, there are cultural and gender barriers that mirror the marginalisation out there in the world. It can feel crushing. We see that now with the climate movement, where indigenous voices who have been leading that movement for generations are deemed inexpert, and excluded from the decision-making table and celebratory headlines. Meanwhile, outside the movement they are far more likely to face abuse and violence online and by authorities for fronting the protest. That is unjust and warrants anger.

But anger has a time and a place. For me, it was okay to be told by a friend that the expression of that emotion was affecting my work. It wasn't the way I wanted to project myself into the world. I could direct it more productively. But that means seeking safe spaces to be angry too, to rage, to be validated and validate others. I think having lived it now for more than two years, I know how to take a breath and save the impulse to strike. I know the difference between the genuine online and in-life challenges to policy, which are satisfying to respond to, even when there is disagreement, and the ones made in bad faith, aiming to degrade us as people.

A conversation I had one night over drinks with a group of women MPs, in the very male space of the parliamentary billiards room, helped clarify the triggers. We were speaking openly about online abuse. Marama said she had been 'lucky', in that she didn't get much abuse to start with, but now she gets abuse the more she posts about race. Labour MP Louisa Wall, who had been instrumental in heralding marriage equality in 2012, said the abuse she experienced during that campaign was awful, but now she has a strong supportive community around her, so posting about LGBTQIA issues is safer for her — though she added the abuse is shocking if she posts about the rights of transgendered people. Julie Anne said she never really got abuse while her public presence was centred around Green transport issues, except for the odd person vehemently opposed to public transport. That was policy-based at least. But now, when she posts about her work as Minister for Women, she experiences misogynistic abuse.

I thought about it and realised that I got abuse almost perpetually. The topic didn't matter. Even when I repeated longstanding Green Party positions, on disarmament, on te reo Māori teaching, on free trade, I was received as a dangerous radical. I realised during that conversation that the worst abuse came to me when I appeared to be confident or knowledgeable, god forbid I appeared to be celebrating a win. The most offensive thing about a female refugee MP, I realised, was a display of self-assurance.

Some of the first very organised attacks came from men dissecting everything I said for any possible inaccuracy and adding comments like, 'Looks like Oxford UN lawyer didn't know as much as she thought she did!' Unbeknown to one commentator, Guy was tagged in one such post. I hadn't even noticed the barrage until he rang me quite distressed. He wanted to know if I was okay. He said he was shaking. It actually didn't bother me much, because it was so petty and about an issue I had strong feelings about.

But what came next was revealing in terms of both race and gender issues underlying most of the angry teardowns I get as a confident-seeming persona. Realising that Guy was tagged, the commentator wrote him a personal message, apologising for the abuse. He said he had become overly emotional, but would hate for Guy to think he was 'just another white man who hates Golriz'. He would hate for *Guy* to think that. Basically: sorry I insulted your woman. Guy suggested that he apologise to *me*. But that apparently made no sense.

A pattern that brings misogyny and race together for Marama and me in particular is the line that constantly accuses us of having 'gone rogue' or being angry radicals. In fact, it is my job and an honour to echo the words of Jeanette Fitzsimons, Keith Locke or Russel Norman on peace, corruption, or protest. But something rings radical and angry when I say the lines said before me by other Green MPs on the same issues.

The connection they see between Marama and me drives home the 'angry black woman' trope. We don't, in fact, have a lot in common in terms of our backgrounds or manner. We do both value dissent, feel better at the coalface. We speak to race and poverty as connected oppressions — caused by the same deliberately unfair economic and political system — underpinning the climate crisis. But that is about where our similarities end.

Yet our attackers hear us speak with the same voice. They often tag James into online complaints that read 'get your women into line'. They make memes portraying him as weak or less of a man for refusing to do so. What seems to upset them is that we do our jobs and use our voices as if we're equal to a white man. That feels emasculating. But how else were we ever going to do this job?

*

I created a Twitter account three months before the election, after a sustained push from every campaign advisor and friend I had contact with over the election year. I didn't want to do soundbites in under 140 characters and I certainly didn't want more social media than the already dreaded Facebook in my life. But 'Twitter is where the Lefties are,' they all said. 'Twitter is where the journalists are. You'll get your message out that way. In fact, you can't do it without Twitter anymore. Look at Trump.' The two championing messages 'It's the Left's forum' and 'Trump does it' seemed wildly contradictory, but I succumbed.

I sat down with Tina Plunkett, a veteran political campaigner with three ground campaigns for Jacinda under her belt. We had known each other in political circles, but mostly shared a social scene on K-Rd and a haughty distaste for watered-down Wellington politics. We poured wine in a mutual friend's kitchen, Tina opened my laptop, and I pointed her to the most recent high-resolution photo of me before walking off to anxiously pace and throw snacks at her. Self-promotion still felt mortifying. She wrote my Twitter blurb and pressed 'Done'. I could barely look at it.

Over the afternoon and evening, Tina sat, mouth agape, staring at the screen as the madness began. To this day, she apologises with every new flare-up of uncanny abuse. Knowing I'm writing about this, she told me, 'I remember you saying, "I just don't need more abuse in my life," and I said, "Oh, it isn't that bad." It was so bad.'

The first couple of attacks were from relatively prominent right-wing commentator types. The focus that first night was why the

Greens wouldn't support a National-led government. I had been on morning TV that day reiterating our commitment to change the government in cooperation with the Labour Party. It was a legitimate-enough attack in the context of the looming election. But the attack was framed differently. It was tailor-made for me. The question I was badgered with was how an immigrant could support the Labour Party, who campaigned on cuts to immigration.

At first that made me smile, because I had an answer to it immediately. I knew bringing up attitudes to migrants in my context would backfire for National supporters. Their sitting prime minister had been caught calling refugees 'leftovers from terrorist regimes' and suggesting Iraqi refugees were associates of Saddam Hussein, in an article on his website dating back a few years, but still online. I knew this because in February 2017, when *Newshub* journalist Lloyd Burr discovered it, Lloyd told me about it. Lloyd hadn't exactly been a Green Party fan, but he was coming to see me for a comment on Trump's Muslim ban, and he had discovered this Trumpish rant by our very own prime minister shortly beforehand, so it seemed sensible to ask me about that too. So shockingly bigoted was English's article that Lloyd and I both had to read it through a few times before the interview, just to process it. My voice is shaking a little with fury in the TV clip. I happily linked that interview as a response to those first attacks by commentators.

The rhetoric of mass immigration cuts, especially during a general election, is often harmful. Not because talk of immigration policy is inherently racist, but unless it is done with nuance and based on evidence, alongside the work of debunking race myths that go with that conversation, it very easily feeds damaging populist rhetoric against already marginalised groups. The idea of immigration cuts is attractive fodder, because it can give politicians oversimplified xenophobic responses to complex socioeconomic problems, including scapegoating immigrants for our housing crisis, road congestions, even our frail and underfunded healthcare system, peopled with migrant doctors, nurses, and technicians at every level.

We often speak about immigrants in terms of economic cost. So while we do, let's remember that in 2016, a study by Business and Economic Research Limited (BERL) had made the economic benefits stark: immigrants to New Zealand had added $3 billion more in a year to government revenue than they took up in spending. A 2018 study by the Ministry of Business Innovation and Employment concluded there was no negative effect of temporary migrants on wages or job opportunities for local workers. These are hardly left-wing sources and are backed up by a 2017 study by the New Zealand Initiative. Even refugee populations, who are a cost in the short term, have been shown to add to the national economic well-being in the mid- to long term, given the relative youth of our refugee intakes. As Murdoch Stephens wrote just prior to the 2017 election:

> While poverty is often characterised as a repeating cycle that spans generations, New Zealanders have little to fear of refugees becoming dependent on the state. When the children of refugees are placed into the New Zealand education system — and more than forty per cent of our new refugees are children — the results are impressive. Instead of being stuck in a cycle of dependency, refugee families have

strong hopes for their children that more often than not lead them to university or to start businesses.

This shouldn't be the way we measure the benefits of the inclusion of those seeking refuge from persecution or war to our society. It should not be the way we look at people who don't appear or sound like us when first we meet them. That's what xenophobia breeds. But we refugees constantly do have to prove our worth — and our worth, including the economic benefits, is rarely included in those opportunistic political debates.

This is not to say that New Zealanders are wrong or racist when they fear immigration, when so many of us already here find it hard to make ends meet. There has been an underfunding in infrastructure over successive governments, most recently with the National Party's extraordinarily short-sighted and cruel selling of state houses when it was clear we should have been investing in more. Tax cuts that meant hospitals were left to literally rot were a conscious choice. It is not that immigrants are not the problem, but without immigration there'd be even less money to spend. The answer is to tax fairly and spend on public services, infrastructure, housing — on the things that help us all live as equals. There would be enough to go around, if only they hadn't prioritised the kickbacks to those who needed them the least.

More than economics, we rarely hear politicians acknowledge the benefits that our country's openness in the past have already brought. I never much liked Iranians talking about what great contributions our culture made to sciences or art as a means of justifying equality (though I do quietly love and lament, given the current state of our affairs, that we wrote the Cyrus Cylinder, the first-ever declaration of human rights). It is worth remembering that shared culture is what humanity survives on. New Zealand wouldn't have our celebrated coffee culture or iconic Vogel's bread if not for the refugees and migrants who made New Zealand home after World War II. The history of the world can be told through conflict, but it can also be told through the benefits of shared knowledge and goods that are seeded by migration.

We all need to get better at talking about immigration because we are responsible for the wellbeing of those communities who bear the impact of xenophobic rhetoric. The Labour policy on immigration cuts wasn't one the Greens supported. The language of blanket cuts should have been more nuanced. The reason it wasn't a deal breaker for me is that I knew a whole lot of people and our planet couldn't afford another three years under National.

Those Twitter attacks by right-wing commentators was the first in a long line of problematic attacks that seemed to suggest I was only there to serve the interests of migrants. That my expertise, political activism and affiliation with the Green Party were nothing. I was seen as a one-dimensional anomaly, defined by my 'foreign' identity. Suggesting my politics would be solely defined by immigration policy was, again, race-based. That framing wasn't being thrown at any Pākehā Green politicians who happened to be first-generation immigrants. Wrong as it was, this was a tidy trap. It degraded my value as a candidate to migrant representation while simultaneously throwing shade at Labour, and by association the Greens, as anti-immigration.

As the abuse grew, it began to hurt. It hurt to know that we — as persons of colour — are not among friends in our broader society.

It hurts to know that you are hated because of your face and your story, which you had very little hand in shaping. It hurts every day to know that if I was to announce a policy, it would have to be messaged more carefully. It would have to be risk assessed. It would receive a different kind of venom. I have to consider whether it would be damaging for me to raise an issue, because the prejudice and hate aimed at me would mar its reception.

In the beginning, my way of addressing the obstacles and the discrimination was to speak about them. But then when the feat began to look never-ending, a deep sense of grief came. Maybe the time and energy I was expending on talking about it meant they had won. Maybe diverting me away from my expertise, the campaign funding reforms, the constitutional conversation, was a loss to me as an MP. Was it a hindrance to have a refugee speak on human rights? But no one else in parliament was prioritising peace issues, or electoral reform, or the constitution. It felt like one part of my experience was thoroughly overshadowing the other: my expertise. The personal toll of that realisation is to be perpetually aware of the injustice at every level. I cried too easily when rom-coms allowed race minority leads, because I knew how much people didn't want us there.

Duelling against the endless gibberish of internet trolls is soul-destroying. You can ignore it, but you know it's there. With you or without you, a flushed-pink, spitting mob of libertines is fighting at the last barrier of civilisation, via misspelled comments you can't look at, lest they win.

Anyone who has experienced online abuse knows it is insidious. It comes into your home, on every device you own. It is there when you wake up. It is there when you lie in bed at night. For me at times it is constant. Unavoidable. And though I have to engage with it to an extent because of my job, it has nothing to do with work or actual debate. It was frustrating to realise that it could not be resolved with facts or reason.

It became, and remains, a daily labour to carry the weight of that continuous stream of hate. Even without looking at it, I know it is there, and every now and then I can't help but see the little eruptions and have to force myself to look away.

The key is to avoid reacting. It was National MP Judith Collins who told me that. She looked me in the eye with a little glint at each corner, leaned in like we were in a girl gang together, and said, 'Don't react. It will be your angry response that will make it a media story. Without that, they're screaming into the void.'

We'd never really talked before, but, our wildly different political beliefs aside, this was good advice.

On an already rough morning or a long night, it's easy to snap and give one nasty detractor some vitriol aimed at the whole lot. It's even harder now, at the time of writing this, only a few months after the Christchurch terror attack. It is harder to carry the grief of fifty-one lives lost with the daily personal grief of knowing we, as a community, remain under attack. The fear is very real for us.

Then came the report that white supremacists were talking about me in secret chatrooms. Joking about how great it would be to lynch me. How funny it would be to see me hanging from a chandelier. There was more that Paddy Gower, the lead reporter in an investigative piece, told me over the phone that could not be played at the show's prime-time slot, because it was far more explicitly violent and offensive even than lynching a woman from the ceiling lights.

A few weeks before, my friend and our then digital campaigns manager, Rick Zwaan, had pulled me aside to implore me to talk to Parliamentary Security. He said, 'You know, the staff are worried too. We feel like we don't want another Jo Cox situation.' I sat silently in my office for what seemed like an eternity after that conversation. My fellow party members were consuming the hate too. They were scared for me. I was grateful for the validation of my own frazzled nerves. Parliamentary Security had long ago set up meetings with me and fitted me for a personal alarm, but it took that news investigation for me to go to them myself and ask for help.

They drew up a security plan assessed by police and I began to be escorted by security officers. It was no relief, though it was the right thing to do. Now I am advised not to speak about security arrangements too much, and I don't, though they are perpetually on my mind.

The difficulty is in holding and speaking to the very legitimate hurt, fear, and anger of an entire community, while resisting the emotions to stay effective as a politician.

I think being forced to talk about prejudice has made me a stronger politician in the end. It has honed my analysis on every other issue. The groups and sectors looking for my voice — echoing it as we echo each other — are always in sharp focus for me. It feels rightly part of my work, alongside all the law reforms I want to lead. But there is no ignoring the fact that it was very much imposed upon me by virtue of joining an institution where I had a minority voice, where I was implicitly expected to shoulder the responsibility of representing some of the most vulnerable voices in the community. Nobody — in any professional situation — should be expected to do this.

*

It was also against this backdrop that the thunderous calls for free speech began, alongside criticism of that thing called 'identity politics'. At its best, this seems to be a call for politics devoid of identity, which is sold as impartial and so fairer. The assumption of course is that politics, as life, is already fair. But before we decide whether politics should ignore identity points like gender or race, we need to answer some hard, or maybe quite obvious, questions: what issues is politics here to address? What issues are we erasing if we take identity out of it?

In fact, the responsibility to ignore 'identity' in politics, as in life, places the burden of impartiality on those who suffer prejudice and marginalisation *because* of their identity. It means we can't speak to our marginalisation in order to even the playing field or have our specific needs met. Systemic unfairness exists because marginalised groups are often under-represented (or unrepresented entirely) in decision-making and lack other platforms to voice their concerns. To actively shut down those voices when they do rise up with cries of 'identity politics' is callous. That is itself the politics of dominant identities retaining their unchallenged dominance.

The reality is that in New Zealand, women are being paid around nine per cent less than men for the same work, so gender is a political issue. Within that group, Pākehā women are paid six per cent less while Asian women are paid seventeen per cent less, Māori twenty-two per cent less, and Pasifika women are paid a whopping twenty-five per cent less than men for equal work — so race is an issue. For the twenty-six per cent of our young rainbow community who are made homeless when they are honest about their sexual orientation or gender identity, those identities are material issues. If, as an MP, I am screamed at online each time I share innocuous policies of the party I represent, often with direct reference to my race or gender, those are very real issues that I can't respond to or change without referencing racism and sexism by name.

The problem is that criticisms of so-called 'identity politics' never seem to count privileged identities at all. No one notices that civic planning by able-bodied policymakers is biased against the disabled. No one seems to realise that, for centuries, straight people aggressively and sometimes violently privileged their sexual identity over everyone else's. I've never had to 'come out' as a cis-gendered straight woman. Majority identity holders get to interact with the world as individuals seemingly devoid of group identity. That is because the needs of cis straight people already silently define the structures of society. But the very thing that facilitates someone's comfortable navigation of the world, their dominant identity points, is the fact that they are well represented in democratic decision-making, which has in turn shaped the world according to their specific needs.

It turns out that only the perspectives of the less-advantaged identity carriers are dismissed as 'identity politics'. Talking from the perspective of privileged status quo identities is just 'politics'. No one ever seems to suggest bankers or big business owners shouldn't be allowed to comment on the economy because of their inherent bias or very real personal interests, in the same way that I am told I shouldn't be able to talk on immigration or ethnic issues. Most blatantly, right now, most of those yelling about 'free speech' and demonising 'identity politics' overtly appeal to identity in those very diatribes. They constantly attack, often in the same breath, groups like feminists, migrants, and Muslims as the scourge of society and the cause of their disadvantage.

When I stood in New Zealand's House of Representatives that first time, I needed to note that the very people in that House constantly contribute to the culture that means people like me are openly attacked, undermined and threatened based on our identity. I wanted it noted that those attacks happen every time politicians scapegoat migrants in that House. We see that in New Zealand both implicitly and overtly.

We saw it when John Key failed to condemn racist jibes made by Paul Henry about Sir Anand Satyanand, joking that the next time Key should appoint a Governor-General who 'looks like a Kiwi' and 'sounds like a Kiwi'. If our New Zealand born and bred Governor-General isn't Kiwi enough in the eyes of Paul Henry, then employers may feel pretty sound in excluding ethnic job applicants. If Bill English, another knighted ex-prime minister, openly called refugees 'leftovers', it must be okay for anyone else to spit venom at us. That is the kind of assurance that normalises bullying in our workplaces, and makes kids with 'foreign' names a little more vulnerable at school. It certainly doesn't feel like 'just a bit of light-hearted banter' when you're on the receiving end. It begins to form the basis of self-hate, degradation, and isolation that threatens our mental health.

Mainstream media platforms are rarely available for victim communities to retort. This barrier was very real for the Muslim community, as they retold their harrowing plight to raise alarm about the kinds of hate and varying levels of violence they were experiencing in the years leading up to the Christchurch atrocity.

At a media function just three months after the attack, one Islamic Council of Women leader, whom I can't name since the forum was held in confidence, spoke powerfully through tears as she reproached members of the media for continuing to take space in commentary about her community. She demanded rightly of one senior columnist who had contributed a piece to the plethora of commentary in the aftermath of the Christchurch terror attacks, 'Why did you write your column about us? Why not invite us to tell our own story, which you did not know? We have been trying to tell you what's happening to us for years. We begged you to listen. It is now all of your responsibility.' She turned, with her raised arm sweeping over the room. 'All of you from the media. Make space.'

She was referencing the campaign by her council to visit police across New Zealand, reporting hate crimes and hate speech, to show that Islamophobia was on the rise and the community was under threat. There had been bricks thrown through windows, verbal abuse and threats against hijabi women, and of course the endless vile accusations and abuse online. But New Zealand had no real way to record hate crimes through our policing, something I now get to work with the Minister of Justice Andrew Little to change.

Later, the minister and I talked about the racist abuse and threats of gun violence that I had raised in my maiden speech eighteen months before, which no one had taken much notice of, while some media had insisted on giving air time to visiting anti-Muslim, anti-migrant 'thinkers' like Lauren Southern and Stefan Molyneux. Unlike me, the rest of our community out there on the streets don't have access to security escorts every time a debate about our right to exist is broadcast.

In 2018, I cried listening to a performance of the powerful Karlo Mila poem 'Eating Dark Chocolate While Watching Paul Holmes' Apology'. It was on the final night of three days' shooting a VICE documentary, where I had been followed by a film crew for hours at a time. The documentary sought to commemorate the 125th anniversary of women's suffrage. The episode was about how far women have come in formal political equality, and the challenges we still face. I had spoken about the strangeness of being the first, and the only, one like me in my role. I had spent a lot of mental and emotional energy talking about the abuse I receive and how it's all 'water off a duck's back', how the platform I have is precious and we're all forging wonderful paths for the others who will follow. The vibe was to reaffirm progress.

When the day was done, I was with friends, my guard down, surrounded by loud, laughing women of colour ready for some provocative theatre. We bought glasses of prosecco and piled into the front room at Basement Theatre. I somehow ended up sitting at the very front, facing the performer, close enough to be at the edge of the glowing spotlight in the otherwise blackened room.

tonight paul holmes apologised for calling kofi annan a
darkie / takes me back

17 years old / do you think they would ever let a boonga
be prime minister / corey p / dreadlocked bob Marley
wannabe / says to me / mocking laughter / he's drunk at
three / in highbury / but we never dreamed they'd let an
indian woman be mayor of Dunedin / so let's sukhi it to

them corey p / we were darkies anonymous then / making
fun of ourselves before anyone else could / revolution in the
bottom of a bong / cutting off our veins to spite our lives /
…
tonight paul holmes apologised sorry / he said / i've hurt
my family / i may have hurt yours /

yes / we scrapped in the car over it / there was yelling /
by the time we got to the end of the mangere motorway
/ i was crying / who is this redneck with the big brown
shoulders sitting next me / anti pc / darker than me /
defending freedom of speech / but i don't want it to be all
right /

i don't want my kids to have stanzas of darkie memories /

Hot uncontrollable tears poured down my face as I heard the
recording of the apology in that performance. I remembered it,
like Mila, as part of an overwhelming fabric of microaggressions
in my own life. The truth is that none of the implicit structural
oppressions or personal attacks are 'water off a duck's back'. As
women, as persons of colour, those tears cost us. We're exhausted
from pretending the indignities are not a big deal, and from
calling them out only to be screamed at for playing 'identity
politics'.

In fact, it turns out telling minorities their collective experiences
don't count amounts to very real abuse. Dr William A. Smith
of the University of Utah coined the term 'racial battle fatigue',
defining racial microaggressions as 'subtle, stunning, cumulative,

verbal and non-verbal insults layered with racism, sexism, elitism, and other subordination'. American studies show the daily toll of microaggressions and discrimination means people of colour experience anxiety so extreme as to be compared with the stress experienced by soldiers in combat. This is not a figment of our collective imagination.

In May 2019, I had the unique pleasure of hearing the great legal scholar Dr Moana Jackson give the keynote address at the Hamilton Press Club. His subject was colonisation and hate speech. I was excited to be there, but as I watched one of my heroes approach the mic, I felt a distinct wave of fatigue and anxiety. I was tired for him, knowing he would have to begin from the start, to prove that racism, inherent in colonisation, exists. In fact, he went as far back as Aristotle and moved up to Kant before speaking about modern-day colonisation, underpinned by white supremacy. He had to prove that it was racist to assume dark-skinned indigenous nations were able to be annexed by way of a flag — when, for example, raising a British flag on the coast of France at the time would have been meaningless. He had to prove that free speech needed protection from hate speech because already disenfranchised groups could not participate equally in their rights with structures that prioritised speech that makes us unsafe. I felt apprehensive knowing that, for the sake of 'debate', a group of known racists had been brought in that day. One raised the debunked Moriori myth 'But Māori were colonisers too'. Dr Jackson simply referred him to research. They can bring up baseless claims, of our inferiority, of our criminality, of our substantive equality against our lived experiences and actual science. It falls upon us to research and disprove these arguments in so-called 'debate' endlessly.

Dr Jackson also retold an anecdote about a time he was a guest lecturer at a law school, speaking about indigenous rights. A few minutes into his lecture, a young Pākehā man waved his arms and asked, 'Excuse me, but what qualifications do you have?'

Dr Jackson is one of New Zealand's most eminent lawyers and legal scholars. He was involved in the drafting of the United Nations Declaration on the Rights of Indigenous Peoples, was a judge on the International Tribunal of Indigenous Rights, and holds an honorary doctorate awarded for exceptional contribution to legal scholarship by the institution at which he was speaking when this particular challenge arose. Being Moana Jackson, he didn't justify the question with an answer, but asked whether the young man would have interrupted a Pākehā man guest lecturing at his law school to ask whether he was qualified enough.

I knew half the audience at the Press Club may be thinking he was being too sensitive, that not everything is a race issue. I remembered US congresswoman Ilhan Omar pointing out that when Republicans attacked her position on an issue, they attacked her qualification to speak at all, not the substance of her point. Instead of 'We disagree,' people of colour have to contend with, 'She doesn't know what she's talking about.' They want to make us feel small.

For us, Paul Holmes' casual little dig at Kofi Annan was a reminder, like all the other daily reminders, that no matter how high we rise, that even if we get to be the Secretary-General of the United Nations (let alone a mere New Zealand MP), they can still just make a joke to put us back in our place.

How is that not identity politics?

*

During the 2017 election, I watched as a Māori woman told her story of being a solo mum on the benefit, forced to take twenty dollars here and there from people staying with her while she struggled to raise her baby on her own. She went on to put herself through law school. She became a politician. She led a political party for a decade, watching as the inequality she suffered ballooned. She told her story as the last weapon in her arsenal calling for change — as only one like her could. That woman was Metiria Turei, former co-leader of the Green Party.

It was moving to witness. It was the first time in a long time that a politician had spoken about poverty — not just 'child poverty', not the 'deserving' working poor, but the real depths of poverty New Zealanders were experiencing. She made welfare an election issue.

Metiria was savaged. Not only was her political work and message about poverty wholly obscured, not only was she painted a criminal and a cheat for what she admitted doing all those years ago, but a frenzied search began to uncover more, to malign her character with new petty exposés each day. Her attackers were right-wing shock jocks on talkback radio, but they were also journalists covering the election in every major media agency. The attacks were done overtly, but also by implication; questions were asked subtly about whether she could ever serve in Cabinet. Could a solo mum who couldn't survive on an income that we know is below the poverty line, who took extra help, raised her child and went to law school, became a politician, and told that story in a bid to eradicate poverty ever be trusted in Cabinet? That the question was asked, that no one bat an eyelid asking it — that hurt.

We knew then that we were never among friends. By 'we', I don't mean the Green Party, I mean the affected communities, the ones who knew instantly why Metiria's admission was the crime of the century — the poor, brown families; the solo mums and their kids living the reality of prejudice and poverty in this country. The harrowing wound of inequality and mass homelessness New Zealand was experiencing was somehow conveniently eclipsed by a Māori woman admitting she had struggled to feed her child without handouts.

It is obvious now, with the benefit of hindsight, that her announcement wasn't managed well. It could have been made clearer that she was not trying to normalise benefit fraud, though she was saying it is a reality and necessity for too many people already. Maybe we could have quantified what help she had received and paid it back beforehand. What she wanted to say was that it is near impossible for people to survive on the benefit without help, that we need to fix it so people don't need to lie.

The obsession turned to finding holes in her story. Had she mentioned she was getting help from family? Yes, I was there, she had stressed that point. But she used her ex-partner's address on the electoral roll! As a result, the Electoral Commission had to ask that people register at the most reliable address for receiving mail, because the witch hunt against Metiria made it a risk that those with frequent address changes, like students and beneficiaries, would stop registering to vote. The fact that the reality of life for beneficiaries was even a shock to anyone became part of the gaping wound she was trying to expose to begin with.

But the fact that a woman with her story got to raise her voice still matters. It mattered to me, as someone who grew up needing and receiving welfare support for a time. I think it shook the

Greens into speaking truth about poverty and compassion. The immediate aftermath of her speech put the party at our highest polling in history. It turns out New Zealanders want real talk. The politics of compassion was suddenly currency. That was identity politics, because politics at its best and most transformative comes from the untold experiences of those who carry the most oppressed of identities. It could have been the true riot of the unheard that we needed.

Still, I look at the vitriol, and the persistence of the viciousness that is a fact of my political life — dehumanising, threatening, and plainly racist:

'Wait until they are punching you in the head and have a knife to your throat.'

'You are the offspring of country shoppers.'

'Go back to where you came from and fix the problem there.'

'Terrorist-supporting tart.'

'Who breeds people like her?'

I know that it is important to combat the prejudice, to forge paths for others like me to follow. But in my most exhausted moments, especially after the rising security threats, I sometimes wonder if dealing with so much abuse is worth it. Then I take a deep breath and think about the last great win we had in parliament, the last warm welcome I received at a community event. It sometimes takes a minute, but the hate never can win.

As adults, if we're lucky and we live in a stable society without war or regular violence in our lives, we forget the visceral feeling of fear. I've felt it again only in this job. The fear for my physical safety. For my family's. I've moved across the world alone, learned to navigate new towns and villages, but walking out of Parliament

House at night is the only time I have felt scared, like a child walking into a darkened basement.

People often say politics is adversarial, that it involves growing a thicker skin. But surely not a thicker skin than the one you grow running criminal trials, or working from prisons or genocide courts far from home. Surely representation should feel safe and equal, no matter our gender, race or place of birth. For most first-time backbench MPs, politics does not involve mass abuse or fear of assassination. So why put myself through that?

Then I imagine the void. I think about the United States Congress without Ilhan Omar and Rashida Tlaib, the two first Muslim women to be elected; or without Sharice Davids and Deb Haaland, the very first indigenous women; or without Alexandria Ocasio-Cortez. Ilhan, a woman, Muslim, refugee, and lawmaker, receives the same kind of relentless scrutiny, abuse, and threats of harm as I do, on a scale befitting Trump's America. That our unapologetic sense of equality solicits such frenzied hate betrays the shocking novelty of our presence in the established power structures of democracy.

I remember Ilhan Omar's victory at state level. It happened with the Trump election. Her victory mattered for democracy, and it mattered to me personally. When we got to spend some time together in September 2019, we laughed about the wild accusations thrown at us and the uncanny parallels in our experiences. We doubled over talking about the persistent suspicion by right-wing trolls that we are both secret terrorists. How deeply incompetent we must be if that were true, how slow and confused, having chosen the hard road of joining progressive political movements and democratic election into Houses of Representatives. Then just waiting around, I guess, doing those jobs publicly.

But we spoke about our purpose too. The sense of solidarity was palpable in my chats with all the first-term congresswomen who now formed this group of 'firsts'. We are there to bring up issues we campaigned for, but also with our voices, as women, as community representatives, to move politics along to a place where it reflects the real makeup of people in our nations. It matters to people like us. For Muslim-Americans, it matters to see a visual representation of their faith, a woman wearing a hijab, engaged at the highest level of leadership in the so-called Free World. But it matters to any marginalised person, whose image is not reflected in those halls of power. To me, it mattered that Ilhan's family, like mine, had fled repression and mass violence. That she had lived through displacement.

For now, I get to sit in New Zealand Parliament, with a few other politicians who are also migrants of colour, with a few members of the rainbow community, a few more women than ever before. We bring our expertise, but we also bring our stories, our perspectives. Our being there means different things to different people. That we get to participate means something for democracy.

The challenge for those of us who are privileged enough to represent marginalised communities is the pressure to be well-behaved and grateful. We are allowed to be there at community celebrations, wearing our national costumes, garnering votes, always with a smile. We are allowed to talk about race, but only in the abstract, so it threatens no one specific. While racism exists, it would be far too aggressive to name the racists, whether human or institutional.

Just as the #MeToo movement found that women advocating for real change, baring their scars, and telling the gory truth will garner backlash in the very institutions we are trying to reform (and not just from thugs on the street or online), if we step out of the confines of what others define as polite discourse, we reap similar repercussions. Worse, we may lose well-meaning sympathisers who find our truths too uncomfortable. We become threatening. We become villains, undeserving of our voice. No wonder then that so many politicians become silent, toe the party lines, assimilate.

So I look to Ilhan Omar, who in a twist of fate entered politics at around the time that I did, to see history being made far more clearly than I see it in Trump's win. That's just a hitch, a sign that we can't get comfortable in formal democracy. A sign that we still have so much more work to do. It is a reminder that majority-rules democracy might at any moment swallow us whole if we don't take our seats at the decision-making table. I see the zeitgeist in global politics is representation, by loud and fiercely independent women. We have been jolted into participation. What is absolutely historic, what we have never seen before, is women of colour, taking our voice in politics.

Christchurch

The Christchurch mosque terror attacks happened only three weeks before I began to write this chapter, on Friday, 15 March 2019. It is still impossible to think about that day without fresh, crushing sorrow. It is the aching realisation that fifty-one human beings, from all walks of life, were murdered together because they were seen as an amorphous inhuman mass. They were seen as different.

For me, the realisation comes afresh each day. As you do after all of life's tragedies, you wake up each morning feeling normal for a minute, then you remember. There is unspeakable hurt in knowing that this happened here.

For those of us who know that we, too, are seen as 'different', the grief itself is different. It is the grief of knowing that our families, our foods and our skin colour are not normal enough. That we are not seen as human enough. We already knew we were not enough to be included in all sorts of ways in our daily lives. People told us that. They screamed it at us from cars, in the playground, online. They tore us down if we rose. But now that knowledge is inescapable. Now, we know they may also kill us. With the grief of the whole nation comes something else. For us, besides the grief, there is now a daily terror.

This was a tragedy that befell people who had already suffered, who were already a little isolated, already overcoming the challenges of rebuilding lives, reclaiming humanity, and feeling safe. It happened in a city that had already suffered unimaginable trauma. It happened here in Aotearoa, where, though the prejudice that underpinned it was known to different communities to different extents for centuries, the magnitude of carnage was a shock to us all.

We all felt its impact, right around the country. We all felt that heartache. But it is important to acknowledge that the target of the attack was a minority group, mostly targeted for their religion, but also because they were seen as outsiders, foreign, and unwelcome. It is that which hurt the affected communities most. Members of the Muslim community, the refugee community, migrants of colour and tangata whenua raised their voices in the aftermath of the attack, all as communities affected by prejudice. The hurt of being dehumanised for your innate difference is what this tragedy brought to light.

The images that marked our collective consciousness that day were of unthinkable violence. The medics described a river of blood. We know the weapons used were military-style semi-automatics, designed to maximise harm, both death and grotesque injury. We each remember certain victims' stories — those we heard first; those who reminded us of the children in our lives because of their ages, their smiles; those who made us think of our own grandparents; those who fought back; those who saved loved ones. The violence was immense and indiscriminate of youth or age, precisely because the murderer did not see his victims as individuals, as human enough. His purpose was to cause terror for the whole targeted community. And he has. It is that feeling of sorrow and very real fear that came flooding to me in messages from migrant and Muslim communities almost immediately after the news broke out.

For me, there was also an immediate sense of guilt. Survivor's guilt. I've seen those threats. Threats of gun violence; calls for me to be taken down, attacked, silenced, put in my place. Calls for rape. Calls for death. I've carried a panic alarm for half my life as an MP. I have fought back against the hate. I have called out racism. I have even highlighted it. I have sat in a place of privilege and relative power while I tore down the sad, angry haters online. I thought that was the right thing to do. I didn't realise that may be a call to arms.

Yes, I was scared sometimes. But as much as I knew the hate existed here, that it had risen up against me because I was different — suspected of being Muslim based on my race — I didn't see the carnage coming. When it did come, I wondered why it wasn't me. I thought maybe it *should* have been me. I had stuck my neck out. I was brazen. I wasn't content to be 'ethnic' quietly in the corner. It should have been me, because I am not a three-year-old little boy, I am not an elderly man finally living a restful life, I am not a newlywed looking to start my life in a city far away from violence. None of those victims had invited a clash with a racist terrorist, but maybe I had.

Living through this atrocity as a 'refugee MP' — a member of at least one affected, targeted community — very quickly felt like an existential crisis. I've been replaying it over and over in my mind in minute detail ever since. Part of the reason I keep repeating the minutiae of the day in my head is that the reactions of the people around me were so divergent and telling. Each minute was a moment in the history of this tragedy and a struggle to shape its legacy that is still being formed today.

I'm still trying hard to process the emotions of the day, but also the politics. At the time of writing, some of what I experienced that weekend remain live social issues, embodiments of the challenges and the changes we need to make at a macro level, as a nation. As a Green MP, I hold every portfolio that was immediately relevant to the attack: Justice, Police, Human Rights, Immigration and Refugees, Security and Intelligence. I was literally in a position to lead that work as a representative of a devastated community. But how does one person shift a tide of understanding? How does one even begin that work?

First, our institutions and leadership need to value community voices. That was already missing. That was why we as a nation missed the signs of danger.

The beginning and end of it for me was the community begging me for a voice, knowing that for the first time in our political history they had representation in their House of Representatives.

The first I knew of the terror attack was when I had stopped on Ponsonby Road for a coffee between work events. It was a gorgeous day and it was glorious to be home in Auckland for it. I was scrolling Twitter while the coffee arrived. The tweet I saw linked to an article that only talked about gunshots being fired at a mosque. It was shared by a friend who had recently moved back to New Zealand from London, saying she had come back 'to get away from this shit'. It took me a minute to consolidate her caption with the headline. I read it a few times over — 'a shooting in a mosque' — but … here. I scrolled through the article, silently pleading for there not to be any deaths. Maybe it was a scare tactic, or the terrorist was stopped before he could hurt anyone.

I knew it was a high-pressure day at our office. It was the day after our party co-leader James Shaw had been punched on the street in an unprovoked attack. It was also the day of the school climate strikes. Thousands of beautiful, hopeful, young people were striking all over New Zealand for action on climate change, and we were focused on supporting them.

Soon there was a second report and it confirmed ambulances at the scene. People *were* hurt. I needed to put out a message, as spokesperson on both the Justice and Human Rights portfolios, given it was fairly clear, no matter the extent of harm, that this was likely a hate crime aimed at the Muslim community.

As I began to interact with the bureaucracy of government and parliament that day, I realised that establishment institutions are not only ignorant of minority issues, they are actively resistant to engaging with them. I realised over the next hours and days that as women and minorities, our struggle to be heard, to have resources supporting our issues in politics, let alone our voices, is still very real. Representation does not come with the mere election of a 'representative'. This was still an institution peopled with those who did not understand the value of a marginalised community's voice, even when that community was under physical attack. If ever I was unsure that this is a live challenge in my work, that day it was made very clear.

The type of questions that came back over the day as I put a statement together, in solidarity with my community and with the victims, and in condemnation of the hate and terror, and fought to put it out were surprising. The bureaucracy didn't seem to get it. They wondered why I would comment on this, since politicians don't comment on every crime. Was I only interested because this happened in a mosque?

For me, the issue was one of ensuring the targeted community didn't feel alone. Just as we speak out loudly when the rainbow community is attacked, as we have done since the dehumanising attacks against the trans community became more organised in 2018, the cries of support and condemnation are vital in sustaining marginalised groups when they are under siege. I was surprised at the suggestion that I, in particular, may be biased in prioritising this issue, presumably because I share ethnic and refugee identity with some of the victim group. I would have thought that could only be a good thing, when a representative speaks.

Accustomed to explaining things to vexed institutions whose routine is interrupted with the inconvenient truth of minority perspectives, I explained what a hate crime is. I consciously kept my tone calm and a little, almost inappropriately, upbeat, to avoid being accused of being overemotional. I kept it technical. I started from the beginning, as we often must, to prove, again and again, that our issues exist and they matter. I said when crime targets a community based on their race, religion, gender, or some other discriminatory identifier, it is more serious than an ordinary crime. The victims extend beyond those directly affected, given the aim is to scare and demean that entire community. That made this a politicised crime, different than a usual act of individual violence.

It would be the same if a church or synagogue was targeted, indeed if a gay nightclub or women's space had been. 'This is likely an act of terror,' I said again and again that day, and it felt like words would form part of the battleground for some time.

It seemed like the extent of the tragedy was not really felt — maybe couldn't be felt — by anyone outside the targeted group. Thankfully, that feeling was very much quashed by night's end. The relief that came when we heard Prime Minister Jacinda Ardern say, so resolutely, that it *was* an act of terror was great. But at that moment, it felt like to 'them', this was any other day, while we were contending with how life would now be forever changed. Would hijabi women still feel safe enough to leave home with a head covering? Would young Sikh men be safe on the bus late at night? Would our grandparents be okay alone out there in their national dress? The effect of a shooting borne of xenophobia is immediate for the targeted people. We didn't need to wait for the body count to know this was a fork in the road. For me, it felt like the rest of New Zealand might just shrug and change the channel. It was important that we didn't, important that we never do. To listen to an affected community is to continue listening.

Still maintaining my surreal calm to accommodate the apparently unmoved world around me, I sat back down in front of my now-cold coffee.

Members of different affected groups began reaching out to me in droves. It was the Muslim community, but also a cross-section of the migrant communities who knew full well that we were all targets when the threat was white supremacy. Refugee groups were asking for details, asking how they could reach their people in Christchurch. It transpired in the wake of the attack that the

272

refugee community there had become isolated from institutional support since refugee resettlement services were wound up after the 2011 earthquake. They sent messages of love. They shared their fears. They wanted me to share our fears out there in public. I said I would as soon as I could. They asked for guidance from someone they saw in a position of power from their community. *How can we keep safe?* I didn't know, but I knew we needed to keep calm. With despair, people were saying, 'We were worried this would happen.' I began the work of responding with words of comfort. But their fears were real. I couldn't tell them otherwise. We affirmed each other. We shared our stories of the warning signs, in a safe space away from the public eye, where it still felt nothing much was wrong.

Then, news came that a second mosque had been attacked, at first passed on privately to me by messages from Jan Logie, who called me from Christchurch. She wanted me to know it was serious, but that we didn't have all the facts yet. She told me to brace myself. She asked me if I was okay.

As I was still staring at the phone in my hand, digesting the harrowing implications of those messages, I got another call from a friend in our office. He asked, 'Are you on your own?' He wanted me to call someone to come be with me, as more news was coming. He paused a lot during that call, trying to keep his voice steady. He was trying to negotiate a tone that was serious without causing me alarm. I realised he didn't want to tell me outright that I may be in danger or that this was going to get emotionally rough for me, but that's why he was calling.

Suddenly, more and more people were in touch to see if I was okay. Some staff, my friends, members of the public. It hadn't sunk in yet that I might be any more affected by the horror unfolding than anyone else sitting afar reading the news. But I quickly realised that people knew the threats I get. They had thought of me in part because they were scared for me. They saw me as a potential target of what might be a series of attacks. For now, that was a possibility I needed to push away.

I stepped outside onto the sunny Ponsonby sidewalk, among the Friday afternoon crowd avoiding work, laughing and chatting about the weekend. That morning, I had been writing the second chapter of this book about my childhood in Iran. I had been writing about the oppressions imposed by the Islamic regime. My mind raced through what I had been writing, searching for what might be taken as demeaning of Muslims as a group. I find it so hard to exhibit deference to any religion that it was very possible my words were capable of affirming general anti-Muslim sentiment. The Iranian experience of having religion forced upon us by a violent regime that purports to enforce Sharia makes it too easy to frame all opposition to that regime's brutality as opposition to Islam. As someone who can be seen as 'rescued' from her culture, it was important to me to give no fuel to that kind of prejudice.

I remembered Ayaan Hirsi Ali, the Dutch parliamentarian and former refugee, whose ongoing campaign for Islamic women's rights sometimes manifested in condemnation of the religion and its practitioners. That rhetoric often doesn't feel like it has the effect of lifting Muslim women to a place of gender equity, a movement they themselves are well capable of leading. Instead it validates hatred and exclusion, antithetical to lasting progress within any culture. For many years, she was the only refugee I knew who had risen to prominence in Western politics. For all those years, I wished she hadn't used her platform in a way that in part legitimised white nationalist rhetoric. Now I was in a position where I had to choose my words carefully, as a matter of fairness but also public safety.

Fifty-one innocent people had just been gunned down, far away from the 'Muslim world', because they were seen as representatives of a dark abyss that had become the portrayal of their culture. In fact, they represented very different cultures. Among the worshippers at each mosque were groups from Africa, Asia, and that ominous construct called 'the Middle East'. They practised their religion in diverse ways even within their small community. Some women wore the hijab, others didn't. Some were highly educated 'career women', while others were stay-at-home mums. Some men wore beards to express their faith, others didn't. It was words, images, and media headlines about 'jihadi brides', 'the War on Terror', and 'threats to our freedom', with no counterbalance, that had done this to them. Their real stories — of motherhood, of their research projects, of the young soccer star who coached women's football in the community — had not been told. Just as Anjum Rahman and others from the Islamic Women's Council, who had sounded the alarm about hate speech and hate crimes for the past five years, they had not been heard. The responsibility now was to humanise a vulnerable, targeted community. That is why I needed to speak.

Finally, I went back into the café, packed my things to leave. I closed my laptop. Looked back to see if I had everything. Very slowly, with the feeling that my mind may not be all there, I walked back out onto the bright footpath. The warm sunlight felt ill-matched to the emotions of the day, and I didn't get far on my walk home. I crouched down near a bus stop and put my face in my hands. The grief finally poured out.

I was near Prego, a bustling restaurant, and people finishing long boozy Friday lunches were spilling out onto the pavement. I could hear a group of women talking and smoking out front. It was a strange relief to find they were talking about the attack. One of them was in a panic, telling the others that her sister was in Christchurch. That the schools were under lockdown and she was trying to find out if everyone was okay. At least by now, people in Auckland were becoming aware. I realised I had been staring up at the women — probably somewhat unsettling coming from a crouched, weeping figure on the footpath. I got up and kept walking.

Guy got in touch to see where I was and said he was on his way home. I was walking down a side street to avoid freaking out the public again, and I could barely breathe. He told me to wait there for him, but I didn't want to stop walking.

By the time I got home, nine people were confirmed dead. Already, this was unthinkable.

Things changed markedly with the death toll. It was clear to me, and — thankfully — to our Prime Minister, that this was a devastating tragedy for Aotearoa. And she did say it.

My focus turned to keeping in close touch with others whose voices needed to be amplified. I knew some columnists would be going out with articles about the attack over the next day or two and I asked whether they could push for voices who were on social media speaking from that all-important lived experience. They were Muslim voices; women of colour speaking about the daily abuse; Māori, very quickly and astutely speaking about the thread of racial supremacy woven into the very foundation of our nation. It wasn't about blame, but if we didn't hear those voices now, we were in real danger of ignoring them forever as the narrative of this atrocity solidified. It would be a lost opportunity for essential change. It felt unbearably urgent.

My solace came by way of a phone call from Marama. I had been calling her all afternoon, but she had been in meetings. I didn't want to call James, given he was in hospital coping with his own violent assault. Marama's voice was out of breath,

She said, 'Wherever you are right now, I will come to you and we will record a video message together and we will post it tonight on our own channels. I promise you, you will get to speak.' The relief I felt was profound and I started crying again. She got it.

We huddled around the kitchen table at Ricardo's house, a halfway point between my and Marama's houses in South Auckland. Marama wanted to speak as tangata whenua, as an indigenous woman both inherently understanding racism and able to welcome migrants now experiencing that prejudice into her ancestral homeland. In fact, the connection between Māori and migrants of colour would be strengthened exponentially in the coming days. The point would be made again and again that colonisation was the start of white supremacy here. An iteration of that old ideology had killed the mosque victims, but it was a continuum of the systematic racism that decimated Māori first.

I was angry by then, on behalf of a community who *had* tried to raise the alarm. In different ways. we *had* tried to have those hard conversations about the rise of violent racism. I knew that hate had been allowed to fester and grow, because it was too uncomfortable to talk about racism and extremism while some of us lived it.

I remembered making the hate speech video in response to Lauren Southern and Stefan Molyneux's New Zealand speaking tour six months before, asking that we de-platform white nationalism. We weren't talking about locking anyone up, just asking that the words which call our humanity to question maybe shouldn't be put on national TV and mic-ed up in town halls. That was because famous racists were coming here. It was a global phenomenon and we were clearly not immune. I remembered the absolute barrage of abuse that came with it. It came from around the world. It was organised.

I remembered my maiden speech telling the House that every time politicians and media personalities scapegoated minorities, we felt that hate out in the streets. I told them then, eighteen months ago, about the calls for gun violence against me as a refugee, assumed Muslim. The narrative of racism and hate speech that underpinned this atrocity could not be lost.

But I also knew that — on that night — I needed to signal it gently, because this was a time for grief.

One thing I knew I had to do, from the very start — what I had been fighting for all day — was to call this an act of terror borne of white supremacy. Words were important. The grief of that day became part of years-long grief at our dehumanisation, which came with our portrayal as terrorists. That word 'terrorist' was central to our suffering as Middle Easterners, as anyone of a race or region suspected of being Muslim, and in particular for the Muslim community across the globe. I hadn't heard the word 'terrorist' used to describe the attacker yet that day. It needed to be said, because it was the truth.

When we are the victims of bombs that decimate entire cities, when our wedding parties are massacred, when a generation of our children are maimed, those acts are almost never described as 'terror'. Mass murder in the West by Westerners — like the shootings in public places and schools in the United States — has rarely been recognised as terror. Shootings by white supremacists at synagogues, at gay clubs, are not charged as terror by police. The very real and ongoing lived horrors of colonisation of indigenous peoples — from mass incarceration to the forcible removal of generations of children from their families — is not counted as terror. In fact, just about every mainstream Western war film focuses on the humanising stories of an invading force, unless that film is about World War II. Where are the films about the young Vietnamese lives ripped apart, their friendships destroyed by war? Where are the stories of complex Iraqi or Afghani lives, filled with individual personalities, hopes, and dreams, ripped apart by US–European invasion? None of these phenomena are as universally and clearly condemned as to warrant the instant use of the word 'terror'. That matters.

The weight of that label is not just rhetoric to me, to us, because it is the very vehicle that delivers and justifies violence against us, and did so on 15 March 2019. To unashamedly call a Pākehā man a 'terrorist' when he commits a quintessential act of terror is only fair. It is one way to move forward toward a world where Muslim lives matter. Aotearoa did that, but at that moment we weren't sure if it would happen yet.

The video was done in a few minutes. We sat on the grass in Ricardo's backyard in the last of the waning sun. We sent love to the victims and acknowledged that there was a broader community deliberately terrorised by this act of violence. I noted the fear, pain, and valid anger being felt by those affected and ended by promising that we would have the hard conversations arising from what had befallen our nation that day.

Putting out that statement seems trivial now, but to us it was everything. It was the start of a series of statements we made off the mainstream grid that weekend.

From Ricardo's, I went to the offices of a radio station covering the shootings. I had been called in to do an interview about the attack. The interview never happened, but, as I waited, sitting in the middle of the newsroom facing a huge TV screen, the broadcast team came to a standstill for our Prime Minister's first press conference since the attack. I remember that speech so vividly that I still relive moments from it at will.

I remember when she first uttered the death toll. It was palpably difficult for her to utter that number. None of us knew it yet. The Prime Minister said the word 'forty-nine'. The number would rise to fifty the next day and fifty-one in the following weeks. A deluge of hot tears silently poured down my cheeks. Each breath was a struggle to take. People started taking notes for stories with wild urgency. They were screaming facts. 'Three are arrested?' 'He's definitely from Australia?' 'How many did she say were injured?'

Then back to silence, and the Prime Minister spoke the word 'terror'. That signalled a thoughtful government response. That showed it was already different than the darkly comedic response to mass shootings we would usually have heard by now elsewhere. That was a good moment.

She also said, from the very first statement, with defiance, 'I tell you now, our gun laws are going to change.' We didn't know it yet, but that would be a uniting call in our parliament and across New

Zealand. Within five days, a seventy-thousand-strong petition was presented on parliament's steps, calling on us to ban military-style semi-automatics. A small group of us in the Green caucus, me as Justice portfolio holder, together with our ministers James Shaw and Eugenie Sage, and Chlöe Swarbrick who went on to the special select committee for gun law reform, pored over the urgent cabinet papers that came through in the week that followed. Our political team were sending analyses late into the night as we all processed the technical information on guns we never had prior cause to know. In twenty-three days, we passed the first of the gun-control laws banning most military-style semi-automatics, as the world cheered us on. Another moment of lasting good.

But on the night, the defining message of our Prime Minister's statement, for most people watching, was all in the line in reference to the victims of the terror attack, 'They are us.' Those were the operative words that kept the country calm. It signalled the unity we would at least strive to live by in the wake of that attack. That soon proved a challenge.

In the immediate hours and days after the initial message from the Prime Minister, it was apparent that her words were received differently by different communities. From communities of colour (and those who work more broadly on race equity), there was fear that in reassuring the nation that the act of terror 'is not us', the message would allow us to move on without deeper reflection. The status quo would feel absolved. They would take from the message what they needed, an identity disassociated from whatever underpinned the extremist attack. We would get to write off the terrorist as Australian. The cause of violence, like its human instrument, was and is to some extent, even now, pitched as entirely foreign. Within that narrative, all New Zealanders, not just the targeted community, were victims. But if racism and Islamophobia drove the terrorist, that simplistic takeaway was disturbing to the communities living the everyday reality of those ideologies in New Zealand. It was a problem if we let that continue.

In those first hours and in her position as Prime Minister, Jacinda couldn't add the complexity of racism and xenophobia to her message. There were grave and very live security threats to consider. The uncomfortable truths were too much to process all at once in the context of already unthinkable violence.

My dad, who sank into a distressed state that weekend, found great comfort in the Prime Minister's message. He saw it as one that would guard against reprisal acts. Like my dad, many in the broader targeted communities — including migrants of colour across the ethnic spectrum — did want to move forward with a uniting message, without raising deeper issues, without showing anger, lest we be blamed somehow for the violence. They were grateful for the invite, finally, to be included in the society they were already part of. This was a contrast to the activist voices in those same communities, but it was the response from a significant segment, the silent majority within our groups.

It was what came in mainstream media soon after Jacinda's words, prioritising Pākehā commentators, that risked erasing the real causes of this attack. Apart from the immediate terror victims speaking to their victimhood, the voices with mass media platforms were only expressing shock that it had happened at all. The narrative of shock was scary, because we had heard it before. 'New Zealand is not racist' was a powerful identity point that erased our experiences of daily racism in order to comfort the status quo. Of course, there was no need to say that New Zealand *is* racist, only to hear that racism exists here and must be fixed to keep us safe. For that, we needed the truth and the details of our experiences to be included in the dominant narrative. I know that acknowledging the existence of societal racism — and indeed white supremacy — within our community and history is difficult. Pākehā may feel attacked by the truth, that this terrorist was driven in part to protect their supremacy, at least was militarised by the belief in that supremacy. It didn't for a minute mean they were responsible for the attack, but might mean a need to actively dismantle the belief system that had allowed it. It might mean they shouldn't have made that joke about the 'towel heads'. It might mean they shouldn't have listened to their favourite shock jock scream each morning about refugee criminals or immigrants in Kmart not looking like 'Kiwis'. I believe we can be jolted to that point of change, which had to begin by making space for the affected community's voices to detail their own plight, frame their own tragedy.

The night of the attacks, after Jacinda's press conference, I sat waiting for an hour or so in the radio offices, listening as regional and local politicians and MPs from across the political spectrum made comment, all Pākehā. Each expressed shock. Some said they didn't believe white nationalism or even racism existed in Christchurch. It was breathtaking to hear that local Pākehā politicians were unaware of the issue on the night of a mass targeted killing of Muslim migrants.

As the programme moved on to interviewing a transport blogger who was being asked to comment on a loud noise heard in downtown Auckland, I knew I had been well and truly bumped. I also knew I had a group of friends — all women of colour — distraught and desperate for support, waiting for me in the backyard at the restaurant Coco's Cantina. I excused myself and said I was available anytime by phone. That phone call never came.

I walked into Coco's, fell into Ghazaleh's arms. Our group talked and cried for hours. We retold our stories of degradation and race attacks throughout our childhoods, in academia, in our relationships. We talked about the responses of the media. We talked about getting our voices out. I told them what had happened to me that day. Did representation mean much if we weren't seen or heard? Was my election a meaningless token? It felt suffocating, but at least we had this safe space. A space to be sad, but also angry and critical without fear of being marked too emotional, too demanding.

The following day, voices within migrant communities went to work on social media, amending the narrative to include mentions of white supremacy. A strong chorus of Māori voices also immediately rose to chronicle race-based violence in present-day New Zealand, directly connected with the brutality of our colonial past.

The narrative of denial centred around the needs of the status quo, which minority communities were well versed in servicing. That is why the largely silent majorities within our communities, our elders, were most comfortable just falling in line. They had learned long ago that avoiding disunity, which they saw as a threat to our safety, was better than fighting for equality. But the catalyst of the mosque massacres meant that others within those communities, joined by tangata whenua, would not be silenced.

As always, it wasn't that the marginalised were voiceless. It was sadly that, even in this moment, they remained largely excluded from mainstream broadcasts.

On Saturday, the day after the atrocity, we gathered at the mass vigil in Auckland. I didn't have a speech prepared, nor did I have any messaging notes from Wellington, but I was ready to speak.

The vigil was truly life-affirming. All of us there will remember it for the rest of our lives. We will be forever grateful to have had each other, grateful to the thousands of strangers who came just to wrap our arms around each other across our grieving nation. We were alive and filled with love, and — away from social media and the loudest voices on the airways — we were good.

It was the most densely packed gathering I had ever seen in Aotea Square, which quickly proved far too small to hold the thousands pouring in. People spilled over onto Queen Street and down the side lanes of the Town Hall. The sun beat down fiercely over the full two hours. We all sat at attention, packing in tighter as yet more people arrived. The communal sorrow fused with so much deep, genuine love was laid bare. It meant everything. It is what we all carry with us still.

We listened first to powerful, emotional speeches from migrant women, an elderly Hindu gentleman who had lost a lifelong Muslim friend in the terror attack, then a dozen politicians from across parliament and Auckland Council. As I waited my turn, I realised only Mayor Phil Goff had mentioned racism by name. He had banned racists from speaking in Auckland's public venues the previous year, citing the measure as a public safety necessity, and felt rightly vindicated. Other politicians, the parliamentarians, didn't touch it. They spoke of grief and unity. It certainly was exceptional to have representatives from both Labour and National parties there together speaking of unity. But the political speeches stood in contrast to the initial words of the ethnic community leaders. Those leaders spoke of the change they needed to feel safe. They *called* for unity rather than declared it. If they celebrated unity, it was the unity coming about now, with the commitment by the people on the ground, to change. It was unity that was possible now because we had come together to name the dark problems, and to solve them. But first we did have to name them.

Marama and I spoke last of all the political speakers. We went onto the stage together, and Marama spoke first, while I stood behind her. She is always an impassioned speaker in front of crowds and in protests. She spoke as tangata whenua sending love and manaakitanga to the Muslim and migrant communities, and in that short speech touched on some dark complex issues about security and identity. She said:

Manaaki and tika — caring for each other in a way that is just and right is what we should be upholding with every inch of ourselves. Upholding my mana, my dignity, is connected to upholding your mana, your dignity …

We will not minimalise this racism and bigotry. We will not ignore that you, your sons and daughters, have been the targets of our surveillance rather than our protection.

We will connect the dots so that people understand that we have to own our nation's historic and modern racism and violence. We will continue having the hard conversations. We will continue to hold up your loving, peaceful families and communities for who you really are. We will continue to celebrate your histories and your stories. We will grieve not just because you are one of us, but because you are you.

She was the first to recall that security agencies, who the Prime Minister had already signalled had failed to monitor the likes of the Christchurch terrorist, had been spying on Māori and Muslims in New Zealand for years. Her words were rousing. The crowd applause felt different than that received by the speakers before her.

It was now my turn. I felt a sense of calm that came with finally having the space to speak. Looking over the crowd, only then did I realise how vast we were as a group. I was angry and I didn't mask it. My arms were either spread open or on my hips for much of my speech, though those aren't natural gestures for me. I was speaking with a voice I had never heard myself use, and without inhibition. It felt like my work had all been building to this.

This is what I said, without the pauses for tears, the audible anger, the aching grief:

E nga mana, e nga reo, e nga karangatanga maha. Tena tatou katoa.

Our nation's heart is broken. My heart is broken today.

But from the bottom of my Kiwi, refugee, migrant heart, I want to thank you. Thank you for being on the right side of history today. It matters. It matters to our community.

We are hurt. We are in shock. And we are scared.

They want us dead. Our nanas, our granddads, our mums and dads, our little kids. We learned that on Friday for sure, but, for some of us, that hate that led to the violence yesterday in Christchurch, we've felt it out there on the street for years.

That hate … that isn't the New Zealand that welcomed me, but it is New Zealand today. It's part of who we are, and we have to fix that, starting by acknowledging that we have to fix it.

We owe them the truth. This was terrorism. It was an act of terror. And it was an act of terror committed by white supremacists. It was an act of terror that had been planned for some time by white supremacists. The killer had the words 'UN Migration Compact' written on his gun.

I know that every time I walk into a room or onto the stage, I do that as a refugee, as the first refugee MP in New Zealand, as a woman of colour, as a woman from the so-called 'Muslim world'.

From the moment I said I was going to stand as a candidate, from the moment I said I might be someone who might deserve to take part in the democracy here, I've been receiving the hate and violence online. I remember that they said, 'It's time to load our shotguns' when I announced my candidacy.

I receive all of your love. I do. And it helps so much, but I do want to acknowledge that there's also the hate and it always has been there. I said it in my maiden speech and I want to say it again here today. We have to hold people to account. From the trolls on the internet, right up to the people who sit in the House of Representatives with me, or on our TV screens. Every time they use the politics of hate and division and xenophobia, we have to hold them to account.

Because we feel it out there on the street. We can't shed our skin, so they have to stop and we have to stop them.

Every time they weaponise the concept of 'free speech' to lie about us, to scapegoat us, we know where that ends. We learned it on Friday, and history has shown us time and again how atrocity begins with cheap opportunistic hate speech against minorities. It has to stop in New Zealand, now.

I do want to say that the fact that you are all here today makes me believe that we will stop them. The fact that you are here today speaks to the strength and the goodness of New Zealand's values. I thank you.

I walked down from that makeshift stage to a flood of warm hugs and tears and shared truths. It took a long time for us to leave, even after all the other speeches were done and the vigil was over. There were so many conversations and embraces to share.

What made the words unstoppable was the rage emerging beneath my grief, which for me came from knowing that politicians — my colleagues — had also fuelled what came to pass that Friday. Rumours had emerged about the words 'UN Migration Compact' on the terrorist's gun. The debate about the innocuous UN Migration Compact had been cynically waged in the months leading to the attack. This was a non-binding agreement between nations to cooperate in devising strategies to address global migration, including to acknowledge the vulnerabilities of migrants and uphold their human rights. The Compact opens by reaffirming the sovereignty of every state party, and preserves their right to formulate national immigration policy.

A coordinated campaign of fear and conspiracy theories about the Compact was started online by European right-wing extremists, described by New Zealand's own security agencies as 'neo-Nazi' groups. They spread deliberate mistruths that the Compact would mean open borders and that the UN would set our immigration numbers, and often shared fake-news stories of violence and chaos caused by migrants. In New Zealand, as in other nations, sadly, these mistruths were picked up and pushed hard by mainstream politicians. It is impossible to say with certainty whether National Party MPs sharing those lines were ever aware of its origin in neo-Nazi propaganda, or if they read the Compact's opening affirmation of state sovereignty over immigration policy, or indeed if they knew the difference between binding and non-binding UN instruments. But we know that politicians have a duty of care. We must all admit that when we rile fear about migration and affirm xenophobia, the most visible migrant communities, migrants of colour, pay for our political gains. This time, they paid with their lives. I could not, and will not, leave that unsaid.

The days that followed were a haze of gathering in different places to speak and hold people. What was extraordinary was that, through this tragedy, so many of us across the nation, for the first time in a long time, maybe ever, felt the same things at the same time. It may have been hard before to imagine the pain that comes with being subject to racism, but I think there was a bond formed in that shared grief, which gives us a little more understanding about each other's experiences. It's what will give us the impetus to stand up against the hate even when we are not the immediate victims. Because now, we know the hurt as a nation.

Then parliament sat. Something truly incredible happened. An interfaith group of religious leaders walked in with the Speaker. They were representatives of the Islamic, Jewish, Buddhist, Sikh, Hindu, Rātana, Catholic, Anglican and Presbyterian faiths and churches. The visual spectacle of their robes and adornments would ordinarily be an uncomfortable sight in that secular place of law making. I flinched for a moment with my deep-seated allergy to mixing religion in state apparatus. But on that day, I was overwhelmed with gratitude that we as a House were strong enough to bring our communities together in that breathtaking act of unity in the face of prejudice. In fact, to open the session a traditional Islamic prayer was first delivered by the imam Nizam ul haq Thanvi. I hadn't heard it in so long. I stood weeping, for everything it meant to the victims who gathered together to hear it last Friday, for everything it had meant in Iran, because a violent regime had perverted it. It was meaningful as an opening of the doors of our House of Representatives to New Zealand's Muslim community, so excluded from mainstream institutions such as this that there was no Muslim MP among us to help with the preparations when the Speaker had inquired. So I wept again, in public, at work, uncontrollably. That prayer was followed by our usual parliamentary prayer delivered first in te reo Māori by Labour MP and Assistant Speaker Adrian Rurawhe and then in English by National MP and Deputy Speaker Anne Tolley.

That day I finally got to thank the Prime Minister, through tears, for her leadership when the House rose that day. We hugged, shaking a little, and I passed on my dad's words of thanks. It meant a lot to me personally that my little distressed dad at home had found so much solace in her words.

The work ahead for me, from that day on, has been to hold people to account for riling hate against minorities.

I wrote to the Police Minister Stuart Nash, asking for police training material on unconscious racial bias. We had already talked a lot about the need to overcome race bias in policing as it applies to Māori and Pasifika peoples, as it was something I had worked on as a lawyer in the only case ever where the Court of Appeal found racial bias in search and seizure. It was time to ensure white supremacist extremism was firmly on the agenda in law enforcement.

I also wrote to the Minister of Justice Andrew Little, who happens to hold responsibility for security and intelligence agencies, asking for the same, and to meet. I wanted to renew my call for a review of our hate speech laws, which had been recommended by the Human Rights Commission in 2016. He was still in the immediate aftermath of the atrocity and — like me — held most of the relevant portfolios facing reform. Still, he made the time to meet, and we did so shortly afterward. I told him that as much I believe implementing hate-speech protections is necessary — in fact, it had been a central focus of my work for at least a year — I didn't want to lead on it.

The truth is, I was scared. I knew now that this would be a call to arms for all the usual groups, the ones that felt white supremacy was worth defending. I knew what vile abuse would pour out. It had done so in 2018 when I first began speaking out about the dangers of targeted hate speech. Even the experts from the

Human Rights Commission who had authored the 2016 paper calling for the review became the target of online abuse. They had their identities revealed by so-called 'free speech' campaigners in right-wing blogs, whose readers then launched threats against them. These were the same blogs, the same abusers, that attacked me daily.

Andrew listened and reassured me that he intended to lead on that work. A review was underway, being conducted by the Human Rights Commission and the Ministry of Justice. I couldn't express the relief in knowing I didn't have to do this alone, because I wouldn't have been safe.

Then the minister, in a low voice tinged with something betraying sadness, said, 'I realise with the privilege that comes with being a Pākehā man, maybe I have tolerated far too much on behalf of other people who were harmed by [hate speech].'

In the end, it didn't matter that the minister, the Ministry of Justice, and the Human Rights Commission were leading this work. I did become a target. I was the only one called 'a threat to freedom in this country' by an alt-right politician. The message apparently sounds different and deserving of extremist reactions when the messenger is a refugee girl.

I remain scared for myself and my family, precisely because I believe hate speech is a weapon that leads to very real violence against people like me. I remember Jo Cox. I remember her every day. I remember that she was killed while politicians deliberately fanned the flames of hate for votes. Hysteria soared. Red-faced and angry, people shook fists, and yelled obscenities. White nationalism took over mainstream life in Britain. They scapegoated a terrified, marginalised community, my community. Jo Cox was killed because she sat with us. Her battle cry was to find commonality. She was killed for her solidarity.

I am scared because the rhetoric of Brexit, the rise of nationalism in Europe, and Trump screeching alarms against migrant hordes — or 'animals', as he calls us — at the border has already leeched into the dark corners of New Zealand's own racist underbelly. Every Muslim woman walking down the street in a hijab feels that fear. Every Sikh dad dropping his kids at school in the wake of the Christchurch attack knows they may be targets for even looking Muslim.

So I clutch my panic button. Double check that it's charged. I pause when I leave the house. Pause before I walk out into the dark, cool night air as I leave parliament. Pause each time I step out onto a podium. I scan the audience for anyone who looks out of place, for lone men, for bulges under jackets. I don't want to feel this way and I try to push those thoughts away. Sometimes, it's impossible to look away from the hate when it is aimed at you. It's impossible to forget that people don't want us — want *me* — here. They hate me because of my story, because of that dazed journey out of Iran, because of the violent Islamic regime I was born under, because of the war funded by the US. We are different. Because of our delicious aromatic foods, because of our dark brows and black hair, because my first language is the ancient, strange Farsi. They don't want us here. They don't care that I am not Muslim, any more than the terrorist cared whether the Muslim victims of his rage were ever a threat to him or his 'way of life'. They weren't. This is about race and xenophobia.

The challenge for New Zealand, now that we know what dangerous prejudice lurks in the shadows of our beautiful island nation, is to be brave.

We have newly committed to unity and equality. Now, we must acknowledge some hard truths. We need to hear and accept the hurt of the dispossessed without judgement. The marginalised can't do it alone. We need everyone to listen to the lived experience of systemic unfairness, of abuse, without the urge to absolve ourselves of blame. Then, we need to actively change what needs to be changed to make our world fair. If that means regulating hate speech to protect the rights of us all to engage freely in discourse, to protect free speech itself, that is a hard and complex conversation we can have together.

For me, beyond legal change sits cultural change. It comes with naming what and who needs to be named, then imagining a world where that prejudice holds no power. This means making space at our decision-making tables, in our Houses of Representatives, for those who are not yet represented equally, whether women or other historically marginalised groups. It means changing the structures that allow discrimination wherever they occur — in media, academics, politics, or science. It means resourcing and prioritising our participation and representation at every level of those institutions. Extinguishing prejudice means we get to tell our own stories in the media and in arts. We get to be journalists, screenwriters, directors, and funding managers, in every arena of that portrayal, rather than only 'diverse characters' where others allow us in. It means we are the researchers, determining the terms of study, designing programmes, teaching courses across every area of study. It means we stand and win seats in elections, at every level of governance, public and corporate. More than that, it means political parties and movements prioritise our participation at the grassroots, in their campaign committees, in their executives, as fundraisers and staff in equal shares, so that politics is geared to reaching and serving our people equally. We need to change the way politics, business, and every institute of power is shaped because diversity is how good decisions are made to begin with.

As the ever-wise Moana Jackson said, 'Nothing is ever unchangeable.' We have never, in our nation's living memory, existed without systemic racism and prejudice, but we are capable of doing so. As Iranians continue to protest for democracy, as women and minorities the world over continue to fight against millennia of oppression, we will fight for what we have never seen but know is possible. As the most marginalised people, women from migrant, refugee, and indigenous backgrounds, rise to positions of power for the very first time, I think a revolution is already underway. I believe Aotearoa can sit at the forefront of that change, because I have already seen so much good in our nation's core. This is already a place where a nine-year-old girl, a refugee, from the so-called 'Muslim world', can grow up to one day enter parliament. That means a lot at this moment in global politics.

I took seriously the responsibility to speak in parliament, once I could, for the first time after one of the worst acts of race violence in living memory, our first deadly act of Islamophobic terror. This was my speech to the House on 20 March 2019, calling for a different kind of politics:

A-salaam-alaikum.
Our nation's heart is broken. My heart is broken today.
Five days on, as the wound is still fresh, as it is still bleeding, we have comfort in all the love, all over our country. As we wrapped our arms around the survivors at

mosques, gathered and held each other at vigils, held our little ones a little tighter as we remembered that little Mucad Ibrahim at three years old was one of the victims on Friday.

The city of Dunedin ran out of flowers on Saturday. They were all at the mosque.

That is the New Zealand which welcomed me and my family when we fled oppression, the risk of torture, after we had lived through war. I will never forget that love as a nine-year-old girl coming down that escalator in Auckland Airport with my frightened parents.

And I want to thank every single New Zealander who held true to our values of love and inclusion this week. You are on the right side of history. It matters to our frightened communities.

I will never forget that a Syrian refugee family were among the victims of this terror attack. Like my family, they escaped the unthinkable and found freedom here. They came here to be safe. They died in Christchurch, New Zealand.

We owe those victims the truth. This was terrorism. It was committed by white supremacists. Planned at length without police interference. Because white supremacy was not seen as a pressing threat, though the Muslim victims had been.

The gun he used had the words 'UN Migration Compact' written on the butt — next to the chilling 'Welcome to hell, refugees'.

Although the man who committed the terror happened not to be born here, the ideology that lead to this atrocity existed here … the communities have been telling us it exists for years. They say they have reported hate crimes for years.

I know it as my daily truth, as a politician perceived to be Muslim, known to be a refugee. I've spoken about the threats I receive, of gun violence, death threats, calls for shotguns to be loaded. Every minority in New Zealand knows this truth. We have to stop and listen to them. We can't afford to turn a blind eye. We can't pretend this was an aberration from Australia. That would be irresponsible.

The truth is that this is a global phenomenon.

It began with hate speech, allowed to spread here online. We know that hate speech begets atrocity and we are behind in protecting against that.

The truth is that we, as politicians — and I mean on both sides of this House — are also responsible.

There sit among us those who have for years fanned the flames of division in here and out there. Blamed migrants for our housing crisis. There sit among us here those who deliberately spread hysteria about the UN Migration Compact.

We've pandered to the gratuitous racism by shock jocks on breakfast TV to raise our own profiles.

No one here is directly responsible for what happened in Christchurch. We are all horrified. But we are now all on notice. We have to change the way we do politics here.

Our most vulnerable communities are hurt. We are scared. They want us dead.

The people at those incredible vigils are watching. They will hold us to account. Their acts of love, their resolve, is the standard we have to hold ourselves to from now on.

The world is watching. We have to get this right. We have to demonstrate to the rest of the world that love, peace, and compassion is a far stronger force than the forces of hate and division. We must be brave as we have the hard conversations we need to have as a country. We must shine the light into the shadows of racism and hatred that exist in pockets of our society. We must weave the incredible outpouring of love for our Muslim and migrant communities that we have seen over the last few days into the enduring fabric of our society.

We have to do this for all the families who have had the lives of loved ones taken from them. We have to do this for little Muscad Ibrahim.

Kia hora te marino.
May peace be widespread.
Kia whakapapa pounamu te moana.
May the ocean become like pounamu.
Aroha atu, aroha mai.
Give love, receive love.
Tātou ia tātou katoa.
Let us show respect for one another.

Forging paths

On 14 November 2019, quietly and without fanfare, a small group made up of human rights activists, literary folk, and just two journalists came together at Auckland Airport to welcome Behrouz Boochani to freedom. For more than six years, the Iranian Kurdish journalist and author had been the voice of asylum seekers imprisoned on Manus Island, becoming the persistent conscience of us all as we learned of the atrocities committed by the Australian Government on its remote Pacific island prisons.

We waited a tense, giddy, agonising hour after his flight had landed until he finally walked into the arrivals lounge. Throughout the wait, we held back tears and spontaneously held each other. None of us had met Behrouz in the flesh before then, but we were all deeply connected with his plight. He was our ally, as we were his. So intertwined are the struggles for equality, for peace, for inclusion in global politics today that we knew Behrouz's fight for freedom was essential to our own.

That night, as we finally met our exhausted, elated friend, the world felt a little freer, a little fairer, and a little more hopeful. Once again, Aotearoa New Zealand got to stand as a counterpoint to the politics of hate and division on the rise elsewhere in the world.

What made the wait at Auckland Airport exceptional for me was the memory of my own walk through that arrival hall as a child with my asylum-seeker parents. My own deeply political, Kurdish mother, and my socialist dad. We had arrived in a nation that recognised our humanity and afforded us a legal process where we could prove our persecution. We were treated as equals, because inherent in the right to claim asylum is the acknowledgement that no one deserves to live with the risk of torture or violence. For all the hurt of growing up alien, some of which drives my life's work for equality, at least I got to grow up free. I was free from that arrival onward from the oppression that Iranians of my generation lived and breathed daily, the oppression they resisted. I escaped that world, while Behrouz grew up in it. He paid a high price for holding on to his humanity under a brutal regime.

'They call us "the scorched generation"; did you know that?' Behrouz told me as we swapped notes about our childhood in that first decade of the Islamic Republic, sitting in the uncanny calm of a sunny courtyard in Christchurch, New Zealand. 'We are the first Iranian generation with no living memory of freedom.' I had never heard that before.

A few days later, my friend Tayyaba Khan told me a Wellington taxi driver had asked her if she was a Member of Parliament. Tayyaba, a community leader and rights campaigner, had emerged as one of the unwavering Muslim voices setting the narrative in the wake of the Christchurch terror attacks. When she asked the driver why he thought she was an MP, he showed her my card. He had given me a ride recently, so he thought she could also be one of those 'young Green MPs'. Tayyaba beams as she retells this anecdote. 'We are normalising diversity. Age, colour, sexuality.'

I realise this must be a warm feeling of triumph felt by women MPs as they put our gender slowly into a different perspective with their mere presence.

There is another anecdote Tayyaba recounts when we talk through the dark side of being a 'first'. This one was passed on to her by an older Pākehā feminist. As Tayyaba tells it, 'Apparently there was controversy in their movement about how hard and how fast some leaders wanted to push for change in the 1970s. At one heated meeting, a nun suddenly stood up and said, 'But some will have to run, so others can walk.''

For us, as outsiders, it proves what we have always known: that by becoming visible in public life, we shape the picture of who looks like a leader, not only within our communities but in broader society and the world.

More than that, we bring our stories, together with our faces, into focus. So, eventually the change is in the humanity with which the world treats minorities and marginalised peoples.

That is the enduring value of voices like that of Behrouz Boochani, who fought long and hard to bring humanity to the way we portray refugee stories. Only then might we all stop and challenge the way governments, our allies, are allowed to treat people fleeing oppression or violence. We need to see refugees as they are: individuals with values, hopes, and dreams, like our own. People fleeing war and persecution have also had birthday parties, created works of art, protested as student unionists, authored award-winning books, like Behrouz. They — we — are complex and diverse. We are all capable of life beyond victimhood.

Before Behrouz took up the task of speaking truth to infinitely brutal power, before his striking image and extraordinary writing brought to light the suffering of detained 'boat people', he was an avid journalist fighting for Kurdish rights under the watchful eye of the Islamic Republic of Iran. As the risk of torture and disappearance became too much, he fled for safety. He was twenty-eight years old.

That backstory may now seem like a footnote, as most refugee and asylum-seeker stories seem to become once we are perceived through the reductive prism of our displacement. We are seen as faceless hoards, victims, or 'queue jumpers'.

How poignant that Christchurch, the city he describes as 'teaching the world kindness' in the wake of a terror attack in part driven by hatred of refugees, is the place to give Behrouz Boochani his freedom. And how perfect that he used the first opportunity to speak with that newfound freedom to remind us that hundreds still languish in Australia's inhumane detention camps. He called upon us to use our freedom to end their torture too.

He said it was the first time he could think of himself as a 'survivor' of Manus Island. During the 2269 days of unlawful detention, in conditions described by the United Nations and Amnesty International as amounting to torture, he knew he may not make it. He began to write his accounts of the prison camp early, but didn't feel safe enough to identify himself as the author until he had established support networks outside of the island. It was the journalists, civil society organisers, and ordinary people connecting with his stories, who used their freedom to give him his voice. That movement made it safe enough for him to speak as himself. It is that movement that we will keep building.

My politics will always be more about securing both nature and human rights from the greed and wanton growth of our broken economic system. Real democracy itself is dependent on that. As a legislator and Member of our House of Representatives, I will keep drawing from my work in justice institutions, from constitutional and human rights law practice, from all those hours writing reports and submissions to hold governments to account. My politics will not be limited to fighting for refugees and migrants, nor even to race equality. But I know now the value of active, substantive representation when it comes to speaking on any crucial issue.

That means now, more than ever, is the time for activism.

So, I look to Ilhan Omar. I look to the climate movement pounding forward with endless fervour, knowing that indigenous voices were its inception, to the unwavering resistance at Ihumātao. I look to the breathtaking courage of democracy movements in places like Hong Kong, Chile, and those still ever staunch throughout the Middle East. It is a privilege to speak to newer or younger activists today, to new and different kinds of outsider politicians. I see history being made there far more clearly than I see it in Donald Trump's win or Scott Morrison's devastating cruelty. The dirty politics that win elections through xenophobia and fear will rise again in New Zealand too — they are tropes, lacking in inspiration as much as integrity. Those are only signs that we can't get comfortable in formal democracy alone. What is important is that we are jolted into participation, that we forge paths.

For now, I sit in the New Zealand Parliament. I bring my expertise, but I also bring my story, my perspective, my face. That means very different things to different people. It brings with it hate and discomfort, as well as unity and hope. In fact, whether I made it in or not, running still mattered. It brought me, and people like me, a little further toward the forefront of public life, where we should be.

References

Chapter 9

215 **'We, as women MPs, consider …':** Zane Small and Anna
Bracewell-Worrall, 'Women MPs urge David Seymour
to apologise for Golriz Ghahraman remarks', *Newshub*,
22 May 2019. Accessed online: https://www.newshub.co.nz/
home/politics/2019/05/women-mps-urge-david-seymour-to-
apologise-for-golriz-ghahraman-remarks.html

Chapter 10

246 **'in 2016, a study by Business and Economic Research
Limited (BERL) …':** Dr Ganesh Nana and Hugh
Dixon, 'Fiscal Impacts of Immigration in 2013', BERL,
July 2016. Accessed online: https://www.mbie.govt.nz/
dmsdocument/4246-fiscal-impacts-of-immigration-in-2013-pdf

246 **'A 2018 study by the Ministry of Business Innovation
and Employment …':** 'Impact of Temporary Migration on
Employment and Earnings of New Zealanders', Ministry
of Business Innovation and Employment, New Zealand
Government, June 2018. Accessed online 14 July 2019:

https://www.mbie.govt.nz/dmsdocument/4241-impact-
of-temporary-migration-on-employment-earnings-new-
zealanders

246 ' … a 2017 study by the New Zealand Initiative': Dr
Rachel Hodder and Jason Krupp, 'The New New Zealanders:
why migrants make good kiwis', *New Zealand Initiative*,
30 January 2017. Accessed online: https://nzinitiative.org.nz/
reports-and-media/reports/the-new-new-zealanders/

246 'Even refugee populations, who …': H Oliver, 'Doing our
bit? The understudied economics of accepting refugees for
resettlement', *Idealog*, 15 September 2015. Accessed online:
https://idealog.co.nz/etc/2015/09/doing-our-bit-economics-
refugees.

Thomas Manch, 'The cost and value of refugees: are
we ready to take on more from troubled lands?', *Stuff*, 30
August 2018. Accessed online: https://www.stuff.co.nz/
national/106406676/the-cost-and-value-of-refugees-are-we-
ready-to-take-on-more-from-troubled-lands

246 'While poverty is often characterised …': Murdoch
Stephens, 'Don't pit refugees against NZ poor', *Dominion
Post*, 11 May 2017. Accessed online: https://www.stuff.co.nz/
dominion-post/comment/92433950/murdoch-stephens-dont-
pit-refugees-against-nz-poor

252 'The reality is that in New Zealand …': 'Pay gaps by
ethnicity and gender, and equal value, equal pay for Maori
and Pacific women', Coalition for Equal Value, Equal Pay
website, last updated 23 August 2019. Accessed online: http://
cevepnz.org.nz/Gender%20pay%20gap/gender-ethnicity.htm

257   **'Dr William A. Smith of the University of Utah coined
      ...':** William A. Smith, Tara J. Yosso and Daniel G.
      Solórzano, 'Challenging Racial Battle Fatigue on Historically
      White Campuses: A Critical Race Examination of Race-
      Related Stress', *Faculty of Color Teaching in Predominantly
      White Colleges and Universities* edited by Christine A. Stanley,
      Anker Publishing Company Inc., Bolton, Massachusetts,
      2006.

Acknowledgements

I recognise that it is an astounding privilege to write a memoir, to be able to analyse any social challenge, personal hardship, joy or triumph at all, and have it published. I know that, for the most part, it is rare for those with stories like mine, whether refugee, migrant, Middle Eastern, 'person of colour', or womankind, to tell our own stories.

So, I thank HarperCollins for coming for this story and providing it a platform.

My eternal gratitude goes to my Green whānau, caucus, and every last comrade in the Green movement. Thank you for giving me, and people like me, a movement. You know that solidarity is to make space, and together we're building a world where leadership includes us all. I would not be heard, seen, nor effective without you.

But there also must be a short, inexhaustive list of humans in my own life without whose direct input this book would not have been possible.

Rosabel Tan, without your insight and sharp wit for reassurance, I would never have trusted myself enough to keep writing. Rachel Dennis, your thoughtfulness, kindness, and literary instinct made editing a relief. Nadine Walker, I would not have the guts to finally release this work out into the wilderness without your wise but gentle counsel. David Cormack, thank you for lending your expertise, time, and nous at short notice and with constant pressure. Damon Keen, I can't begin to thank you for your unique genius in design, and saintly patience.

My friends, family, and life partner, you saw less of me, saw me stressed, exhausted, and weirdly euphoric. You understood. Thank you.

For creating a safe world for our shared joys, hurt, righteous anger, and unflinching validation, I am grateful to the solidarity between women, women of colour, and marginalised peoples who reach across our divides. Thank you for sitting with me, talking it all through, always messaging back. I am grateful to the activists and revolutionaries for pushing me forward, as we lift each other up.

Again, I acknowledge, as we must, those whose stories and perspectives have not been told, published, or broadcast. Those who did not escape oppression or were not afforded the opportunities that I have been lucky to have. You deserve a voice, and the world would be vastly better off to hear your full truth, in your words.